HOW TO
WRITE LIKE AN EXPERT
ABOUT ANYTHING

HOW TO WRITE LIKE AN EXPERT ABOUT ANYTHING

Hank Nuwer

WRITER'S DIGEST BOOKS

Cincinnati, Ohio

Library of Congress Cataloging-in-Publication Data

Nuwer, Hank.
    How to write like an expert / Hank Nuwer.
        p.   cm.
    Includes index.
    ISBN 0-89879-645-8 (alk. paper)
    1. Authorship. I. Title.
PN147.N88   1995
808—dc20   95-20232
                                                                              CIP

Edited by Diana Martin
Cover and interior designed by Brian Roeth

Grateful acknowledgment is given for permission to quote from *Arctic Village,* by Robert Marshall, University of Alaska Press, 1991. Copyright by George Marshall. To Rodale Press for permission to quote from *The Prevention Pain-Relief System* (1992) and *The Prevention How-To Dictionary of Healing Remedies and Techniques* (1992). And to *Arts Indiana* magazine for permission to quote from Hank Nuwer's columns and articles (1993-1995). Copyright by Hank Nuwer.

Dedication

For Irwin and Christine Howard who gave me a treasure—
their daughter, my wife.

And for my godmother, Marion Nuwer,
who bakes rhubarb pie each time I visit the family farm.

ABOUT THE AUTHOR

Hank Nuwer is the author of fifteen books, including *Steroids*, the "Bounty Hunter" fiction series and *Broken Pledges: The Deadly Rite of Hazing*. He is a journalist and has written for *Human Behavior, Inside Sports, Gentlemen's Quarterly, Saturday Review, Sport, Outside, Success* and *Writer's Digest*. His books have been discussed in the *New York Times, Boston Globe, Denver Post, Chicago Tribune* and *USA Today*. He has also appeared as a guest on *Joan Rivers, CBS Night Watch, Tom Snyder, CNN Sonya Live* and the *ABC Home Show*. He was a consultant on the TV movie, *Moment of Truth: Broken Pledges*, that aired on NBC in 1994. As a journalist he has played minor league baseball in the Montreal Expos organization for manager Felipe Alou, flown with a rescue pilot in Idaho's River-of-No-Return country in midwinter, and written about his own experiences hazing and being hazed as a fraternity member. He has interviewed thousands of people as a journalist, including Kurt Vonnegut, Deion Sanders, Bo Jackson, Pete Rose, James Dickey, Rosemary Rogers, John Jakes, Boomer Esiason, Joe Paterno, Bill Walsh, Bobby Bowden, George Brett and Felipe Alou. He lives in Henry County, Indiana and commutes to Indianapolis to edit *Arts Indiana* magazine, whose national board includes novelist Kurt Vonnegut, designer Bill Blass and artist Robert Indiana. He has been an assistant professor of English at Clemson University, an associate professor of journalism at Ball State University and a senior writer for Rodale Press's *Prevention* magazine health books. At present he also teaches arts writing at IUPUI (Indiana University-Purdue University at Indianapolis). He is a professional lecturer who has spoken at dozens of colleges and universities, including Cornell, Indiana University, the University of Colorado and the University of Pennsylvania.

ACKNOWLEDGMENTS

How to Write Like an Expert About Anything was written in the dead of night even as I led *Arts Indiana* magazine through the growing pains of a new editorial direction and a redesign. It could not have been written without the encouragement and understanding of Jack Heffron, William Brohaugh and Diana Martin, my editors at Writer's Digest Books. I also would like to thank my wife, Jenine, and sons Chris and Adam for permitting me to take time away from them to write this book. Time to have fun again, guys! Ready for some romance in Paris (with me!), Jenine?

TABLE OF CONTENTS

INTRODUCTION

If you're not doing research at the highest level and delivering information in a compelling and entertaining style, you're not half the expert writer you can and must become. Decades of exposure to literary journalism and investigative reporting have made readers and editors intolerant of run-of-the-mill prose and faulty reporting. If you're a clear thinker with good work habits and a love for words, let *How to Write Like an Expert About Anything* help you become a superior reporter, researcher and literary stylist.

As the editor of an Indiana-based regional magazine, a college professor, and a freelance writer since the sixties, I have concluded that the only barriers to publication are inside the heads of writers. If asked to pick one field in which the gap between top-notch and mediocre professionals is the widest—outside the worlds of sport and dance—I'd select the writing profession. Doubt what I claim? Think again. If you need a medical procedure to save your life, you can call any number of specialists current in the field and give them your trust. If you need to find your long-lost baby brother, you need only look to the yellow pages for investigators with the know-how to find him. If you need an attorney to prepare a civil suit, you have dozens of equally competent professionals willing to foresake sleep and recreation to win the case.

But as an editor, when I have a terrific idea for a story that requires a freelancer capable of deep digging, penetrating thinking and superior writing, my list contains no more than three or four names. Thousands of people proclaim themselves to be writers, but only a handful have the gumption and savvy to perfect their research skills, interviewing techniques and their voice on paper. The rest coast.

The author in me takes advantage of the marketplace, knowing I'll be employed until I'm nothing but carbon and ashes. What I've done in this book is to address you—a writer with the desire to do it all and do it right—and to give you the know-how that has helped me write fifteen books and fill six portfolios with specialty articles for diverse publications such as *GQ, Compu-Serve* magazine, *Satellite Orbit, Saturday Review, Outside, The*

Nation, Writer's Digest, Success, Child Life, Arts Indiana, Inside Sports, Sport and *Boston.*

How to Write Like an Expert About Anything is a practical, no-frills guide to help you help yourself become a top-notch writing professional—and that's true whether you're an undergraduate writing student, an expert in your field with a graduate degree, or a self-starter taking the practical road to success. This book tells you what you need to know to write with the skill of an investigative reporter, as I did while writing *Broken Pledges: The Deadly Rite of Hazing*—an exposé of deaths occurring in fraternity initiations. It shows you how to get up-to-date information from specialists in any field, as I did while writing *Steroids* and contributing to four *Prevention* magazine health books. It gives you the tips you need to get the answers. And once you can do that, you become one of those experts I—wearing my editor's hat—want to call when I have a feature assignment.

If you're ready to stop reporting at the surface level, to take any paper trail without becoming lost, and to become a writing star, turn this page and get started. You've been waiting for this book since the first time you knew you were a born writer.

I need look no further than the *New York Times* to know that I'm an expert. The *Times* recently carried a major article on hazing deaths in predominantly African-American fraternities that attributes a statement to me and mentions *Broken Pledges*. Will a major newspaper quote you and your writing tomorrow?

CHAPTER ONE

The Elements of Expertise

Over the years I have written about varied subjects such as the arts, computers, education, the environment, food, health and fitness, sports, travel and writing. I published my work in national and regional magazines as diverse as *Outside, Saturday Review, GQ, Saturday Evening Post, Inside Sports, Sport, Success, Men's Fitness, Satellite Orbit* and *Equinox*. Like all freelancers who tackle a wide array of topics, I had to become an instant expert on these topics, because I have no academic training that otherwise qualifies me as one. Every time I begin a piece, I find it necessary to compile tremendous amounts of information. My job is to transform this research into easily understood prose for general audiences.

In time I became expert enough a sportswriter to work seven years as an *Inside Sports* contributing writer, enough a health and fitness expert to work for Rodale Press as a senior writer, and enough an expert on the literary, performing and visual arts to obtain my current job as editor of *Arts Indiana* magazine. Four of my fifteen published books are novels, a testament to my acquired ability to give readers information while telling them a good story. Five are on sports-related subjects, including my book, *Steroids*, which remained in print four years—a dog's age in this era of on-the-shelves-and-off-again publishing. The book that has earned me the greatest national exposure is *Broken Pledges: The Deadly Rite of Hazing*, shelved most often in the sociology section of your neighborhood library. Because of my research, I have become a national clearinghouse for keeping track of the number of fatalities in fraternity and athletic initiation practices.

Once you gain similar expertise—you can and will—you will increase your writing income many times over with profitable sidelines from your writing. I supplemented my freelance income from 1985 to 1989 by teaching graduate and undergraduate courses in writing as head of the magazine sequence in Ball State University's journalism department. From 1991 to early 1994, I held the title of official historian of Cedar Crest College, writing that Pennsylvania all-female institution's history and becoming knowledgeable about women's education. I also taught extension courses on writing at UCLA and Temple University's Ambler, Pennsylvania, campus. In 1995, the journalism department at IUPUI (Indiana University-Purdue University at Indianapolis) hired me to teach a course on writing about the arts. Moreover, after my book on fraternity hazing deaths appeared in 1990, I began delivering up to twenty lectures (at up to fifteen hundred dollars a talk) annually on the topic of fraternity hazing, at universities such as Cornell University, the University of Pennsylvania, the University of Colorado, the University of Richmond and Indiana University. In short, I learned firsthand that people with an expertise almost always find a need for their services.

The task of writing like an expert is simple to conceptualize, but not always easy to execute. Become a recognized specialist in one or more areas, and you're on your way to the top. Fail, and you sink without a ripple.

The concept of writing like an expert has a logical starting point. You must quickly and comfortably acquaint yourself with specialists in a particular field, interviewing them and perusing what they have written in professional journals, scholarly books and various popular periodicals. Each source inevitably leads you to at least one other source and often to multiple sources. Every time you interview one of these specialists, your own expertise increases exponentially, but so does the danger that you can become overwhelmed by your material if you don't make maximum use of your organizational skills. Professional writers realize that there comes a point when they must stop researching and actually write their articles and books.

As a side note I should point out that once you become known as an expert, other journalists come to you for information. I have been quoted as a hazing expert by the *New York Times*, *Wall Street Journal*, *Chicago Tribune*, *Boston Globe* and scores of other publications; I have appeared on talk shows such as *Joan Rivers, CNN Sonya Live, ABC Home Show* and *CBS News's Night Watch*. I have been paid as an expert witness in a hazing death trial and as a consultant for *Moment of Truth: Broken Pledges*, a 1994 NBC made-for-television movie about a hazing death described in my book. Perhaps the ultimate compliment to this expertise occurred in 1992, following the hazing death of a rookie lacrosse club member at Western Illinois University, when an Illinois circuit judge, in lieu of sentencing twelve veteran lacrosse players to jail for giving alcohol to a minor, ordered them to tell a hazing expert the story of what happened as part of their community service. I was the expert chosen by the judge.

THE VOICE OF AUTHORITY

If your work is to gain similar credibility, you must write with a resonant voice of authority. This voice comes across every page of your manuscript. Without this voice of authority, writers come across as uncertain and befuddled. They swamp readers with extraneous information that leaves them frustrated or, worse, gives them misinformation that could even harm them. In short, writers who sound as if they know what they are talking about sound like experts. When you know your subject thoroughly, and you've taken every precaution to assemble flawless research, your writing ability will help you produce books and articles comparable to what the best writers among your sources might publish.

Some people spend years in graduate school because they think this is the only entrance into the specialty writing field. While formal schooling is usually a plus, it often isn't a prerequisite for writing like an expert in one or more fields. I wasn't required to earn a medical degree to write health-related chapters for four writing projects—including *The Prevention Pain-Relief System*, a top-selling book for Rodale Press and Bantam Books on pain-alleviating techniques. Instead, I interviewed dozens of doctors who revealed hundreds of tips, thoroughly researched the literature in the area of pain relief, and wrote with sensitivity, clarity and wit. Voilá, suddenly I was *the* expert on the subject, with the combined advice of all those specialists safely stored inside my notebooks and tape recorder cassettes. Moreover, I knew I had the capacity to do something that most of those experts could not do: I possessed the writing and organizational skills to transform the most arcane material into deathless prose. No, I wasn't qualified to set up a shingle to practice medicine, but I daresay I knew as much as the average general practitioner about the latest medical pain-relieving techniques.

COMING TO TERMS WITH TERMS

If you want to be taken for an expert, you must learn to use concrete, specific terms. All writers must recognize the difference between concrete and abstract words—and learn to forsake the latter. Whenever I give lectures on writing at university conferences, I invariably direct students to heed the advice found in the bible of writing, Strunk and White's *The Elements of Style*, that admonishes writers to arouse and hold readers by using prose that is at once "definite, specific and concrete."

Using the exact terms, particularly if they are colorful, helps jump-start your bid to establish your voice as an expert. Sometimes these specific terms used in one area of expertise are never or rarely used when writing about other fields. For example, when I wrote two articles on lumberjack sports totaling 7,000 words for *Country Journal* and the now defunct *Fireside Companion*, I gave these pieces the voice of authority by learning the lingo of loggers. I didn't describe a lumberjack's tool-of-trade as a mere saw. That term was too unspecific for readers to visualize. Instead, I talked about the merits of a "crosscut saw"—otherwise colorfully known as a "misery whip" in the parlance of loggers—to establish a claim to expertise with readers.

Each new subject, in effect, is like treading pell-mell into a brand new battlefield. But you can take comfort in knowing that the bullets flying around you are familiar and, with experience, easily dodged. In every assignment you are given, you must adopt the language of those you're writing about—to a degree. I attach that caveat because you must set limits, never overusing the terms. After a while, all writers intuitively recognize how far to go with jargon. Basically, a touch of jargon, well-explained and defined, is good for authenticity. Too much confuses both you and your reader.

One of the main reasons—besides superb marketing—that Rodale Press has been so successful in the health-book line is due to the clear material it makes available to readers who have long been dissatisfied with the high-blown way that their own doctors have talked to them. Based upon my interviews with several hundred doctors to write health-book chapters, I can state with certainty that few physicians possess the knack of putting their knowledge into everyday terms. They talk down to their patients as a consequence. Rodale Press, by taking medicalese and "translating" it into simple, conversational English, has become one of the wealthiest publishers of health books. The same premise holds whether you are writing articles or books for laypeople on automobile repair, computer software or any other topic. Keep it simple.

Be aware that even writers who understand the advantages and virtues of simple prose can fall into the trap of talking, in print, like the experts they interview. Thus, those who write about health must refrain from echoing the dry prose of medical journals. Those who write about law must purge all traces of legalese. The same is true of writers who write about sports, science, the outdoors, crafts, gardening, computers, and yes, writing. Authors who can write clean, simple prose in convoluted verbal swamplands such as wellness, psychology, sociology and education are cherished by editors.

THE WHOLE TRUTH AND NOTHING BUT

The best writers understand that those who succeed create a dream in the minds of readers. Once you create an atmosphere of authenticity in your prose, it follows naturally that what you write has the unwavering semblance of truth. Readers must believe they are getting the truth in order to be convinced of the worth of what they are reading, and, in effect, to put their trust in you, the writer.

How do professionals establish that credibility? One way is to use anecdotes and examples to illustrate and simplify complex material. Each time you do this you score important points with your readers. Using anecdotes makes something magical occur on the page: These concrete examples stay in your readers' minds.

For instance, in my book *Broken Pledges: The Deadly Rite of Hazing*, one of my major theses is that dangerous initiations aren't confined to fraternities, and therefore must be confronted and solved in society at large. At the end of the book's 340 pages, readers have digested considerable anecdotal evidence about scandalous hazing incidents in the military, adult secret societies, youth gangs, high schools, athletic organizations and in business. Readers no longer have a vague concept of what the term *hazing* means. The damning examples of silly, or demeaning, or dangerous acts required for membership in an organization or group not only offer incontrovertible evidence that hazing occurs in all strata of society, perpetrated by both men and women, but that the only way the age-old problem will ever be eliminated is if society wages an all-out attack on the practice. These examples lent strength to my voice of authority, informing readers that the problem is far more widespread than they imagined.

Using information gleaned from interviews and classified military records, *Broken Pledges* charged that dangerous, lewd and disgusting initiations take place on many U.S. Coast Guard ships. Here is one dramatic paragraph from that chapter:

> *[Joe] Branson's nightmare went on and on. [The hazers] sprayed his genitals with purple surgical dye. His pubic hair was discolored for two weeks. They packed black bearing grease into his ears, hair, and genitals. That disgusted even some of the sailors.*

Remember, in most instances, simple stating is not enough. To get across their points, the best nonfiction writers create prose that can be compared to a dramatic presentation. Such writers are like dynamic teachers and seminar leaders. Those writers who fail, like incompetent teachers, merely report facts.

By way of example, I once wrote a chapter in a health book for Rodale Press stressing the concept that hypnosis can have an enormous impact on relieving pain. Stated alone, very few readers would have been convinced what I said was true. Therefore, I bolstered the statement with a dramatic presentation, introducing Dr. Louis Dubin, past president of the American Society of Clinical Hypnosis, who successfully underwent radical cancer surgery, without complications, using hypnosis to get him through the ordeal with minimal anesthesia. His personal experience likely convinced the most skeptical readers that hypnosis was worth considering.

BACKGROUND

The best writers, both of fiction and nonfiction, know how readers hunger for verisimilitude. Consequently, such writers provide readers with sufficient background to make them feel comfortable, but don't overload them with details.

In fiction, for example, authors of gripping detective novels from Dorothy L. Sayers to Patricia D. Cornwell know the value of heightening interest in a good murder by setting one in a world unfamiliar to the everyday reader. Sayers's 1931 classic, *The Five Red Herrings*, details life in a Scottish artist colony. Cornwell's entrancing novels about her supersleuth, chief medical examiner Dr. Kay Scarpetta, achieve the heretofore unimaginable accomplishment of making readers right at home in a morgue. Cornwell's readers feel "the familiar blast of cold, foul air" that greets her heroine when she opens the morgue for business, and in time become familiar with every procedure that Dr. Scarpetta uses to do her job well and to recognize clues.

Nonfiction writers such as John McPhee, who write the literature of fact, present background information with equal success. Whether bringing readers into the world of a Maine birch-bark canoe maker, or that of a geologist making his appointed rounds across the high country of Wyoming, McPhee creates background like a weaver bird makes a nest. Every book is a marvel of construction, woven fiber by fiber with small details and solidified throughout its framework with facts that make up the bigger picture.

In McPhee's *Rising From the Plains*, he masterfully takes readers a hundred million years into the past, showing how Wyoming was once a shelf in a great salt sea. With such a background, readers have little problem visualizing how things were as the waters receded and created the great Cretaceous swamps. Yet, rarely does he overdo these details. Writers who pile on more knowledge than the reader wants or can handle are viewed as pedantic, not authoritative.

You must put yourself into the mind of your reader. Why is the reader paying to get the information you provide? What is the reader likely to want to do with this information? *New Yorker* readers have an insatiable appetite for particular, precise details, while *USA Today* readers want summation and a little titillation. We've all had the frustrating experience of having people tell us more or less than we want to know about a topic. If you have any doubts about who you are writing for, consult your editors. Their jobs depend upon knowing their readers, and megacorporations such as Rodale Press spend fortunes to pinpoint who buys their books and publications.

ACCURACY

Nothing gives readers greater confidence in a piece of writing than when they trust that the author has every word, name and fact correct. One of the worst experiences I had as a journalist was having to fire an assistant who mangled the spellings of the names of a half-dozen then-unknown athletes from the former Soviet Union in a story on the Summer Olympics. My own last-minute fact checking kept the information from appearing in print, but my trust in him was shattered.

Author Louis L'Amour was hardly the equal in prose of classic western author Walter Van Tilburg Clark; nonetheless, L'Amour was a fine storyteller and assured his popularity by painstakingly earning a reputation as a never-erring researcher. Readers knew that if he placed a lone cottonwood hanging-tree along the banks of the Colorado River in Utah, they could count on the fact he'd verified the location of that tree. While reviewers faulted him for writing too many books too fast, his passion for scrupulous detail guaranteed him a committed following.

Don't rely on a publisher's fact-checking staff to spot an error. True, your hide may be saved because the mistake won't see print, but then again, you may never get an assignment again— and deservedly so. A few years ago I adopted the practice of re-contacting my sources after completing a manuscript to go over quotations and facts. The ground rule I establish ahead of time is that I am contacting them to ascertain facts only; in no way do they have story approval. On numerous occasions the sources have pointed out inconsistencies, misleading nuances and flat-out mistakes. When a topic is complicated, and a deadline is at hand, the most careful, seldom-distracted writers can misinterpret something; it's also common for sources to add something that could be crucial to your story once they hear how you've paraphrased what they've said. Often, a source can suggest a more precise and colorful way of saying what needs to be said.

If a subject is vague about some information—a date, for example—go to a reference work to check for specifics. In fact, check all dates you're given as a rule of thumb. For example, I recently interviewed a young playwright who had learned some of what he knew while working as a driver for Harold Clurman, the director of the Group Theatre which included many important playwrights such as Clifford Odets. The playwright said Group Theatre had flourished "about forty years" ago; however, a visit to the reference section of my library demonstrated the movement had started in the thirties—some twenty years before my source thought it had started. You can't expect a source to recall every detail. You can't, so why should they? Make them and yourself look good by verifying dates, spellings and facts.

Moreover, by calling these sources to go over the facts and to correct any errors they might have made, I have built a relationship of trust with them so I can call them another time. Once you've misquoted someone or attributed an incorrect fact to them, the working relationship is gone and rarely can be retrieved.

It's always a good idea to fact check what experts tell you by going to other sources. You need to make sure sources haven't mistaken opinion for fact, or they haven't had some hidden agenda for what they've claimed.

PRESENT CONFLICTING OPINIONS

Tell your sources you are eager to present every side of an issue, and ask them for the names of sources who would have opinions opposing theirs. Editors and readers alike appreciate information containing several points of view so they can make informed decisions. You, the writer, must make it clear whether sources are merely speculating or if their various analyses are based on hard facts. On occasion, you will make informed judgments of your own.

For example, in the January 1994 issue of *Arts Indiana*, I wrote a 7,000-word essay on the controversial topic of whether Indiana—nearly the worst state in the union in terms of funding support for the arts—was a good or bad place for creative artists to work. The artists I interviewed had very strong opinions either way. But when I had talked to enough sources, a very definite pattern began to emerge. Those playwrights and painters who incorporated Indiana themes and subject matter into their work inevitably said the state was a good place to work; many of those who did not incorporate Indiana into their work were dissatisfied with the state as a place to create art. That was a distinction several sources indicated to me was very astute, and was something these artists themselves had never considered.

In your books and articles, identify conflicting opinions for what they are. Professional writers gain credibility when they present conflicting viewpoints so readers can make up their minds about issues. If you don't point out that they *are* conflicting opinions, however, you will confuse your readers.

Remember, experts in all fields disagree, sometimes vehemently. One of my writers from *Arts Indiana* phoned me, confused and frustrated, because she had contacted several experts to get their professional opinions of the vocal quality of an Indiana opera singer named Angela Brown, and their opinions ran the gamut from future star to a never-was and never-will-be.

"Whose opinion do I quote?" she asked.

"All of them," I said. "Readers will love you for your honesty, and they'll see how hard it is to make it in the world of professional opera. You're doing a great job. Just evaluate what they've given you and write a piece in which you trust your own conclusions." She did, too. And got a wonderful letter of praise from Camilla Williams, one of the first African-American opera singers to break into the field, who was an expert quoted in the piece.

GIVE CREDIT WHERE DUE

Expert writers treat their sources fairly and honorably. They always give sources credit for original ideas, but they don't muddy their prose by giving attribution to specialists who have merely provided well-accepted research as background. When in doubt, simply ask your sources if what they say is original or derived. More often, however, you won't need to ask. When you start hearing the same information from two or three sources, you don't need to credit them for such common knowledge—with a couple important exceptions.

Whenever offering your readers tips tantamount to advice from experts, attribute the information to these specialists and list their credentials. For example, when imparting medical advice from physicians, I attribute the information to them, even though I may paraphrase their words. For your legal protection and that of your source, as well as for the well-being of your readers, make it clear that all medical tips being dispensed come from doctors, not from you or other sources such as satisfied patients. Also, when you write books or articles including medical tips, you must always have a disclaimer somewhere in the text that tells readers no book can serve as a substitute for medical advice, urging readers to seek the counsel of their doctors for help with specific complaints.

In short, always follow the old adage about giving credit where credit is due. One of the most difficult things any writer is called upon to do is to blend material from sources into the text so it combines well with your own work without plagiarizing someone else's ideas.

This becomes especially difficult when I am called upon to write books such as *Broken Pledges* that take material from many sources and yet must never sound pedantic—the kiss of death that makes a book unable to compete in a commercial market. Later in this book I'll cover source notes in full detail, as well as specifics on using end notes for attribution.

LEARN TO ANTICIPATE YOUR READERS' QUESTIONS

Writers who wish to be considered experts must be alert to hidden dangers that can trip them up and cause both editors and readers to question their credibility. For example, they must anticipate every possible question that likely will arise in the minds of any nonexpert who reads an article or book. Likewise, any claims or assumptions that writers make must have solid material backing everything up.

One tip that has worked for me is to keep a file of questions that I've asked sources. A year or even a couple days into a project gives you a wholly different perspective from the one that you had when you first began work on a particular topic. Writers, like experts in any field, can fall into the trap of taking far too much for granted about what is common knowledge and what needs to be made clear. When you recheck those questions during the draft process, you'll be less likely to write over your readers' heads. By rechecking the question sheets that I keep in my files, I can take readers through the same learning process that I myself went through to understand difficult concepts.

Readers don't need a tremendous amount of explication to

feel comfortable with all sorts of intellectual and complex subject material from atomic energy to zoology, but they do need things explained in a clear and readable fashion. Moreover, when you're explaining complex information to them, it is important that you don't skip any steps. I proceed from the notion that nothing is over the heads of my readers unless I put it out of reach by my own ineptness.

When something is difficult for me to understand even after talking to one expert, I sometimes have to glean such information by looking at the material from several different perspectives and from the viewpoints of many key sources until all is clear to me. When trying to convey especially complex material, I find it useful to pay special attention during the writing process to areas that once tripped me up, assuming that my readers—"generalists" like myself—will need to be similarly coached through obtuse and arcane material, a common situation when writing about health and science matters.

By way of example, I had to write an entire chapter on how a relatively common medical technique called biofeedback is being used to treat patients under stress. After phoning several doctors, I found myself confused by their jargon and assumptions that I knew more about what they were talking about than I actually did. So, I persuaded a physician to let me undergo a couple biofeedback sessions at a local hospital. I brought along a tape recorder and taped everything that went on. I saw an instant change in this doctor who heretofore had been treating me on the phone like a fellow expert instead of the novice I still was. Suddenly the doctor saw me not as a writer but as his "patient" who had to be walked through every step lest I incur stress and lose confidence in his bedside manner. By the same token, suddenly everything became clear to me as I visualized the biofeedback equipment and saw how to alleviate stress in my own life through the principles "my" doctor was teaching me.

In short, I was able to write a smashing chapter for a *Prevention* health book and gained some information that helped me relax under pressure as well. In fact, while writing the book in your hands, I also had to cope with the demands of a commuter marriage after leaving Pennsylvania to take over as editor at *Arts Indiana*; the biofeedback techniques that doctor taught me got me through more than one bout of stress.

VISUAL AIDS

Like many people I've learned that I'm a visual person, meaning that I can understand something and write about it much better when I see it clearly in my mind's eye. Before I write about artists for my own magazine, I have them show me their work, slides of their work, and portfolios. Before writing a chapter for *Prevention*'s health division about an electronic method to destroy kidney stones without resorting to invasive procedures, I drove fifty miles to see a test run of the fabulous new machine. Phone interviews are time-savers that no writer can do without. But when the material is hard to understand, I conduct my interview in person, or ask my sources to send me all the visual aids they can.

Much of my job as a writer comes down to watching and observing. I ask questions—maybe too many if you ask the people I follow for a story—but I also spend hours on assignments simply watching what is going on while saying nothing, or very little. When writing a feature on a potential champion racehorse named Timely Writer—what a great name!—for *Boston Magazine*, I spent half my time, often forgotten by stable boys and trainers, in the company of the horse to absorb his personality, mannerisms and quirks. Here, in part, was the prose that resulted:

Timely Writer is an impressive creature viewed up close, except for his ridiculous idiosyncracy of keeping his tail dipped in his water bucket. Although not a pretty boy, his profile is noble. The bay colt's wide forehead is marked by a falling star that looks more like a meteor. Thick veins line his head like tributaries. His eyes are full and dark, the flared nostrils are wide and hairy—signs of intelligence and breathing capacity. The mane and tail are thick and black. Red bandages, wrapped perpetually around the legs to prevent injury, cover a white splash of color on the rear left leg. A little over 16 hands tall, he possesses breadth and conformation that far surpass his rivals. He looks a year older than most three-year-olds, the kind of "router" that thrives on distance courses such as the Belmont Stakes, and can spring like a jackrabbit even on a muddy course. His loins are shockingly muscular—"close-coupled" as they say in the barns—and his chest is solid as a bulwark. The horse is built like a boxer.

THE RESPONSIBILITIES OF BEING AN EXPERT

Just as all successful magazines have a mission statement to guide their key decisions, policies and daily operations, so too writers need to come up with a written or unwritten mission statement that keeps them from swerving off course. Readers buy nonfiction books and articles because they believe they will benefit in some way. If you keep their concerns and needs uppermost in your mind during a writing project, you'll satisfy your readers and do your job. As an editor, time and time again I see articles in which the writers have forgotten their readers. They've gone on a tangent or have written to impress their friends or—even worse—the people they interview.

Make it clear to readers how they can benefit from the information you have gleaned from many experts. For example, in a piece I wrote for *GQ* on guidelines for buying craft goods, I cite ten ways potential buyers can save money on their purchases and be reasonably certain that what they buy is of good quality. "Never be reluctant to discuss prices," I wrote, and then summarized the fine art of negotiating with those who sell their wares. "When bargaining, simply take the initiative and tell the craftspersons if you like a product, but that you think it's overpriced. They'll either explain their reasoning behind the price or, since prices are always somewhat arbitrary, come down to a point that's mutually agreeable."

That suggestion—to negotiate—came from several craftspersons I interviewed. Prior to doing the piece, I had purchased several small craft pieces and had paid the full price on the tags. At that time, I would have no more considered bargaining with the seller than I would have considered bargaining with my editors for more money to write an article or book. That *GQ* article gave me a lesson in getting more money for my writing as well. Everything *is* negotiable, I learned.

EXPERIENCE COUNTS

Whenever applicable, establish your credentials and the life experiences you have had for writing on a particular topic—and/ or those of the sources you interview. Degrees earned from educational institutions are important to list, but readers always want to know that they are getting input from experts with life experiences, too. Thus, in that aforementioned chapter that I wrote for a

Prevention book chapter on kidney stones, I interviewed doctors versed in all the latest techniques and medical equipment, but I also talked to doctors and ordinary people who once suffered with kidney stones. I know that I made points with my readers when these latter people—trusted sources by dint of their experiences—explained with precision and somewhat gory detail what the pain of a kidney stone attack feels like. Here is the description I wrote:

> *AAAAARGGGHHHH! There you were having a wonderful time on vacation in the Bahamas when suddenly your side felt as if someone spiked your planter's punch with ground glass. AAAAARGGGHHHH! No matter what you do or what position you assume, the pain remains the same—simply unbear-AAAAHHHH!-ble.*

Convinced now you don't want kidney stones? I was—and started drinking water by the quart ever after to guard against acquiring them.

Likewise in *Broken Pledges*, although I quoted sociologists, psychologists and educators, I also took the time to interview hazing victims, families who had lost a loved one during an initiation, and young people who had been members of a fraternity that experienced a hazing death. The latter had a perspective that the academics could not possess, making for a book that provided not only information but also conflict, high drama and insights that might serve to keep other young men alive.

AVOID SOURCES WITH HIDDEN AGENDAS
Ask all sources probing questions that will warn you if these people are giving you information in their own best interests.

For example, if you're writing an article about osteoporosis and doctors insist that one type of medication works better than competing brands, be sure it's because they really believe it is so through repeated trials, not because they're earning fat consulting fees from a pharmaceutical outfit.

As a matter of course, I ask key interviewees to give me copies of their vita. Resumes serve as good background material, but of greater importance, they reveal what boards people serve on and what allegiances they may have. I rarely publish the quotes of people who have self-aggrandizing reasons for telling me what they do, and if for some reason I do use them, I make it clear to my readers what I've learned about the background of such sources.

Sometimes you learn about such things only by accident. In 1993 I had to research an article on computer clip art. One graphics expert I talked to had me convinced that personal computers were far better than Macintoshes for integrating clip art into brochures, newsletters and so forth. It turned out, during the conversation, that he designed clip art for one company whose art packages were not available for Macintoshes, only personal computers. Consequently, I ignored his denigrating comments about Macs, but did not throw out his tips for using clip art with IBM machines and their clones. He really knew his stuff and proved quite useful. On the other hand, if I thought his knowledge of personal computers was suspect, I would have discounted everything he gave me. As a writer you'll make similar judgment calls again and again.

Also, when interviewing people who are highly critical of someone or something, find out if they have an axe to grind. In 1993 I excised highly negative comments about a curator at the Indianapolis Museum of Art that I'd gotten from a respected local artist for a piece on the flight of creative talent from Indiana. Upon further questioning, the local man admitted that he was upset with the curator because she had invited a major artist to put on a show at the museum, and had not invited him to meet the star, thereby ending his opportunity to expand his network of connections. The local source no longer had credibility for me—or for my readers. His judgment of the curator was, in my opinion, not worth mentioning.

The point is that you learn it can be a trap to take people's comments and criticisms at face value. Always probe, probe and probe again until you're sure you've uncovered any hidden agendas and buried vendettas that your subjects may be bringing to your interviews with them. On the other hand, when your questioning uncovers true professional conflicts and genuine differences of opinion, this is your chance to rejoice. Readers love tension and conflict. You should give it to them whenever you can. For example, in a 1986 interview that I did with Kurt Vonnegut, reprinted four times, the author provided his estimation of his severest critics, book reviewers Jonathan Yardley at the

Washington Post and Peter Prescott at *Newsweek*.

One of the marks of expertise, as a matter of fact, is a willingness to take a stand, to make strong (but well-supported) statements, and to cause waves to come crashing down on someone else's beach. Who wants to read a review by some wishy-washy critic that says, in effect, it's too early in Such-and-Such's career to judge his or her art/book/performance? Readers know they've been handed a crock. First of all, it's never too early, and so the reader knows that Such-and-Such's work wasn't superior. The only other thing the readers can conclude is that the writer hasn't the expertise to make a critical decision—what he or she may be saying, in effect, is, "Let me read the reviews by real experts, and then I'll tell you what I think after they tell me what to think."

In a piece for *Arts Indiana* that I co-wrote with an expert art appraiser, I chided people who were throwing away up to twenty thousand dollars for inferior paintings by Hoosier impressionists because they got caught up in the hysteria of investing. "It is one thing to yearn for the romantic environment of white picket fences and oldtime Hoosier hospitality," I wrote. "It's quite another to be taken for thousands of dollars for the privilege of hanging a second-rate picket fence on your wall." I'd like to think that I saved several readers the price of a lifetime subscription to my magazine in just that one article.

VALUE INTELLECTUAL HONESTY

To write like an expert you must first think clearly and organize your thoughts, then put those thoughts into words. Some writers who think quite clearly and who are well-organized, however, fall apart on the third step because something within them prevents them from saying what is on their minds. They are afraid someone might think them confrontational, pushy, uncollegial. Or they worry that someone might retaliate, hurting their careers or their pocketbooks with a lawsuit.

But just as artists confront the world around them in their work, so too must writers possess the professional integrity to speak the truth. They must get their points across with strong nouns and verbs, few qualifiers, and a tone that leaves no doubt in their readers' minds about how they feel. In my opinion, to think one way and to write something else is intellectual dishonesty that belongs in the same boneyard with plagiarism. The best writers feel an obligation to work with their editors to serve the wants of readers. They go to whatever lengths are necessary to get the information in their stories to the people to whom they owe their livelihood—the readers. Those who write as a form of therapy or to attain star status and a table at Sardi's can never know fully the joys of pleasing their audience, because they're too preoccupied with pleasing themselves.

As an editor, not only do I read and publish letters in my magazine, but I also answer many of them personally. Whenever possible, I take phone calls from readers, too, to hear what is on their minds. The point is that editors and writers can never forget that their readers are the people really paying their salaries.

The other thing I do as a writer and editor is cultivate and keep the sources I interview, staying in touch from time to time to let them know that I value them as people and as experts. That way I don't contact these sources only when I need something from them. They are a part of my life as I am a part of theirs.

I also avail myself of the minds on my editorial board at *Arts Indiana* which includes a journalist, a professional art critic, college professors, an artist, a musician and so on. While I can write well on the arts, I have my limitations when it comes to subject knowledge. I use the talents of these people to fill in gaps. That's precisely what I do before writing my books and articles: I seek out the best minds and ask question after question until I'm confident that the information I'm about to provide is as accurate and thorough as it can be. As a writer, I regularly keep in touch with experts such as sports information directors, doctors, psychologists, behavorialists and educators who serve the function of editorial consultants for me. In return I have helped several of these people by agreeing to read their manuscripts for book proposals and presentations. The bottom line is that you need to cherish and keep good sources if you plan to write consistently good articles. Admittedly, sometimes you feel you are using people, milking them for information as it were. I try to overcome that by trying to connect with people as people, and I make a special point of staying in touch with those who become aged or infirm, letting them know that they meant more to me than mere information. Once a writer loses empathy and starts regarding sources as less than human, that writer ceases to be of much value as a writer and ought to leave the profession. I truly believe that.

CHAPTER TWO

Ideas Under Construction

My nine-year-old son Adam has been drawing horses and sailboats, his special loves, for four years. His first drawings were unrecognizable, although as a proud father I found something to praise in each one. About two years ago, however, his horses really did look like horses, and his sailboats had become so lovely that I wanted to frame them instead of consigning them to a file folder. Practice, advice from his art teacher, and studying models had begun to pay off for him. When I came up with the idea of having a fellow writer's nine-year-old boy review a children's book for *Arts Indiana*, I assigned Adam the job of illustrating the other child's comments to give one layout in our section of reviews a different look.

Writers who wish to improve their ability to write about any topic must go through a process similar to the one that my son went through—and will continue to go through for as long as he wishes to draw.

As the editor of an arts magazine with the limited budget that plagues many niche publications, I often need to contract the services of inexperienced freelance writers to write articles for me. Consequently, often I work at my office until late at night, going over third, fourth, even fifth drafts with these writers. As with Adam, in time most of these writers improve, some of them dramatically so, making them far more valuable to my magazine, and imbuing them with the confidence to query other publications as well.

Some of these writers never had written about the arts. Consequently, many had fears and reservations about accepting assignments on such topics as opera, ballet and classical music. I had to sell them my conviction that they could, indeed, write on topics that they never before had tackled.

Once these writers see the results of their hard work in the form of bylines on articles and their names on the magazine's checks, they usually gain the confidence to work on subsequent articles on their own. They see that they have the ability to write about any topic. Once they get the essence of a particular topic, they are eager to tell readers what they themselves have learned. The best of them can communicate the sense of excitement they experienced while doing research for the piece.

Every story is like a hurricane with an eye at the center. Writers who would write like experts succeed in finding the means to become transported into that eye, seeing everything clearly once they've gotten past the initial chaos experienced upon entering that hurricane.

I felt similar insecurity when I went to work at Rodale Press, because I found myself in the company of people who had written health and science articles all their professional lives. When we went out to lunch, I talked about literature and sports, while they talked about cholesterol, symptoms and hormone levels. It took me a while to fit in, but in time I left, realizing that I felt more comfortable working with colleagues committed to the arts and education than with people who wrote exclusively about health and fitness.

THE FOUR THINGS EVERY SUCCESSFUL WRITER DOES

Nonetheless, I'm glad I had a chance to work for Rodale Press, because I learned some lessons that have helped me both as an editor and writer. The most helpful lessons came from the teachings of Mark Bricklin, then Rodale's Group Vice-President and *Prevention* magazine editor. What I learned at Rodale applied subsequently when I accepted a freelance book project to write about women in education, as well as when I began writing arts articles and editorials for *Arts Indiana*.

My time at Rodale taught me to do four things as a writer:

1. Display leadership. Bricklin wanted Rodale writers and editors to perceive themselves as authorities in the health field. I've taken that philosophy to *Arts Indiana* magazine, looking for writers willing to acquire expertise in the visual, literary and performing arts—or at least one of these areas.

If you choose to write regularly in any one field, you must keep current with what is happening in your area. You must read, cultivate pertinent sources, and do frequent computer searches in your area to assure yourself that nothing important has slipped past you. For example, knowing that I soon will write a second book on hazing, I collect and file information on every instance of initiation abuse I can find, as well as keeping abreast of whatever doctoral research on hazing is being done. I lose no opportunity to be interviewed as an expert on the topic, because it is important to maintain the public's perception that I—as the only author of a full-length study of hazing as of 1995—am *the* person to call for information on the topic. Editors and readers alike are drawn to authors who are seen as leaders in their field, and my staying current assures me that I'll continue to influence public policy in the area of hazing.

2. Become tip conscious. Unless readers receive tips they can apply to their own situations, the most current and enlightened health-related information is useless to them. Even profiles tend to show readers another way to live. The nineties are the era of service journalism. Everything you write must serve your readers in some important way. If what you write doesn't give readers some short-term or long-term benefits in the form of tips they can use, what you write has no value. Presenting these tips in a lively, captivating way is just as important as the information itself. Hundreds of health publications put out health-related information every day in the form of magazines, pamphlets and booklets. Information is everywhere. But Rodale Press's health books make millions of readers come back again and again, because the writers put information in the form of tips rendered in a way that *entertains* and *enlightens* people. No matter what you write, your tips must do both.

3. Always be professional. Rodale expected its writers to perfect all skills and work habits. Bricklin likened us staff writers to brain surgeons because it was our job to insert ideas into the heads of readers. And who wants to go under the knife with a less-than-professional brain surgeon operating?

Professionals, no matter what the field, work five or six days a week—not when the urge strikes them. They read the literature in their field (just as you are reading this book) that helps them learn new techniques and perfect old ones. They calmly assess their weaknesses and devise a plan to make those areas strengths. Before coming to Rodale Press, I had done these things intuitively—as you yourself may be doing them—but my stint there taught me that I had to concentrate on little details and go back to fundamentals every now and then. It's only human to develop sloppy tendencies, and I knew that honest self-evaluation was a must if I were to become what I wanted to become—a professional that professionals looked up to.

4. Empathize with your readers' needs. One of the things I routinely do as an author to help me do my job right is to talk to people interested in the topic I am writing about—in other words, to potential readers. Talking over the piece with acquaintances gives me a sense of direction and a feel for the overall scope of the writing project. Otherwise, trying to plunge ahead and write anyway is not only frustrating but futile. In my opinion, the questions that potential readers ask, the fears or apprehensions they express about some project I'm considering, and the comments and criticisms they make are almost always necessary to help me narrow my focus. For example, I talked to a female friend in her twenties who had battled incontinence for a decade before I outlined an important chapter on that subject for a *Prevention* health book.

Almost as important as learning what information she needed to obtain was the empathy that I developed for her as a person. Her condition was psychologically and physically painful, and in her case, career-threatening. My notes on our meeting helped me find the narrative voice that I needed to use in this particular chapter. If you write as though you are talking to a particular person, your readers will feel they have been personally addressed.

MINING YOUR IDEAS

Writers of Rodale's health books—many of them under the *Prevention* magazine imprint—quickly learn that the company is in the "idea business," as Bricklin and my boss, editor in chief William Gottlieb, always emphasized in meetings and company handouts. Rodale's management made a practice of putting enormous amounts of time and money into developing specialized ideas such as the incredibly successful *Doctor's Book of Home Remedies*—a project that made more money for Rodale than most publishing firms earn with their entire lists.

Rodale takes an idea like *Home Remedies* and gives it a strong service slant. Readers get practical advice in the form of tip upon tip that they can use to improve their health and daily lives. *Home Remedies*, for example, takes the results of interviews with dozens of doctors and boils them down into more than two thousand tips that imaginatively lick everyday health problems. People with arthritis, for instance, learn which vegetable oil is best for them to use. The book heavily depends on using ordinary household items to lick health problems, such as using baking soda to thwart athlete's foot.

All writers can learn the secrets of publishing success from examining Rodale's veritable library of health books. I myself learned that the best ideas for Rodale books are concepts that are "so well focused and particularized"—in Bricklin's words—that readers and writers alike should have no trouble visualizing them. Not coincidentally, Rodale writers are taught that the word "idea" hails from the Greek word for "picture."

At Rodale's home base in Emmaus, Pennsylvania, I was taught that to succeed in publishing it was important to get beyond thinking that I was merely in the information business. I learned that information in itself is useless. What is useful is the ability to take information and to weave it full of ideas in the form of practical tips and commentary. The ability to examine mere facts and to create something valuable—an idea—from raw data is a skill in employees that all employers crave. The ability to come up with idea after idea is what distinguishes writers who are experts from writers who are merely confused—in spite of all the information in the world at their disposal.

SHOWING READERS WHY THEY SHOULD CARE ABOUT YOUR IDEAS

I learned long ago that my writing success depended upon giving my readers new ideas in a context that was somehow familiar. Readers—being human and naturally skeptical as humans are— will only accept a new idea if it is in a context they can understand. For example, many years ago when I wrote an article for a men's health magazine about the warning signs of alcoholism, I had to inform readers that their ability to drink their peers under the table was a bad sign—indicating growing alcohol tolerance—

not the manly attribute they had always boasted it was. To get the readers' attention, I constructed a scene in which a heavy drinker had come to the point in his illness when he began getting drunk on just a few drinks because his body's natural defenses had begun to break down. The scene wasn't pretty, and I received several letters from young men who said my article had made them question the wisdom of cultivating drinking prowess.

LOOK FOR AN EVENT'S LARGER SIGNIFICANCE

A Louisiana photographer I met some years ago while I was on a magazine assignment was incensed because the Marathon Oil Company had just bulldozed a historic Old River Road plantation home. When I heard that fact, I buried him with lots of questions. Was it possible that industry posed a threat to Louisiana's architectural treasures? Why hadn't preservationists intervened? Was this part of a pattern, and would more homes come down? In short, I wanted to get beyond the simple fact and investigate why this event had happened and its larger significance. In short, I had an idea for an article.

After spending some time in southern Louisiana, I uncovered certain facts that led me to believe that industry posed a threat to these historic homes along the Old River Road. The results of my investigation went into a piece titled "Louisiana Plantation Homes: On the Road to Destruction." I concluded that these proud dowagers of the Deep South no longer lived in a state of grace. Here is the lead and a small section from that piece:

> The secret execution was scheduled for dawn. The victim was Welham Manor, which for 144 years had held dominion along southeastern Louisiana's historic Old River Road. The still-elegant brick and cedar structure had once served as the plantation home of sugar king William Peter Welham and all he begat.
>
> The ravages of time, angry hurricanes and the oft-rampaging Mississippi River could not budge the manor, but family fortunes had declined, so the property went up for sale. Bidding $5.3 million, the new owner was the Marathon Oil Company of Findlay, Ohio, which decided a pipeline was needed precisely where Welham reposed. Consequently, in May of 1979, while local preservationists slept,

bulldozers surged ahead, cables pulled taut, and another visible part of the Old South went down, never to rise again.

During the 20th century, particularly in the last two energy-short decades, Louisiana plantations along the Baton Rouge-to-New Orleans section of the Mississippi's great River Road have become a vanishing species. The problem, essentially, is that the petrochemical giants have taken over in Louisiana, a state rich in resources and a complacent concubine of Big Business. Thus, a stately 1840s plantation named Three Oaks is now the site of the America Sugar Refinery's parking lot. A roof blew off an otherwise lovely home named Helvetia, and it was demolished. Seven Oaks, an 1830 heavy-columned building with sloped roof and belvedere, was abandoned to the elements. Armont and Riverton were sold for scrap; Belle Helene is soon to follow them to the junkyard.

By taking an idea—Louisiana's historic properties are being abused—and using specific examples to illustrate my contention, I gave cohesion and substance to what had seemed to most residents an unrelated series of demolitions. There was some risk on my part. It's unlikely that I would have had a national story had the Welham incident been the only one of its kind, and I would have wasted some research hours, but that's a fact of life that comes with the territory for writers. Namely, not all article ideas pan out.

JUST HAVING IDEAS ISN'T ENOUGH

My dentist comes up with dozens of ideas for me that he thinks would make great articles, and he's often right, but rarely do I pursue them. Why? Because having an idea isn't enough; executing the work necessary to present that idea to the public is required. Expert writers are deluged with ideas. They pursue only those that experience and instinct say are worth pursuing, given the constraints of time and cost factors.

People with good ideas are people who ask good questions. If, for instance, you're the type of person who is always questioning authority and wants to go past the face of a matter to find out what's really happening in city hall, the queen's palace, or wherever, you're already a man or woman of ideas. The challenge is to present your ideas and inform your readers in the story format they demand.

There is another challenge, too. As *Arts Indiana* editor, again and again I receive query letters from writers who wish to write about a particular subject that strikes them as perfect for my magazine. Some of these query letters are all over the map, showing no ability on the part of the writers to develop a complex idea. For example, a writer from northern Indiana wrote to ask if I would be interested in a piece that showed that the artists' colonies of the nineteenth century in the Dunes area along Lake Michigan were being replicated today by an influx of great artists from Chicago.

This might be a great idea for *Arts Indiana*, and I was intrigued. Unfortunately, the examples of contemporary artists she cited were run-of-the-mill crafts makers, not people doing truly quality work. I phoned to tell her that she had lost a sale unless she could substantiate her contention by proving that some outstanding visual artists were creating work in the Dunes today.

Here's a tip to keep in mind. Never send in a query that claims something you cannot substantiate (or that you haven't substantiated). When proposing an idea you have to dig, research, and use your best reportorial skills to show an editor that you can produce what you say you can.

THERE IS NO SUCH THING AS A GOOD NOTION

Many would-be writers are stopped before they start. They possess only vague notions about the articles and books they desire to write someday. Writers must get past these notions if their projects ever are to see print. I learned at Rodale that notions are unproductive and the opposite of ideas. Notions are too general and unparticularized to capture a wide audience of paying readers, according to Rodale's Bricklin.

Given what I learned at Rodale, how do you tell the difference between a notion and an idea? Simply stated, if you can picture or visualize the project you wish to write, you are well on the way to carrying an idea to fruition, according to Rodale's philosophy. If, however, you find yourself stuck and unable to clearly see in your mind what it is you want to produce in your prose, chances are a mere notion is bogging you down.

The trick, therefore, is to take a notion and give it shape until it has the heightened status of an idea. For example, say you want to write an article or book on fashion for women. Sorry, that's not enough to interest an editor; "fashion for women" is a mere notion in Rodale terms.

In contrast, a book that I co-wrote with *BBW: Big Beautiful Woman* founder Carole Shaw sprang from a true idea that she had. The idea was that large-sized women deserve access to the same top fashions that their petite sisters wear. Our book told readers what they needed to know and do to force manufacturers to provide all women with high-fashion clothing. Written in 1981, the book was the first of many books by large-sized women for large-sized women; ours was relatively militant in tone. Hefty people, said the stereotype, were supposed to be jolly. Shaw, instead, showed the world that large people had had enough and would take no more abuse from the World of Fashion— which, as a result of Shaw and others, has begun to offer better options to women size sixteen and over.

TAKE A FRESH LOOK AT YOUR REJECTED QUERY LETTERS

This concept of an idea rather than a notion sounds easy to grasp, but it's actually quite complex. Many people had ideas for inventions that would replace kerosene lamps, after all, but only Thomas A. Edison perfected a filament to make the light bulb work.

Thus, if you're a writer whose queries to publishers have been collecting rejection after rejection, perhaps you might do well to reexamine your rejected proposals to see if your projects were doomed because ideas were not there (or were presented in fuzzy prose that obliterated them). If you are convinced that you have had bankable ideas, the job ahead of you is to polish your presentations. If you've had only notions, either scrap them or use them as a starting point to add flesh to those bare bones.

True, some genuine ideas get rejected by publishers. The reason is often good economics, not an international publishing conspiracy against you. Not all ideas have the potential to earn back authors' advances, let alone become blockbuster sellers. Some may be too derivative of other books and articles already in print. But unless you write a proposal that highlights a bona fide idea, your submission won't even make it to a publisher's ideas meeting for discussion. Once you have a bona fide idea clearly in your head, it is much easier to write a proposal. Until you think clearly, you cannot write clearly.

When is an idea good enough and narrowed down enough to sell? It's when you are sure that the readers of a particular magazine would pay the cover price to get what you offer. That is my criterion for buying a piece for *Arts Indiana*. If I, as a reader, wouldn't shell out the money to buy a writer's idea, I, as an editor, won't shell out hundreds of dollars for that dubious privilege either.

THE IMPORTANCE OF STRUCTURE

After coming up with an idea, it is important to highlight that single idea in your piece, not letting it lose its impact because you've strangled it by putting it in the company of too many other ideas. Offhand, I can't think of a single manuscript I've received at *Arts Indiana* that had to be killed because there was no way to expand it. The problem with professional writers and amateurs alike is usually the opposite. They tend to present more ideas than readers can chew in one sitting.

Writers that include too many ideas leave readers reeling and feeling overwhelmed. Idea-laden pieces are sketchy, hard to follow and maddening to edit. For me, as a reader, it's as if I had sent a server to get me food at a banquet, and my plate came to me with every course piled one on top of another, making the meal unappetizing at best, unpalatable at worst. Just as I would send back the server to start over again, so too must such writers go back to their raw materials and begin anew.

An article, like a good meal, must be arranged properly. There should be just enough of each portion, not too much or too little of this one or that. Any reader, like any diner, wants to savor what's in front of him, not tear into everything in a frenzy—or be overwhelmed by too much of one portion or another.

WHAT IT MEANS TO NARROW YOUR FOCUS

I tell writers again and again to narrow their focus. I'll define that term in a moment, but first let me say what I do when I write an article.

First, I give hard thought to my word count. When editors give writers assignments, they assign a specific number of words. Not only does this help you see the scope of what you must do, it also helps the editor and art director assign space in the issue of the magazine in which your piece will run. If, however, you're writing a piece on speculation, carefully consider the number of words at your disposal based upon what your target magazine usually runs. If pieces run 1,500 words, you must approach what you write in a different way than you would for magazines that regularly run 3,000-word articles.

For example, the lead in a 1,500-word piece is tighter than the lead in a longer piece of 3,000 words. The latter gives a writer more freedom to speak. There is more summation in the shorter piece instead of piling on anecdotes. The pacing is much brisker.

Nonetheless, some things are the same. It's likely you would interview the same number of sources for both a short and long piece, collect nearly the same amount of data, and spend almost as much time on the first as the second. Writing "tight" prose is a time-consuming job.

In both pieces you begin by making readers a promise that you will deliver certain information. When readers have finished your article, they should walk away thinking that you've made good on that promise. For example, in a piece I am now writing for my magazine on master's degree programs in creative writing, my premise is that there are ways for people to know in advance whether or not the graduate degree is worth the pursuit. I cannot publish that article in *Arts Indiana* until I've given readers an almost infallible way of knowing whether or not they should put their time and money into earning a master's degree.

Finally, the way I'd define "narrowing your focus" is making an editorial decision to shape your material into one particular slant and delete whatever research that fails to fit that slant. When editors demand to know your "angle" or "hook," they're really asking you to show you've narrowed your focus so that your articles are manageable.

Remember, good writers not only include information—they know what material to *exclude* as well. Then they take the material deemed essential and fashion it to sound like a piece that readers of their target publication would want to read. This is called "knowing your market," or being able to visualize the personality of the publication you are trying to hit. It's knowing in advance the values, prejudices and preferences of the people that will be reading your article.

Think of your material as bolts of fabric. You, the writer, are like the fashion designer that must shape and sew that fabric in a way that pleases particular buyers.

THINK LIKE A CHESS MASTER

No editor likes telling writers to junk what they have and do it over. I prefer working with writers who work like master chess players and get things right the first time. Master writers work several moves ahead. They know how to compose leads that draw readers into the story. They know what pieces of concrete information they wish to get across and have a sense of the right place in the story to drop this element or that. Sure, it troubles them to have space limitations that force them to excise perfectly good details they've obtained during the process of research, but true masters reason that some pawns have to be sacrificed if the game is to be won.

Moreover, a master is going to add his or her sense of style to every piece of writing. In spite of the limitations that an article's word count imposes, the best writers exercise their creativity to not only communicate information in the form of usable tips, but to surprise and delight their readers (and editors) time and again. Sure, writers start from an outline, but they never let themselves get locked into it. They always add surprises to delight and instruct their readers.

Nor do they panic when they're temporarily blocked. They make themselves a cup of coffee, perhaps, or chew on an apple and figure out solutions with the skill of a sleuth. Experienced writers who have solved the mysteries of dozens or hundreds of articles will find some way to make a piece work—just as a veteran mechanic will figure out some way to get a stalled car running again.

Getting (and Staying) in the Mood

When the best writers conceive and write their pieces, they choose one tone—be it conversational, formal, impersonal or (rarely) flippant—and rarely, if ever, ask the reader to get out of the established mood. The best writers write their pieces using a single tense, never shifting tenses or only when there is no other way to say what has to be said. Finally, whether a piece is

750 words or 3,750 words, writers work hard to get across one single idea to the reader. Here are some examples:

- Do these exercises and you'll have an abdomen hard as sheetrock.
- Follow this advice and you can survive in Alaska on fifty dollars a day.
- Travel outside your state and you can buy the work of your state's artists for far more reasonable prices than you'll likely pay in-state.

Making Sure Readers Get the Idea

Emphasize one idea—*that's* another thing I mean as an editor when I ask writers to "narrow" a topic for me. I prefer that writers slant their pieces in such a way that everything—from headline to closing paragraph—can be reduced to a single, well-shaped idea. In a query letter, when writers try to get me to assign a piece, they should be able to tell me what they are writing in one paragraph. If they can't do that, if they flounder when they describe the piece, I suspect that what they're going to turn in will ramble without focus. In that case, I won't commit to a contract. The best I'll do is invite the writer to complete the piece on speculation, guaranteeing only to read it.

BANISHING ANXIETIES

Is it sometimes frightening when I write about subjects I've never tackled before? No—it's *always* frightening to write about them.

In college I feared taking math and science courses. One of the worst experiences I had in college was having to take a physics course without ever having taken chemistry, and I broke my back just to get a passing grade. Now I routinely write articles and book chapters on health, medicine, computers and drugs. Maybe, at first, I wrote because I needed the money, maybe the fear of failure (discussed at length later in the book) spurred me to succeed, but I no longer hesitate to accept assignments to write about topics that frighten me or are out of the range of my normal areas of expertise.

In my opinion, that old dictum about writing only what you know has probably killed the careers of countless writers before they had a chance to get started. Whether in high school or college, beginning writers ought to be challenged to write about all subjects—bar none. Part of the challenge of writing is to find the answers to what you don't know, and once you find them, to write coherent sentences, paragraphs and pages until you've written all you intended to say. All of us must cultivate the ability not only to think on our feet, but also to think on the page. There is tremendous satisfaction in writing about a topic that you thought impossible. Writers who only write about what they know run the danger of finding out, early or late in their careers, that they know very little. Natural writing talent goes only so far. Perseverance, dogged curiosity, reasonable intelligence and the ability to think on paper must accompany that natural talent if you're to succeed as a writer.

The Mechanics of Expertise

If you wish to write like an expert, you must see yourself as a pacesetter in any and all fields you write about. For beginning writers this occurs when they publish several articles—or one major article—on a particular subject.

Without question, publication gives professional writers tangible proof of expertise. For example, the very first article on fraternity hazing that I wrote for *Human Behavior* in 1978 let me inside the door to achieve my current status as a hazing expert. Educators, people injured in hazing incidents, the survivors of people killed in hazings, and others writing about the topic began to contact me by phone and letter. The number of phone calls I get every week has inspired me to start a publication of my own. By the summer of 1996 I expect to complete research to see whether there is sufficient demand for a newsletter on the subject of hazing, and also will be deep into research for a second book on hazing.

I find after talking to writers at various conferences that many of them seem apologetic about claiming expertise because they lack academic credentials—not knowledge in their particular area or areas. I'd like to hammer home the point that you don't have to possess a doctorate to write with a clear, respected voice for specialty magazines or book publishers. All that counts is your knowledge of a subject.

For example, I write articles for many specialty magazines that are outside my areas of expertise. In a decade (1983-1993) spent as a contributing writer to *Satellite Orbit*—a sort of *TV Guide* for satellite dish owners—I wrote only three technical articles. I did, however, contribute more than sixty pieces on sports, unusual networks (the Silent Network for deaf viewers, for example) and issues affecting the satellite communications industry such as con men posing as dish salespeople.

DEVELOPING IDEAS FOR SPECIALTY PUBLICATIONS

Freelance writers must always take the time to analyze a variety of specialty magazines to see what their editors are buying. Instead of writing a publication off because it is a specialty magazine, I try to find ways to make editors buy pieces from me that connect with their readers in some tangential way.

Let's say, for example, that you think you have no mechanical ability and you avoid electric tools of all kinds lest you lose a finger or worse out of sheer klutzery. That isn't sufficient reason for you to avoid writing for the many so-called "mechanical" magazines. The editors of such publications routinely purchase articles that have nothing to do with technical expertise, such as pieces on health, money matters and household affairs.

You may find it helpful to know that nonservice veterans have written for *American Legion Magazine* (one of its editors is a nonveteran—Doug Donaldson, an "A" student of mine when I taught at Ball State!); and that confirmed couch potatoes have written for *Men's Fitness*. One of the best writers for a major publisher of health books is a lovely woman who weighs over two hundred pounds, seldom exercises, and eats the very foods she advises readers to avoid. On the other side of the coin, I've met editors at *BBW* who are ultra-thin. It is my contention that any writer worthy of the name can write with flair and gusto about diverse subjects such as antiques, history, camping, backpacking, collecting, pets, firearms, sports, conservation, fashion and computers. Since the early eighties many magazines have repositioned themselves to survive in this age of specialization, and writers who formerly wrote for fast-dwindling, general-interest publications had to adjust or die in the marketplace. Like it or not, *Look* and *Collier's* and a slue of airline magazines have gone to that Great Remainder Pile in the Sky. In addition, even the handful of general-interest publications have absolutely narrowed their focus. The *Saturday Evening Post*, for example, has found a new niche with health articles; airline magazines for the most part run a high percentage of articles directed toward business travelers.

Identifying Their Needs

How can you identify the needs of editors with specialty magazines?

One way is to write a brief letter to the editor directly, briefly outlining your particular skills. For example, if your particular expertise happens to be sports, you might study a dozen magazines in a variety of niches and then write to the editors to suggest ways that you might prove valuable to them and their readers.

Be creative. Perhaps you could review books on sports for *Library Journal* or *Publishers Weekly*. You could offer articles on preseason sports predictions for one of the many weekly satellite television guides such as *ONSAT*. For the latter magazine I even visited remote parts of Alaska for a 1993 article on rural Alaskans (like Dick Mackey, oldest person ever to win the Iditarod dogsled race), who keep in touch with the world through satellite TV programming.

In effect, you are creating a need for yourself and your work by showing editors how you can serve their readers.

Another thing I strongly suggest is that in your letter you ask if the editor might inform you of any particular needs such as special issues planned far in advance. My magazine, *Arts Indiana*, runs theme issues on occasion such as an issue devoted to education.

In addition, at present, my best dance writer is only available summers in Indiana, because she teaches at the University of Missouri nine months out of the year. I have been scrambling to find someone in Indiana who knows the dance scene and is a good writer. Other editors have similar needs from time to time, and, like me, many don't mind polite inquiries asking them to briefly outline the needs of their respective magazines.

GETTING THE CONFIDENCE TO WRITE ABOUT SPECIALTY TOPICS

Although I had heavy experience in the literary arts and theater in almost every area when I came to *Arts Indiana* in 1993, I had far less experience in the visual arts, opera and dance.

If you have similar deficiencies in one or more specialties, you might consider immersing yourself in those topics just as I did. First, I purchased a wide variety of books and periodicals on the subjects, reading well into the night and sometimes waking in the morning with a periodical flat on my chest. I also made a point of meeting with performers and arts administrators across the state of Indiana, asking them what issues were of concern to them and what things they were trying to get across to their audiences and potential audiences. No matter what the subject, you're sure to find well-informed people who love to talk about themselves and what they love to do best.

In short, immersion in the topic is the fastest way to acquaint yourself with any area of specialty, allowing you to write with confidence and giving you professional contacts who can proofread your stories to make certain any deficiencies in knowledge haven't slipped into your prose.

HOW TO GET UP AND RUNNING WITH NEW TOPICS

Even in elementary school I was a magazine junkie. Mr. Novak, the late owner at Novak's Drugstore on Buffalo's East Side, had no idea that he was cultivating a future editor and writer when he kindly allowed me to sprawl after school in front of the magazine rack with copies of *Saturday Review, True, Esquire, Police Gazette, Sport, Time* and *The Sporting News* spread out before me. I could be a wild kid on occasion, but not in Mr. Novak's store. My parents paid for my cherished subscription to *Boys' Life*, but there was no way they could afford all those adult publications I read voraciously even in the sixth grade. Mr. Novak chased away all the ill-behaved boys, particularly those he recognized for the shoplifters they were, but he let me read for hours at a time.

If you would write for magazines, be prepared to haunt newsstands and to subscribe to as many magazines as your pocket will bear. Study the annual *Writer's Market* and write for copies of magazines not generally available from your dealer—particularly well-paying association magazines such as *Kiwanis*.

Don't just read a magazine, analyze it. Look at the ads, the mission statement (if there is one), the features, the columns and the editor's message to get in touch with what that publication is trying to be. Early in my career, I took notes on magazines and memorized the names of editors and recurring authors, knowing more about those publications than probably some of their job candidates for staff positions knew.

Familiarity with a publication helps you get the right tone into your queries and cover letters. Not only that, it helps you make reference to things you've noticed in the magazine, making the editor aware that you've taken the publication seriously. Nothing irks an editor more than to get a query on a piece that ran just three or four months earlier. If you don't read the publication, you can't write for it.

Sure you will compete against a lot of freelance writers, but I assure you that many of them are lazy and careless. If you act like a pro, and you can write at all well, you will crack markets in all specialties almost at will.

Hooking Readers With Celebrities

In addition to doing your homework by studying the markets and writing as well as you can, there is one more thing you must do. You must cause editors to want you to join their team because of the breadth and depth of the ideas you present.

Are there ways to enhance your ability to find ideas? Absolutely.

For example, editors and writers often take advantage of the fact that this is a celebrity-fixated world by yoking celebrities and concepts. If the article is on beating an addiction on your own, support that point by using stories about movie or sports figures that overcame alcoholism, gambling or drug use on their own. If the article is on walking forty minutes a day for weight loss, find celebs who stay fit by doing just that. At a time in my career when I was writing a celebrity piece almost monthly, I cultivated the acquaintances of celebrity publicists and sports information directors who put me in touch with their stars when I needed full-length interviews or quotations by phone.

After you've done celebrity pieces for some time, you'll form relationships with some of them just as I did. I found it helpful to keep files on all the sports stars, authors and celebrities that I interviewed regularly. Whenever I read an item about these people, I would add it to my files.

These files, in turn, sparked ideas. If I saw, for example, that a well-known figure's child had overcome a dread disease, it could spark an article proposal on ways to cope with such occurrences. Or, if I saw that a well-known celebrity had shed thirty pounds, I could almost always count on that person being willing to share secrets with readers of almost any women's magazine or fitness magazines for men or women.

Choosing Fighting Words

Like celebrities, controversies always provoke interest from editors on behalf of their readers. For example, regional magazines always have articles on national issues and situations, personalizing these for their readers by getting local people (the more well known the better) to speak for or against them. As an editor, I know that my readers in Indiana's community of artists and art lovers like to make up their own minds on issues. By giving them views of people like themselves, they can have more informed opinions.

City and other types of regional magazines frequently find new ways of working old standby hotboxes such as abortion, gun control and crime into their features. Sometimes the quotations their authors get actually flame or quell controversies. Always remember that whatever you write about has to still be a hot topic four or six months ahead. Technology is changing the speed with which a magazine can be put out, but for now, there still is a lead-time factor to consider when you write your articles. No editor is going to buy a piece that readers will consider old news at the time it runs.

What's Fresh? What's in the Future?

Another type of sale stems from the idea of easing readers' anxieties about the future by informing them about what they can expect in those areas that concern them the most—their health, their finances, their families, their environment and so on. You don't have to guess that publishers are going to make small fortunes on books and pieces that tell readers how to survive the coming century, that predict how life will be when the twenty-first century ends, that, in short, prepare them for the inevitable.

What inventions just patented will have the impact that computers had on life in the twentieth century? What diseases will go the way of smallpox? Which retirement plans for the future will be obsolete? How will our children's children be governed? What is going to happen if crime, poverty and ignorance continue unabated? Interview experts in these areas—or better yet, become an expert with the right answers yourself—and you'll find publishing house after publishing house waiting for you with contracts ready for the inking.

In the short term, look for isolated incidents that taken together constitute a trend. For example, I've recently noted a spate of horrific gang initiations from Florida to California in which would-be members are asked to kill, mutilate or rape strangers in order to join the club. If I yoked all these incidents into a single piece, it would make a chilling and revealing trend that would alert the public.

Lists: The Most, the Best and the Worst, the Strangest

David Letterman isn't the only one who loves lists. Readers love ideas for categories that rank people, things and places. The most mail—much of it angry—that I've received on a single article at *Arts Indiana* was a list of people "who matter" in the arts.

These are good articles for beginning and young readers. If people didn't love ratings, we wouldn't have book, TV, movie and food critics. Readers love to compare and contrast. They love to go to places that are in and to take pride in the fact that they shun places that are out.

The construction of such articles is simple. Come up with a concept. Establish some criteria for making your point. Choose examples that satisfy, or fail to satisfy, those criteria. Prepare to defend your choices. That's it.

LEARN FROM THE GREATS

There are ideas and then there are blockbuster ideas. That's my philosophy as I try to put together a magazine every month. The best ideas—the ones that bring in mail, signed new subscriber cards, and fresh advertisers—are the blockbuster pieces that get the big blurbs on the cover and the most prominent layout space. In the world of books, they are the ones that get preferential rack space at bookstore chains across the country.

Be able to succinctly summarize the appeal of a particular article or book. Why do so many people swarm to buy *The Celestine Prophecy*? Answer, millions are looking for fulfillment in their daily lives and want the insights in this best-selling work of fiction. What about *In the Kitchen With Rosie?* Answer, people identify with Oprah Winfrey's weight loss and want to learn from the cook that helped the talk show host get svelte. *Men Are From Mars, Women Are From Venus?* Both sexes want to improve their relationships and want to know why they themselves so often have been misunderstood.

Here's a great exercise. Take a best-seller, any best-seller. Read it, study it. Then try to reslant the book's main premise without stealing the idea, putting your own experiences and particular expertises into a fresh new project. That is precisely what many Rodale Press writers must do. They are to look at the health books that earned millions for the company, repackage health information in some fresh new way, and write up proposals for future books.

Try to develop the qualities that enable the best book and magazine writers to consistently come up with blockbuster ideas. Like creators of inventions, such writers always ask, "What if?" What if I yoked that concept with this one? What if I went to every city and town in America named Buffalo and wrote about it? (I did the latter about fifteen years ago.) What if I spent a season with a particular coach and his team? (John Feinstein's book about Bob Knight's Indiana Hoosiers, *A Season on the Brink*, had many imitators.)

To see what is unique, first figure out what is unique about you. Make a long list of life experiences that have made you the person you are and make you see things in a way different from someone else. Here, for example, is my list:

- Reared Catholic and attended a seminary for priests.
- Flirted with delinquency as a youth and was expelled from high school.
- Have traveled extensively in forty-nine of fifty states. (Any one care to send me to Hawaii?)
- Have been divorced and had children by two women.
- Have known people who were murdered.
- Have been present as a reporter at the first Woodstock and a Washington peace march (where I was caught in an area where teargas was released).
- Have interviewed many notable sports figures.

- Have worked in steel mills and a printing plant.
- Have a passion for going off the beaten path in winter on snowshoes.
- Have helped my wife through my son Adam's birth.
- Have once lost sixty pounds in a two-year period and didn't regain them.
- Have a fear of heights.
- Have been homeless.
- Have formed a collection of authors, poets and playwrights on postage stamps.
- Have been stomped by plainclothes detectives in Buffalo, New York, when I tried to help an elderly suspect they were kicking.
- Have seen someone severely injured in a hazing incident.
- Have been painfully shy. For example, in the sixties I refused to approach Olympic athlete Jesse Owens when he came to a gymnasium at Buffalo State College where I was working as a student-athlete, because I was intimidated by his accomplishments.

Each of these individual experiences suggests ideas for magazine articles for me; the last two experiences have resulted in books—*Broken Pledges* and a future biography on Jesse Owens for teenagers.

Make no mistake about it: You have had experiences that will give you insights only you can have, and that other people would pay money to read about. Look beyond the obvious. Have you written a dissertation or a senior honors thesis? Do you love reunions? Are you an expert tea taster? Have you overcome an addiction? Do you have access to a famous personality? Were you a part of history in some way? Self-awareness is the first big step toward awareness in general, in my opinion. Knowing why you think as you do because of the experiences you've had is the first step toward identifying potential great ideas.

Because I'd never taken a writing class and self-help writing books were far less sophisticated in the late sixties, I began to teach myself to write by studying great writers who were my contemporaries. The nonfiction writing of Truman Capote, in particular, made me breathless, and for a time, I thought *In Cold Blood* was the most perfect book ever written. Having taught the book to both undergraduate and graduate students many times, I've come to see the book's flaws. Nonetheless, Capote's ability to set a scene, to create suspense and a mood of horror, and to make his villains accessible to readers has seldom been matched.

From time to time I teach classes such as one on writing about the arts at IUPUI (Indiana University-Purdue University at Indianapolis), because it reminds me how important it is to read the work of my betters to see how they take a single big idea and carry it all the way through a book. I never fail to marvel, for example, at author John McPhee's ability to establish and keep reader attention when writing about offbeat subjects like oranges and birchbark canoes.

I'm not recommending that you copy the style of McPhee or any of your own literary heroes and heroines. To do so wouldn't work anyway and would make your writing sound forced and unnatural. What I am recommending is that you take apart a book and examine the stripped-down parts to envision how a paragraph relates to the work as a whole. Compare the writing in the beginning of the book to the writing at the end. Be able to identify the author's style of writing and check what you've observed against the writing in the author's later books to see how even brilliant writers like McPhee or Gay Talese get better as they age.

These are some questions to ask yourself when you study the better writers:

- What does the author want to do in a particular chapter?
- How does an individual chapter relate to the larger work?
- When did you start to feel yourself get really involved? How did the author make you feel so involved?
- After marking five paragraphs at random in a book, ask yourself what these sections individually accomplish in the book. Can you find anything superfluous? Where is each particular paragraph headed in the book? Is it in there for drama, suspense, information, character revelation?
- Focus on two or three individuals who appear in the book. How does the author introduce major and minor people? Is there a change from how they are first presented and the way you view them later in the book? If so, why is this so?
- Catch yourself when you start to nod off in a section. What

has failed to keep your attention? Be specific. Is the writing aimless here? Has the author become long-winded or preachy? Is there too much exposition or description without action verbs?

WHAT IF YOU'RE NOT THE FIRST TO HAVE AN IDEA?

Some people worry needlessly that they cannot write a book or even a magazine article unless they are 100 percent certain that an idea they have is theirs, and theirs alone. That is self-defeating and wrong to boot. Because Dave Thomas didn't invent hamburgers didn't mean that he couldn't make millions off them. Because several people have an idea for conquering the AIDS virus doesn't mean that no one else should contemplate a cure.

It is infinitely more important to perfect an idea than to be the first with an idea. Untold billions of ideas have been born and died in the minds of people who failed to take their ideas past the concept stage. There is always room for a better diet book, for example, even though thousands have already been published.

STUDYING INDUSTRY TRENDS

Rather than lament the publishing days of old like some hard-drinking, latterday Miniver Cheevy, the writers who survived the magazine industry shakeups of a decade ago were those who saw a way to turn the trend to their advantage. For me that meant becoming an expert in areas such as health, fitness, sports, entertainment, education, writing and performance-enhancing drugs.

You too must think like an industry professional, devouring publications in the industry such as *Folio:*, *Writer's Digest* and one of several newsletters for writers. Keep up with hirings and firings on the editorial side, knowing that ground-floor opportunities for writers always present themselves when a new team comes aboard at a publication.

Similarly, keep an eye out for freelance opportunities at start-up publications. I subscribe to the *New York Times*'s city edition (not national edition), not only to keep up with the arts, sports and news, but also to read the publishing want ads from new and forthcoming magazines for freelance writers and editors. In fact, one of my first magazine freelance opportunities back in the sixties came from responding to an ad for humor writers from Dell Publishing's magazine division—a relationship with its *Cracked* magazine ended up lasting four years and did much to help support me in graduate school.

National trends in other areas also have an effect on publishing. The increase in the number of households owning Macintoshes and personal computers has led to the proliferation of computer periodicals and giant computer book companies such as Indianapolis-based Que. The mania for sports and the market for sports paraphernalia and trading cards is reflected not only in the wide number of sporting publications for adults, but also in the popularity of magazines for juveniles such as *Sports Illustrated for Kids.* The problems with the economy have caused a boom in the number of magazines that offer investment advice. The fact that airlines get so much traffic from business travelers has caused in-flight magazines to stop emphasizing general-interest subjects and to offer service pieces slanted toward businessmen and -women.

You must become a creative thinker. Read the news and know how current events likely will cause reverberations in the world of publishing. When a publication folds or loses circulation, ask yourself why and come to informed conclusions. The satellite television industry was in dire trouble in 1988 through 1990, putting satellite magazines in danger and causing several editorial changes. However, with the proliferation of cable channels and smaller low-cost dishes, the industry again became strong by 1993. That fact translated into hard dollars for writers who had kept abreast of publishing developments.

With Democrats in power and their history of supporting the arts, I thought it was a good time to come to *Arts Indiana* in 1993. However, as this book goes into its final stages in 1995, the new Republican majority in Congress is making growling noises about slashing funds to the National Endowment for the Arts (NEA) and similar government-supported agencies. This ripple effect, most certainly, could have a deleterious effect on arts magazines such as *Arts Indiana* which—in addition to subscriber and advertising dollars and the generous support from its publisher and other benefactors—depends on the funding it gets from the NEA-linked Indiana Arts Commission. While it is too early to predict what will happen here with certainty, I can say that our publication is doing all that it can to support the NEA and to bring awareness of the need for the arts to the public at large.

What do industry trends mean for you and other writers? You can lament changes in the publishing industry, but you must react to them in order to survive and prosper. As a freelancer I have attended several farewell parties sponsored by publications that had gone out of business. I now have adopted a "forewarned is forearmed" philosophy. So should you.

MASTERING THE ART OF SPIN-OFFS

Every time you tackle an assignment, try to visualize three to five other magazines that might buy a "spin-off" of the original article from you. A spin-off means selling material unused in your primary piece to another publication for additional moneys.

For example, a 1986 visit with then-San Francisco 49er coach Bill Walsh for an *Inside Sports* profile also resulted in an article on the team's conditioning program for a health magazine, a piece on Walsh's coping with changes in the game at midlife for *Dynamic Years*, a humor-heavy profile of Walsh for the *Saturday Evening Post*, and a television tie-in piece for *Satellite Orbit*. One visit to the coach meant $3,500 in the bank—not counting the money I would later get using the material in my *Strategies of the Great Football Coaches*.

You can increase your freelance income many times over if you are willing to wrap and rewrap the presentation of words in metaphorical new gift paper and bows. Some specialties will always be in vogue at certain times of the year. Your research on changes in tax legislation, for example, theoretically could appear in dozens of different magazines come April simply by changing the slant of each piece to the requirements of the various readerships. Whether the magazine is geared for writers, antiques dealers, airline travelers, doctors, service veterans, fraternal or service organization members, or regional publication subscribers, there is a way to reformat a piece on taxes to make it appeal to specific readers.

The same possibilities for spin-offs apply, to say, an article on ways to avoid carpal tunnel syndrome, the bane of many persons who use a computer, and therefore a natural for the readers of a plethora of publications for computer users in any number of fields. That's for starters. You then also could sell spin-offs to any number of trade publications whose readers are susceptible to carpal tunnel syndrome. Ethically, the only thing you must do is make certain your article doesn't appear in competing magazines until the original buyer has run it.

Exploring Secondary Sales

If there is one thing better than getting paid for writing an article, it's having a second or third publication pay you a fee to reprint the article. Some writers, such as Idaho-based Louis Bignami, have turned the art of selling a piece multiple times into a profitable sideline.

The possibility of an article being reprinted by a magazine or an electronic reprint corporation such as SIRS is why writers always should only sell "one-time rights" to a publication. If you sell all rights to a piece you write, you cannot turn around and offer it to other publications who, with slight changes in the manuscript, would want to pay you small fees to reprint what you've written for someone else.

Ethically, you must be upfront about offering pieces for sale that have appeared elsewhere. If a magazine buys only first North American rights, you should not waste that magazine's time or yours by trying to get it to reprint what's appeared elsewhere.

SHOWCASING YOUR WORK IN A PORTFOLIO

The writer who develops several specialties, as I have, needs to have several portfolios on hand. A portfolio is a sturdy binder containing see-through sheets. Any supply store for artists, architects or engineers should contain a well-stocked selection of portfolios.

These binders keep examples of your work protected and reduce the chances that you'll lose something or see it damaged. More important, a portfolio serves as an oversized key to unlock the doors at national magazines that have never heard of you. I use these portfolios on my visits to editors along with a folder filled with article ideas. Over the years I've visited publications in such farflung locales as Emmaus, Pennsylvania (Rodale Press); Hailey, Idaho (former home of CommTek's *Satellite Orbit*); Columbus, Ohio (*CompuServe* magazine); and Dublin, New Hampshire (*Yankee Magazine*), as well as the traditional publishing centers of New York, Los Angeles and Chicago.

Portfolios provide instant credibility with busy editors who can assess your range of coverage, writing ability and expertise at first meeting. I also find that the portfolio helps me to get story assignments that an editor has been hoping to give to the right writer. Time and again something clicks when an editor sees my clippings, and I'll get an assignment then and there—or a phone call down the line—to do an assignment that requires my particular expertise.

Never Put Your Work in a Scrapbook

Let me note what a portfolio is *not*. A portfolio is not a scrapbook. Don't make the mistake I made early in my career by pasting your hard-to-replace clippings in a scrapbook. You'll need to slip these in and out of protective sheets for easy photocopying when you send writing samples with your queries.

A scrapbook looks amateurish and earns you the treatment that editors reserve for amateurs. The sooner everything you do is done in a professional way, the sooner editors will treat you with the respect they reserve for pros.

I own six binders. Some have handles so that they are easier to carry. All of them have the best quality sheets I can buy, because the cheap ones tend to tear after a couple dozen people have thumbed through them. I use one portfolio for sports pieces, another for health and fitness, another for the arts, one for scholarly writing, and one made up strictly of profiles. I also have one portfolio that I keep blank and fill with computer articles, education pieces, or general-interest features—depending on the idea I'm pitching to an editor during a personal visit.

Opting for Oversized Portfolios

My personal recommendation as an editor and writer is that you purchase oversized portfolios. For years I carried a small 9″ × 12″ portfolio, but I noticed something untoward happening again and again. Editors flipped too quickly through my book without pausing even to read my leads. Their eyes left the words, drawn to the art and layouts that *Outside, Inside Sports* or some other magazine had used to make my pieces jump off the page. That did me no good whatsoever. I needed editors to slow down and actually *read* my work or I had little chance of their giving me an assignment or two.

My solution, made out of desperation, was to purchase an oversized portfolio. This worked far more to my advantage. The eye-catching spreads still intrigued editors, but now they were able to see an entire article instead of just the opening pages. I found myself rarely leaving a new editorial office without some kind of commitment from an editor.

Here are a couple more portfolio tips:

• Stop clippings from slipping in the portfolio sheets (thereby making them harder for editors to read and less visually appealing) by keeping them in place with easily removable hinges available at any store that sells stamps to collectors. Never glue your clips to a page. Editors frequently pull out pages to photocopy so that they can read them after I depart. Samples glued to oversized portfolio pages are hard to fit in many copiers.

• Be sure to get an extra magazine when you publish a piece and keep a separate set of clippings in a safe place outside your office in case of a fire or flood. In the event of a catastrophe or in the unlikely event that an editor loses a portfolio you've been asked to leave for a day or two (a practice I dislike immensely as a writer), you'll be able to construct a new portfolio.

• Put your address and phone number in a prominent place inside the portfolio in the event it does get separated from you.

• Replace plastic sheets if they get torn or soiled. Damaged sheets jump out like clothes stained with food. Neither are appropriate at interviews with editors.

• When you have the money, buy portfolios that look impressive to you. If you feel good about the way you've showcased your work, chances are you'll be more animated and confident during presentations to editors.

Having well-organized and professional-looking portfolios is important to project the image you wish to create of yourself as a poised and prepared professional.

THE ROLE OF PHOTOGRAPHY

Although I find that carrying a camera interferes slightly with my note-taking and concentration when interviewing someone, I nonetheless will bring along a 35mm camera on an assignment to take color slides or black-and-white photographs as needed. Many small magazines, including *Arts Indiana*, like to use writers who can supply pictures with articles. In fact, for many outdoor magazines, writers who can't take decent pictures find themselves at a distinct disadvantage with editors.

At *Arts Indiana*, in addition to saving the costs of sending a photographer out with a writer, I like the fact that I'll be getting photographs that have direct bearing on the story I've assigned. All too often, when photographers accompany writers or go out on their own, they send back pictures that seem to have no relation to the story that's been assigned. When writers take the photographs, they may not be as technically proficient, but at least there's no question that the photos they take belong in a particular piece.

Now and again it happens that when I go out on an assignment a photographer will accompany me. I've had the poor fortune to work with a couple of boors who worked against me on the piece, distracting my subjects and interfering with my note-taking. More often, however, I have worked with famous photographers like Max Aguilera Hellweg who enhanced my own performance. From them I learned that ideas can be visual. I learned to see people and places from odd angles and different perspectives. I became sensitive to the way a mountain or field of sagebrush looked different at various times of the day. And most of all, I was sometimes shocked, a week or so after finishing an assignment when I viewed his photographs and saw all that I had missed.

Working with a photographer can teach you the value of appreciating subtleties and nuances while you're on an assignment. Looking at a story from different camera angles can teach you new ways of focusing a story, too. Moreover, more often than not a photographer will ask a subject a question that is crucial to understanding that person. In such cases, I feel terribly humble, but that's all right—having a little humility makes you always aware that there is a need to improve your professional techniques.

CHAPTER THREE

Research and Interview Like an Expert

Duman Behavior,uring my tenure as a senior health writer for Rodale
Press, I conducted research on such esoteric topics
as osteoporosis, cystitis, Crohn's Disease and other
maladies that I could hardly define at the outset, but
ended up writing about with authority. I've written about the
dynamics of group behavior for *Human Behavior*, on the dangers
of electromagnetic fields for *The Nation*, and on various sports
medicine topics as a contributing writer for *Men's Fitness*.

What I do to make a living as a freelance writer is what you
must do no matter if your subject is in the area of science, health,
psychology, sociology, religion, sports medicine or any other
field you care passionately about. Bit by bit, nugget by nugget,
you must educate yourself on the subject at hand until you know
as much as anyone else—and preferably more. The only way to
do so is to conduct research and interview authorities until you
feel you could write an article or book on the subject—then
you do. Because your writing will contain your own unique
experiences, perceptions and knowledge—in addition to the
facts you uncover—you will have the satisfaction of knowing
that no one can inform and educate your audience in quite the
same way that you can.

RESEARCHING UNDER THE PRESSURE OF A DEADLINE
Research is always—repeat, *always*—slow and laborious (but
not unpleasant) work. Eventually, as you will learn later in this
chapter, you must streamline the process by taking advantage of
print and electronic sources to make the most of your limited
time. If you are writing for publication, you must deal with the
demands and pressures of performing with a deadline hanging

over you and your keyboard. I won't patronize you by trying to say deadlines are our friends. They are a source of stress for all of us. But you can and must work without letting them paralyze you.

The best way to beat a deadline is to set up many small deadlines for yourself. There are two ways to do this. One way is to set a per-hour rate for your work. If you demand twenty-five dollars per hour, and an editor offers you one thousand dollars to write an article, that means you can spend forty hours total on research, writing and rewriting. If it takes you eight hours to write a piece, and you allow two hours for any rewriting your editor may require, you are left with thirty hours to do research and conduct interviews. The deadline your editor has given you, plus the demands of whatever other assignments you've undertaken, will tell you how to apportion your time.

If you want to make a business out of your writing, you must get editors to give you fees that reimburse you for time spent doing research, or you must forsake assignments that give you too little financial return for your working hours. It is important to know roughly how much time is required to do a piece prior to sending a query article to a magazine. If an editor gets a proposal for a piece from you, the understanding is that you know how long it will take you to get it done. By having a ballpark estimate of the amount of time you'll need to get the necessary information, you'll better be able to negotiate a fee with an editor, as well as prevent the possibility of taking on more assignments than you can do justice to.

Estimate all of the time you'll need for research, including phone calls, library and computer work, interviews and tape transcriptions, tracking down photographs and illustrations (unless the publication does that for you), and so forth. Add to that the amount of time you think you'll need for writing and doing at least one rewrite. You'll find that it all adds up fast, but if you have any doubts about your ability to give time to a project, it's better for you to deal with your misgivings prior to giving a commitment to a publisher.

It's even more crucial to keep track of the Big Picture when writing a book. It is, of course, immensely easier to write one if you're a full-time freelance writer, as opposed to being a freelance writer by night and a wage slave by day. But I've written books under both conditions, and so can you.

It's important to break a large project into manageable segments. Give yourself a series of deadlines for research, interviewing and writing, claiming small rewards when you meet them. Ideally, writing full time, I would ask my editor to give me one full year start-to-finish for a self-help book, and two-and-a-half years for a biography or book-length work requiring investigative journalism. Your pace may be faster or slower than mine.

Whether writing an article or book, I construct daily goals. For example, I might tell myself, today I'll write 1,500 words, or I'll interview five subjects. If you're like me, you'll function best if you give yourself small rewards for meeting goals. The rewards you give yourself depend upon your own circumstances. Maybe it's nothing more than the freedom to visit the mall and buy a book. Maybe it's a telephone break or a chance to take the dog for a run. Or, when you're really successful and have finished a project, maybe it's a vacation trip somewhere. Whatever suits you and works.

I should note that the time I allot to a project is never exactly what I'd planned it to be; estimating writing and research time isn't the same as planning to lay a floor or paint a room.

Sometimes it will take you a little less time to do a piece than you had estimated, sometimes a little longer.

The occasions when I've found myself under severe stress as a writer occurred when a project demanded far more research than I had thought it would, giving me about the same pay I might have made peddling hot dogs at a baseball game. With experience, however, I've learned to acquire better instincts and have shown the courage to say no to projects that show evidence of being less than cost-effective.

You will find it enlightening to keep track of the time you spend doing research so that in the future you can make educated estimates on the amount of research you'll need to complete a project.

Always look for ways to save time. For example, keep file cards (or a computer entry) on reference books you've consulted to reduce the amount of time you spend online at the library scanning the card catalog. Prior to going to a library I arm myself with notecards so that I can go straight to the stacks to pull out reference books that I've used on prior occasions.

You'll come up with your own ways of streamlining your research, and it's very important that you do so. You must consider the number of hours it will take you to do research before you send out a query or accept an assignment an editor offers you. Never offer to do work you cannot realistically accept if it is assigned you.

Unproductive Research

Much of the time spent doing research may seem unproductive. You read a lot of background material that you never put into your own work. But the time spent getting a handle on your subject is usually not wasted. The acquisition of facts, statistics and knowledge is necessary before you can begin to see insights and trends that will make your piece different from all that have come before.

I suggest that you keep notes about your responses to important new bits of information. Later, this will help you put yourself into the place of your uninformed reader. For example, let's say that you're writing a chapter on the benefits of exercise for a health book aimed at aging baby boomers. In a notebook keep track of key pieces of information as you find them. Then, when you are in the process of writing, you can look at these notes and put yourself in the mindset of a reader. Otherwise, without such a control, you can make the mistake of writing over the head of your reader, something that experts who are not professional writers primarily have a tendency to do when they write for a general audience.

Almost certainly you'll spend far more time doing unproductive research in the beginning stages of your career. Until you get a sense of the library reference books you consistently need, for example, you'll waste time going to the wrong shelves and perusing the wrong reference books.

ENVISION YOUR TASK

No matter what the topic, my starting point to obtain information is always the same. I envision how much labor actually has to go into the project—as well as budgetary limitations depending upon the size of my book advance or the expenses I've negotiated with a magazine editor.

For instance, I intend to begin research for a novel for the young adult market about a Borzoi and his young master, a serf who trained him, that is set during the bloody unrest in St. Petersburg, Russia, in 1905. I'd love to be able to take a costly trip to the former Soviet Union to visualize everything I write about, but the expense would be too great for the return. No matter, I am confident that I'll be able to give young readers a book that will have nearly the same authenticity as if I had spent a year abroad. By carefully using the research facilities at the Library of Congress (in one or two trips to Washington, DC), the wonderful public library in downtown Indianapolis (a few blocks from my *Arts Indiana* office), and the reference books at Indiana University, I am certain that I can get a vivid picture of cataclysmic life in St. Petersburg in 1905.

Other writers on a budget often write about places they've only visited in their minds. For example, historical romance writer Rosemary Rogers was a secretary when she set her breakthrough novel, *Sweet Savage Love*, in Mexico without actually traveling there. "I talked to several close friends who were born and brought up in Mexico," she once told me in an interview published in my *Rendezvousing With Contemporary Authors*. "I just got a feeling for the place. I looked up books, old maps, geographies, and I found that the coast of Mexico was very similar to Ceylon [her birthplace]. Several people have asked me, 'Oh, when did you live in Mexico?' I say to them, 'I didn't.' [But] I was very careful, even to know what plants were growing there [and] geography, what the climate was like, as many pictures as I could find."

THE WRITING BEGINS

If I had all the money in the world and no day job, I might have another problem to deal with as a freelance writer: researching too long before putting a word down on paper.

Many writers freeze up and find themselves over-researching. If you wait until you know everything there is to know about a subject before you write it, your project is in trouble because you'll never know everything. You'll either be emotionally incapable of starting, or will start and restart the same project over from new angles until you lose interest in it.

It has been my experience that trying to complete all research before beginning a first draft inhibits my writing rather than enhancing it. You probably know people who have told you they have been researching some subject for years, but who have yet to get a word down on paper. The halls of academia are littered with untenured professors who never seemed to be able to publish a word in their fields after earning doctorates, even though they knew their subject thoroughly and held their classes spellbound with the knowledge they possessed.

All of these people—at least those who are clear thinkers—could have completed their respective writing projects had they not self-destructed by either over-researching or by convincing themselves that they were unworthy to write word one until they read just one more authority's book (and then another, and then another). I'm not mocking such people, I have a tendency to over-research myself. The difference is that I do eventually write my books because I know that I can be conscientious without being conscientious to a fault—that being professional suicide.

REASONABLE EXPECTATIONS

Even if I were doing a nonfiction book called *All About Vegetables*, I'd know before I started that there is no way I can possibly know it *all*, in spite of that imposing title. Even if I could exhaust the topic in a single volume—which I couldn't—I know my readers wouldn't want to wade through a four-thousand-page horticultural version of the Torah just to plant cukes and zukes. Put another way, no "Complete Guide" to any subject is ever really complete—otherwise writers would never actually complete such projects.

On the other hand, I do have a "dream" project that I want to write that could take three full years to research properly. It's a biography of a major American figure who lived to be nearly one hundred and was active all his life. Nonetheless, after I've gotten two or three months into the research, I'm certain that I would already begin putting words down on paper, getting the facts of his birth down, for starters.

Do begin writing some text once you've found materials that you see as essential to include in the book. Don't wait until you *are* an expert before you begin writing like one.

On a happier note, I have found that quite often the over-researching I may do on an assignment gets used in some future assignment. By keeping good files, I'm often able to sell future stories on the basis of research I've already done. For example, much of the information I gathered on the binge drinking of adolescent and college students during my research for *Broken Pledges* wasn't used in the book, but I've saved it all because I intend to do some magazine pieces on the subject.

Whenever possible, though, I try to be realistic with my time while doing research. Because my book *Steroids* was to target only the adolescent market, I could keep it relatively short—only 125 pages. It took two months of intense, full-time research, far less than the years of research required to write the far-more demanding *Broken Pledges*. The writing took me ten months in between teaching and writing approximately thirty magazine pieces during the same time period.

BACKGROUND READING

After I made a realistic estimate of how much work my project on steroids was going to take to research and write, I began looking for what was currently available on the topic of perform-ance-enhancing drugs. I conducted such research via an online computer base and at the library, eventually coming away with several thick folders of articles that doctors, researchers and other health experts had written. Then I made myself comfortable, made sure the coffeepot was full, and read and reread all I had gathered.

The second time through the material, I began outlining the chapters that I intended to write. I also began scribbling question after question that I later planned to ask the medical experts who wrote the papers in my folders.

Much of this information I culled from journals was remote and technical—often poorly written and organized—seemingly fashioned by experts who thought writing clear prose was be-neath them. On the other hand, a few journal articles were clear, concise and marvelously structured. I took no shortcuts here, reading the badly written and the well written, afraid of missing some nugget that might be the highlight of the book I was writ-ing. I scanned all the material, reread whatever was pertinent, digested it and set up interviews with the journal authors—the mechanics of which I'll discuss a little later.

WHERE TO GET INFORMATION

To achieve the status of expert, you must have access to many sources of information to become as knowledgeable as you can. Think of your article or your book as a gigantic puzzle with all the pieces spread, not on a table in your living room, but inside miscellaneous databases, the Internet, CD-ROMs, library reference and publications rooms, government information agencies, research universities and in the minds of those who possess information you need to obtain. Some pieces are in plain view; others are in obscure locales. To miss some of these pieces is to frame and hang a puzzle with holes everywhere for your readers to see. Writing pros have too much pride to accept such humiliation.

Something magical happens each time you do a new book. You gain knowledge and confidence and expertise. Your prose starts to get tighter and your style shines through. You have connected with other experts, librarians and fellow researchers so that you can claim a network of sources—primary and secondary—that you can plug into for knowledge. In time you find, after you publish your work, that other writers are calling you for help to find information. When that happens, you begin to feel like an expert—and you are.

Libraries: Books and More

Twice I've been to the main Indianapolis public library this week to do research for *Arts Indiana*, and neither time did I check out any books. In one case I needed information on Ross Lockridge, Jr., the Indiana author who committed suicide in the late forties while his *Raintree County* was atop the fiction bestseller lists. In the second case I needed to find background on screenwriter Angelo Pizzo (*Rudy*) to send to a writer who was interviewing him for us. My solution was to ask to see the library's "vertical file"—a collection of news clippings, pamphlets and miscellaneous documents—on "Indiana writers." The same vertical file on writers produced eight or ten usable clippings about Lockridge and Pizzo. The point is that it isn't enough to do research merely by reading books as you may have done writing college research papers.

Public, academic (college and university), and one-subject libraries are repositories of many types of information. There are thousands of one-subject libraries in the country, like Rodale's health and nature/outdoor/gardening libraries; the Domino's Pizza corporate library in Ann Arbor, Michigan; and the Baseball Hall of Fame library in Cooperstown, New York. For their listings see reference books by R.R. Bowker (*Subject Collections*) and Gale Research (*Subject Directory of Special Libraries*). A few, like the Rodale library in Emmaus, Pennsylvania, are off limits unless you are a freelancer or staffer doing work for the company.

Corporate libraries such as Domino's evaluate requests to use their facilities on an individual basis. Most university libraries allow you to come and go as you please. Some, like the Vanderbilt University library in Tennessee, charge admission for nonstudents to use the facility. Others, particularly private institutions such as the Cornell University library, require visitors to explain their research needs and give access if the research is deemed legitimate. On occasion I have even visited the libraries and morgues of large newspapers to seek information, writing the librarians to explain my research needs instead of popping in uninvited.

Rarely will you research a magazine piece (and never a book) without using the facilities of one or more libraries. In addition to accessing vertical files and checking out books at libraries, you can access periodicals, use interlibrary loan services, do CD-ROM and database searches, examine government publications, and pore over manuscript collections. If you're having trouble finding specialized information, you can phone or write the Chicago-based Association of College and Research Libraries, a division of the American Library Association, 50 Huron St., Chicago, IL 60611, (312) 944-6780, for assistance.

If you need information from a library outside your area, don't despair. Simply write the reference librarian with your question and attach a stamped envelope with your address on it. I've never failed to get a quick, courteous, informed response. I always put in a note saying how much I am willing to pay if I need something photocopied. Of course, common courtesy demands that I never ask a librarian to do something that can't be done in five, ten or fifteen minutes tops. I often have had to drive or fly to perform research in the Library of Congress, for example, because I needed materials that took me days to locate and photocopy.

Some libraries publish guides to their facilities, holdings and manuscript collections and will give or sell you one upon request. The University of Colorado Norlin Library, for example, publishes a guide to its Western Historical Collections.

Paper and Electronic Chases

Back in caveman days like the late 1980s, searching for information in various print sources was a long, laborious process. No more. Many library reference rooms now carry a wide variety of indexes and source materials on CD-ROMs so that you can get information efficiently. There are a number of useful books available on the topic of research. Particularly useful to me while teaching research methods to Ball State University journalism students in the mid-eighties was a reference work called *Knowing Where to Look: The Ultimate Guide to Research* by Lois Horowitz.

Also, if you have much to learn about research methods, you can reduce your frustration by asking a reference librarian to assist you in locating some indispensable sources of information such as the *Readers' Guide to Periodical Literature* (which indexes nearly 250 magazines), *Business Periodical Index* (a guide to what's in some 350 magazines), and specialized indexes (*Art Index, Biography Index, Education Index, Engineering Index, General Science Index, Humanities Index, Index to Legal Periodicals, Social Sciences Index*, the *New York Times Obituaries Index*). There also are thousands of special directories on subjects such as journalism, law, and arts and entertainment; Gale Research Company's *Directories in Print* gives you the addresses and phone numbers of nearly sixteen thousand directories.

Other valuable reference books are the various Marquis Who's Whos, containing thumbnail sketches of the lives of prominent persons. Look up a name in *Index to Who's Who Books* and you'll find out if it is located in one of the more than a dozen Who's Whos such as *Who's Who in America* and regional compilations such as *Who's Who in the East.*

Many of the country's large newspapers put out indexes that are useful in looking up keywords like someone's name or a specific subject; the granddaddy of them all is the *New York Times Index*, particularly useful because your librarian likely can provide you with a microfilm to read whatever articles you've selected. However, I also used indexes put out by the New Orleans

Times-Picayune, the Los Angeles *Times* and the Chicago *Tribune* to get important information used in *Broken Pledges*.

For business articles, my two indispensable sources are the *Wall Street Journal Index* and the Funk & Scott Index, the latter indexing a wide range of industry periodicals. Other important reference books about business and industry are the Dun & Bradstreet *Million Dollar Directory*, providing alphabetical information on any company you're likely to write about, and *Standard & Poor's Register of Corporations, Directors and Executives* and *Ward's Business Directory*, useful guides to anyone who is anyone in industry.

In trying to track the more than thirty authors I've interviewed such as George Plimpton, playwright David Mamet and Norman Mailer, I've found it useful to examine a number of reference books listing authors such as *International Authors & Writers Who's Who* and Gale Research's *Contemporary Authors*. The latter publication lists personal information such as date of birth, education and marital status, a current address, writings, work-in-progress, biographical and critical sources, and quotable quotations.

The entry for one Hank Nuwer, in Volume 128 of *Contemporary Authors*, reads as follows: "I've never taken a journalism or creative writing class in college, but I took several literature classes from Professor Fraser Drew at Buffalo State College. Drew was not only a fine teacher but a scholar who went to Cuba to interview Ernest Hemingway and to Vermont to interview Robert Frost. Drew's classes electrified me and gave me direction, and when he also liked and encouraged my embryonic scribblings, my life's course was set. I either had to become a writer or an outlaw. Every other career seemed too tame."

Finding Experts

It isn't very difficult to learn where experts work so you can contact them. (The hard part is using all your resources to convince busy people to give you their valuable time.) Their research papers and books list their professional affiliations with universities or other institutions. Even if the person has left an institution, you can call the personnel department or their former division to get a forwarding address. Another good starting point for finding experts is to contact professional associations listed in the *Ency-*

clopedia of Associations. All of them have staff members trained to assist authors and journalists who need to contact people in their profession. Another method is to contact the public information bureaus of universities that grant doctorates in the area you are researching; all have to be familiar with the research specialties of professors on their campuses. Another helpful way to find scholars, particularly those at the beginnings of their careers, is to go to a research library's reference room to see what doctoral research has been done on a particular topic. Not only can you get the names of researchers and their topics through a service provided by University Microfilms International (UMI) Dissertation Information Service, but you also can purchase the dissertations themselves from the company. They can access almost every doctoral dissertation accepted by a legitimate institution in North America since 1861. You must, of course, respect any copyright restrictions that a particular dissertation writer may have imposed on the doctoral research.

COVERING ALL THE (DATA)BASES

In today's world of rapidly emerging technologies, you have no choice but to learn how to locate and extract information as quickly and skillfully as you can. At the risk of stating the obvious, you must acquire computer skills to perform research today. Any time you save during the research process is all the more time you'll have to polish your prose. For example, it behooves you to have the most powerful modem (an invention that converts computer digital signals to telephone line analog tone signals) you can afford to enable you to access databases from libraries and private information services to get information quickly and efficiently while you're working in your home office.

Be it facts, charts, statistics, biographical information, legal statutes or whatever, writers-cum-researchers must know how to get what they need. While writers always run into experienced reference librarians (Bless 'em!) to render help, having the good fortune to locate these people is far too much a hit-or-miss process to rely upon throughout one's career. You have no choice but to become an expert researcher. I happen to love research, but I don't know that you have to love doing it to do it right. You do need to be methodical, thorough and unrelenting.

Few libraries in major cities today are found without computer terminals containing CD-ROM drives to run laser-coded discs similar to the discs you have at home for music. The library CD-ROMs can store the equivalent of one thousand books more or less. Some have the full text of periodical articles, while others have abstracts. As you get comfortable using CD-ROMs, you no doubt will find some that you rely on more than others.

Costs now have come down to the point where you will want to purchase a CD-ROM reader and compatible CD-ROM discs. Most likely you'll start with a multimedia encyclopedia put out by one of the mega-companies such as Grolier, Inc., or a reference tool like the U.S. Government Manual containing valuable phone numbers for agencies and departments. A valuable library reference book is Gale Research's *Gale Directory of Databases*, updated frequently, which will introduce you to some fifteen hundred CD-ROMs.

Even if you have trouble running a computer software program, you should have no trouble extracting information from a CD-ROM. You select a CD-ROM title and read the description that comes onto the terminal screen to make sure you have the right database for the information you need at the moment. You choose a term from the index or enter appropriate keywords such as "melanoma" and "research." A few keystrokes later your search is over and the items are displayed, ready to be printed. You also can just print bibliographic entries and go to the periodicals themselves.

All libraries of any size today use a computerized information system on CD-ROMs put out by Information Access Company under the name of InfoTrac. These CD-ROMs on InfoTrac help researchers investigate what has been published in a wide variety of academic, technical and popular newspapers, magazines and journals. The list of InfoTrac indexes is expanding all the time, but I used, in particular, the *Health Index* and *Health Reference Center* while I worked for Rodale Press, the *Academic Index* while I wrote scholarly articles as a college professor, *Magazine Index Plus* to help me do basic research to write query letters, and the *National Newspaper Index* to help me track hazing incidents.

Another maker of CD-ROMs, University Microfilms, has been useful, allowing me to purchase doctoral dissertations in hardcopy form (your librarian has an order blank) which would otherwise be difficult for me to obtain. The company also puts out

CD-ROMs that index, abstract and provide full text of many newspapers, magazines, business publications and journals on their line of popular databases.

Many libraries carry *Online and CD-ROM Review*'s "*Online Information Retrieval Bibliography*," which has news you need on advances in database retrieval and information that will assist you while doing searches. There also are dozens of satisfactory books available in any library or large bookstore that will take you step by step through the fundamentals of online searches.

What Is a Database?

A database is nothing more than information in terminal-readable form, so don't let the term intimidate you. I use a modem to access an online information network called CompuServe that allows me to search several databases.

I use one database to get the lowest airfares I can, another to find the telephone numbers of potential experts and sources, and several others to do research for the magazine I edit, for my freelance articles, and for my books. These powerful computer searches provide instant responses, whether you need indexes, abstracts, statistical information or directories. Some are put out by private, for-profit companies, others by government institutes and agencies and miscellaneous associations and organizations.

In the early eighties when I first needed database searches done, I always went to libraries and had a reference librarian do the search for me. This was expensive, and as I learned to do the searches, I saw that I often could do them as quickly and sometimes more accurately than the librarians. These libraries would charge me the cost of computer connect time plus a surcharge for items printed out for me. For the hazing book, to find articles on the subject, I did several keyword searches on ERIC, a database of educational research reports, periodicals and other materials collected by the National Institute of Education's Educational Resources Information Center in broad subject areas such as urban education, reading and communication skills, and higher education.

By 1987 my wife—then freelance writing herself—had convinced me that it was cheaper and more convenient to subscribe to an online information service that sold access to various databases than to run off to a library to have searches done. I already had the telephone line and personal computer, all I needed was to purchase software to let me hook up with an online information service, and a modem powerful enough to reduce online time and online usage bills. (However, if you've never done a database search, you may wish to begin by using a library to get the hang of things.)

My only regret is that I didn't hook up with an online vendor sooner. Online information services give me access to international sources that can provide in seconds or minutes information that heretofore required days of laborious research in the library. In addition, I can search at two or three A.M. when I fall out of bed, since I'm not forced to do research during library hours.

Plus, online research is incredibly up to date. For example, my online vendor has a news service that allows me to put down keywords like "fraternity," "initiation" and "hazing." The service automatically routes news stories from wire services, the *Washington Post*, and other papers into a file I've created to keep me abreast of breaking hazing stories. These stories remain in the computer file until I print them and file them for use in future books and magazine stories on hazing that I plan to write. I can also receive stock quotations, getting them a day before I'd get them in a newspaper.

Online Information Systems

For your first online experience, you'll want to choose an online service from one of the large corporations quite willing to bombard you with promotional materials to read. Rather than make a recommendation, I suggest that you read this chapter and perhaps call customer service representatives at the online service companies to get your questions answered before you decide to "subscribe"—that is, pay a monthly fee and additional charges based on usage. Most likely the consumer services that you'll contact will be America Online, CompuServe, Delphi, GEnie and Prodigy. I've given America Online and Prodigy a whirl but have stuck with CompuServe since 1987. From 1988 until 1994, I contributed many articles to *CompuServe* magazine, a service-oriented publication the company sends to its subscribers. Because I have interviewed so many experts, celebrities and writers on CompuServe, I have developed an extremely valuable system of professional contacts through a communications system known as e-mail (electronic mail). (CompuServe and some other online services also allow you to use your account to send electronic mail to Internet members.)

Only by reading the literature of each information service can you decide which one is "best" for your specific needs; you may wish to subscribe to more than one service if you have full-time research needs. You access these systems from your home or your office by dialing their local number via modem, using low-cost software available in all computer shops. The meter starts ticking the minute you dial, so it would behoove you to take advantage of free instructional time that all these services offer their customers.

I also participate in literary debates, on occasion, in Compu-Serve's Literary Forum, Journalism Forum, and miscellaneous forums devoted to health, Macintosh communications systems, and so on. These forums contain an incredible wealth of professional and amateur experts willing to share their expertise online—as I share mine—on a daily basis. I also have assigned several *Arts Indiana* articles to freelance writers in CompuServe's Literary and Journalism forums. In fact, our Atlanta correspondent and main poetry reviewer, Gloria G. Brame, has become a close friend as well as colleague—even though I've never met her in person.

However, because *Arts Indiana* is making expansion plans and our reference needs are becoming more and more complex, I also am looking into more comprehensive, although pricier, systems used by many experts in the fields of journalism and corporate communications. I have used vendor systems such as Dialog and Nexis/Lexis for my freelance career with the assistance of reference librarians, always paying a connect fee for the privilege, and will be using Nexis to perform arts research for *Arts Indiana* soon.

I must stress the importance of using precise keywords when doing an online search to keep from needlessly wasting dollars on extraneous research. With the online meter ticking, you can waste hundreds or thousands of dollars over the course of a year. Always make it a point to do library research before attempting an online search.

Here are the addresses and phone numbers of the major online communications companies. My suggestion is that you write to each for information and choose the one that best serves you in your areas of expertise:

- America Online, 8619 Westwood Center Dr., Vienna VA 22182; (703) 448-8700.
- CompuServe, CompuServe Information Service, P.O. Box 20212, Columbus OH 43220; (800) 848-8990.
- Delphi, 1030 Massachusetts Ave., Cambridge MA 02138; (617) 491-3393.
- Dialog Information Services Inc., 3460 Hillview Ave., Palo Alto CA 94304; (800) 334-2564.
- GEnie, P.O. Box 6403, Rockville MD 20850; (800) 638-9636.
- NewsNet, 945 Haverford Rd., Bryn Mawr PA 19010; (800) 345-1301.
- Nexis Mead Data Central, 9443 Springboro Pike, Dayton OH 45401; (513) 865-6800.
- Prodigy, P.O. Box 791, White Plains NY 10601; (914) 993-8000.

In addition to mastering the new technologies, writers must perform research the old-fashioned way—by digging in libraries. There are many times when crucial information is not found in databases, for one thing, because it fails to show up in keywords. For example, a database search I conducted during the research stages of writing *Broken Pledges* turned up only thirty-three citations on hazing incidents. A great deal of the problem was that the word "hazing" wasn't given much prominence in 1976 when I began my research. It was because of the work of anti-hazing spokespeople—and my book and an NBC-TV movie inspired by my book—that "hazing" became part of the public's vocabulary in the late eighties. In conducting research to publish almost forty pages of hazing incidents in the book's appendix, I relied on traditional methods to uncover deaths and injuries—one at a time—by checking in various sources related words like "initiation," "fraternity," "secret society," "Greek-letter organizations" and so on.

The bottom line is that database searches are important, but it is also necessary for you to perform routine searches in the nearest good public library. I am very budget conscious both as an editor and a freelance writer. I don't believe in paying forty or ninety dollars for information that I can obtain in five minutes by driving to the public library. I do believe in paying for whatever information sources that would otherwise be unavailable.

Moreover, while databases are important to provide facts and analyses, they are next to useless unless employed by writers with the skill to use them in the context of a well-written story.

DRAGGING "THE NET" FOR INFORMATION

Like most professional editors and writers, I depend on the complex and useful web of electronic networks in the world, Internet, linking universities, libraries, database communications vendors and government agencies. As an information link and exchange it is incredible, connecting nearly fifteen thousand networks and more than twenty million people at this writing. Maybe you're more sophisticated than I am, but it boggles my mind to think that my computer in Indianapolis can connect with any one of more than a million computers around the world that are plugged into Internet. Unlike online vendors such as Prodigy and CompuServe, Internet has no home office where all online connections come to roost.

Internet is a direct descendent of a US Department of Defense project begun in 1969 under its Defense Advanced Research Projects Agency [formerly known simply as Advanced Research Projects Agency] branch. Gradually research scientists in universities climbed aboard, as did more and more users who wanted to communicate as well as exchange technical information.

Best of all, most Internet services—including many software packages and services—are free, although there are some pay services you'll find indispensable as well. You also have access to international experts through Internet's online bulletin board via its USENET system. Unfortunately, while it's relatively easy to use CompuServe and other electronic commercial vendors, it takes some people years to feel truly comfortable on Internet. Yet, logging on and off computer connections is no harder than being a traveler on many flights as you make your way around the world.

Signing up on the Internet varies from individual to individual. If you are connected to a university or government research agency, you are aware that all you have to do is get a password from your powers-that-be. If you're not, you'll need to sign up with Delphi or some other online vendor offering Internet access for a fee. Do some shopping and be a smart consumer.

Internet use is too broad a topic to cover accurately here. My local bookstore has two full shelves of books (many of them simplified and easy to understand) devoted to Internet. Because Internet is expanding at such a rapid rate, I hesitate to name one of the half-dozen books I consult regularly, because I'll be using other books even if you read these words six months after this book is published. Be sure to open the book to the copyright page and be sure it's no more than one or two years old before you make a purchase. Also be sure to purchase an elementary book like *The Internet for Dummies* (IDG Books) before you buy a book that the rocket scientist down the street is cribbing from. Things *are* changing that rapidly on Internet. Be sure to familiarize yourself with the following Internet terms to minimize online discomfort:

- Archie: a utility for gaining access to files by name
- Gopher: a utility for giving you a "menu" of options
- Veronica: a means of searching the Gopher menus by using keywords
- WAIS (Wide Area Information Servers): a utility to perform database keyword searches

NARROWING YOUR RESEARCH

Online services provide writers with another benefit. Many of these electronic services, ironically, put out magazines printed on paper that they send to their subscribers as part of the sub-scription package.

Today a magazine editor approved a story idea I submitted a full year ago on professionals who use online forums to get ad-vice on ethical issues. (In the magazine business, such a delay is unusual, but I once had an editor assign me a piece on author Kurt Vonnegut three years after I pitched it.) The editor has given me a deadline, some direction on the piece, and a request for me to create a sidebar to accompany the main piece's word count of two thousand words.

I know that my audience will be made up of highly educated professionals who congregate online in forums devoted to law, education, journalism, healthcare and so on. This tells me the tone and level of the vocabulary I'll use in the piece. My main sources in this article will be those professionals as well. The experts I know in journalism and health care who do not belong to online networks are only of service to me here for background or quotations if they are truly experts in the area of ethics. I plan to "visit" a dozen to twenty forums and leave an online message that asks members in each of these forums what ethical issues they've discussed and resolved after online debate. In a day or two I can count on having fifty to seventy messages waiting for me to read. Some will be cutesy, some insulting, and perhaps ten or fifteen will contain information that I can use in the article or can use to ask additional questions. Anything goes online, and I'm always surprised by the brilliant, foolish, sweet and bitter responses that turn up in my messages when I leave a question for all to read.

In brief, what I'm doing is what all researchers do—I'm narrowing my search, excluding some sources, contacting others. I'll also use various CompuServe databases to do searches on ethical issues in a wide variety of professional fields. I expect, for example, to learn what restrictions photographers have in an era when any digital image can be altered so that photos do, on occasion, lie. I may hear from journalists who are concerned with the ethics of using unnamed sources in their stories, or doctors who want to know whether they should even try to save the lives of brain-dead cardiac victims. The relatively short length of my article means that I won't focus on too many issues since I could never cover them all. If I were doing a book on the topic, however, my database searching would be exhaustive.

The relatively short length of my article and the short deadline of thirty days to finish the piece also helps me limit my search. There is no need for me to do follow-up interviews with fifty professionals on ethics issues when I can likely only quote nine to twelve people in a piece this size. Likewise, I will quote no more than two or three people in a particular profession, since this article is a general treatment on online ethics, not a specialty piece for say, journalists and doctors. However, I definitely have the option of using the information I obtain to write article proposals on online ethics questions for specialty magazines like *The Quill*, a publication put out by the Society of Professional Journalists.

Once I have identified the nine to twelve people (in about six different professions) I'm going to interview online and by phone (in person if they live within fifty miles from my home), I've made the organization of my piece a cinch because my choices naturally break my piece into sections. Remember, if you look at a book or even an article in one big lump, it's harder to envision and write the piece than it would be if you break your book into chapters and your chapters into sections—and your article into sections (or sections and charts and sidebars, if appropriate).

HOW TO FIND EXPERTS

Not until the early eighties did I learn a simple tip from a librarian that saved me considerable time and long-distance expenses in locating experts in various fields. Instead of knocking myself out calling university after university in a sometimes profitable, more often frustrating attempt, I learned that it made more sense to consult Gale Research's *Encyclopedia of Associations* to contact representatives of various associations whose job it is to connect experts in their field with writers, journalists and other interested parties. I have used some of these associations over and over again for assistance in writing my books and articles. A few of these I called repeatedly while with Rodale Press are the American Association for Marriage and Family Therapy, the Academy for Guided Imagery, the Scientists' Institute for Public Information and the Laughter Therapy association.

If you are having trouble locating the precise name of an association, contact the American Society of Association Executives in Washington, DC, at (202) 626-2723, for assistance. If the public relations department of an association can't seem to locate the information you need, ask them for the phone number of the editor of the association newsletter or magazine; as a professional courtesy, these editors often will help you with your quest. Your library reference department also will be helpful in locating state and regional associations for sources you can visit in person.

In the few cases where I have been unable to locate an expert or a vital piece of information with the help of local librarians, I have phoned the New York Public Library's 455 Fifth Avenue branch at (212) 340-0849, and they have always been professional (if not particularly fast, because of the volume of calls they handle). In writing about theater, dance and opera for *Arts Indiana*, I have also phoned the John F. Kennedy Center for the

Performing Arts' library (202) 707-6245 and have always been given prompt assistance when trying to find experts to write on the arts for me.

If you plan to write investigative articles, it's a good idea to join a professional organization called Investigative Reporters and Editors (IRE) which is housed in the journalism building at the University of Missouri at Columbia. Their staff is very helpful in providing print and broadcast materials that relate to your subject. The IRE also puts out a directory that is useful in case you need to call a reporter who has done a story similar to yours. As a professional courtesy, most reporters are eager to oblige when you call them with specific questions, but they get testy fast if you're vague or expect them to do your work for you.

Authors are experts that are fairly accessible—unless they are in the final stages of writing a book themselves, when it is quite possible you'll get a turndown or no reply at all. To track one, I usually look at a book jacket to see if the author's hometown or affiliation (say with a government agency or university) is listed. In the case of authors who write for trade and popular periodicals or scholarly journals, I check the contributors' box or author's bio at the beginning or end of a piece for information on the writer. Then I check directory assistance to see if the author's home phone is listed and/or to get the number of the institution the author is affiliated with. I also have found it helpful to talk to book, magazine and journal editors. If not experts themselves, they often can put you directly in touch with their authors (unless it's against their policy) or experts these authors have cited in their books and articles.

Don't overlook the experts cited in books, journals and popular magazines. Authors rarely make the mistake of identifying experts without listing their place of residence or affiliation. Often there is enough information to get you on the phone with an expert or the colleague of an expert in a matter of minutes. You have to become an expert yourself in moving from person to person in a bureaucracy until you reach the person who can best help you talk to your expert.

I've also found it very helpful when talking to the public relations departments of various associations to request brochures about upcoming conventions. These conventions invite top people in their respective fields to speak, and most contain bios that give you enough information to make a contact—if you can't do so through the public relations department itself.

I also sometimes phone federal government agencies or large corporations without the name of a contact, but by being polite and resourceful, I often can ferret out the names of experts who can be tapped for information.

Many experts in various fields also make a living as consultants. They often ask for a fee when you phone, but I've rarely had anyone insist on a fee when I explain that it's against my policy to pay for information. I remind consultants that it is in their best interest to be called an expert in print. Most consultants send copies of clippings to potential clients as a means of obtaining future business. In that case, you're as important to the experts as they are to you.

CONTACTING EXPERTS

Once I have the name of an expert I have two ways to go. I can either go through the public information office of that expert's association or educational institution, or I can try contacting the expert directly—something I'm not shy about doing. Once the expert is on the phone, I identify myself, the project and the name of the magazine that I'm representing on a freelance basis (or the working title of my book). I make my request succinctly, and I answer any questions that the expert may have. If the tone of the expert's voice tells me that I am calling at a bad time, I ask for a specific time when I can call back. If I am on a tight deadline, I reveal my time frame for completing my research, or if I am fairly flexible, I say that, too. Also, if I have spoken to other prominent people in the field, I drop these names to the source in an offhand way, getting across my desire to be thorough.

In the event the source is able to talk with me right then and there, I have a notebook full of questions before me and a tape recorder ready to be switched on—as soon as I'm granted permission to tape. I always begin to record as I'm asking for permission so I have the source's "yes" on tape. If the source does not wish to be taped—it rarely happens—I immediately turn off the recorder and jot down responses in a notebook. It is against my ethics to tape someone without permission, and in many states it is illegal.

INTERVIEW PROTOCOL

The first thing I do when beginning a new research project is sift through the unfamiliar material without letting myself be intimidated by the sheer amount of what's available. The contents of many journal articles and technical books—in the area of health, for example—are sometimes too difficult for me to assimilate. In such cases I read for general understanding, filling in the details later when I interview the authorities who wrote those articles, asking them to put their material into the language of a layperson.

Caution: It is *essential* that you have a grip on your subject before you begin the interviewing process. To phone authorities without some knowledge of the subject gained from perusing materials in print is to invite these sources to express scorn, frustration and anger. Do your homework first. Most sources are so in love with their subjects that they display pleasure when a writer shows real interest in writing about what they know best. However, when a writer calls unprepared, it can be taken for a lack of interest, even disrespect, and sources may be unwilling to speak for fear of appearing in an article riddled with errors. Refrain from calling your "big-gun experts" until you've gotten your feet wet speaking to minor sources of information.

Here is a tip I learned after being chided by a doctor who asked me if I believed everything I read in print. Don't assume that news articles you've read are 100 percent accurate. Almost always will experts take exception to some or all of what has been written about them. In effect, you are protecting yourself and the source by fact-checking what you've found elsewhere in print before using it. Even if something was accurate two years ago, it may no longer be accurate, or timely, today. Always verify the spelling of sources' names, their professional affiliations and their titles. People constantly change all three—particularly their titles. I also jot down Internet and CompuServe numbers, if the experts have them, so I can follow up with a question by electronic mail if need be.

Never try to bluff by pretending to be more of an authority than you are. If you don't know something, or you need a fuzzy point explained, be honest and direct with the experts. Also, don't let them get away with using jargon you're unfamiliar with—insist on getting explanations and definitions.

Many experts like to think of themselves as entertaining as

well as knowledgeable, so don't take them for granted. When they say something that amuses or informs me, I respond with appropriate laughter or appreciative comments. You'd be surprised how many journalists rattle off a list of prepared questions and do not react to what the experts are saying, because they aren't really listening. Don't be so locked into your questions that you fail to establish rapport. You'll never get experts to go beyond terse official statements and open up to you unless they feel you're really listening to what they're saying. Don't let them get away with vague or unsupported contentions of the "everyone knows" variety. If a doctor insists that all men with prostate cancer need surgery, ask him how that will help someone who has been diagnosed late and is now riddled with the disease.

Listen for exceptions. If a source tells me that something is true in almost all instances, my ears perk up at the words "almost all." Those exceptions make for interesting reading.

If a source cites a study or a statistic, come back to it later to get a source so that you can ascertain the accuracy of what has been claimed. I've done so many interviews in which well-meaning experts have incorrect figures, dates and so on that it's become routine for me to verify *everything.*

Also, I don't try to bury the hard questions as I used to. I usually say something like, "As you know, there has been some controversy about your work, and I'd like to see the situation from your viewpoint." Don't hem or haw and stumble or sound guilty. You're asking a question, not defending yourself of Murder I on the witness stand.

Be direct. Say, "In interviewing Professor So-and-So, he made the allegation that you . . ." or, "Correct me if I'm wrong, but wasn't your decision to quit the prestigious University of So-and-So an indication that you had gotten fed up with the lack of state funds being funneled into your program from the legislature?"

Often you need to establish rapport to get experts to give you the names of "ordinary" people who have had experiences that make them important sources for you. For example, at Rodale Press, while writing a chapter on kidney stones for a health book, I needed to get stories from people who had stones. Doctors would not violate doctor-patient confidentiality ethics to give me names of patients—nor would I want them to do so—but often they did take my name and number and actually contacted a few patients themselves who then phoned me to be interviewed.

Near the end of an interview I seek suggestions for further reading and always ask the sources if there are competent people in their fields who may have opinions that differ from theirs. Some of the liveliest articles I've written have come about when I've obtained the names of an expert's peers who don't agree with what the original source has said. I always ask what research or project my interviewee is doing now; sometimes a bell will go off in your head and you'll be able to tie in some very current research or possible future development to what is happening now. This happened to me three or four times at Rodale Press when I learned that research scientists were working on experimental drugs. This enables you to write a "Someday human beings may take a pill to prevent Alzheimer's disease, but for now . . ." lead.

Always be polite and professional. At the end of the interview I offer experts a soapbox to state their views, and I conclude my questioning by asking them if there is an important line of questioning that I've overlooked. If the responses I've gotten suggest to me that a source has a hidden agenda (say, a basketball coach insists the players play better in Brand X shoes), at the end I try to probe to see if I can reveal the true agenda (the coach gets $200,000 a year from a footwear company). If I'm unable to do so and my "BS" detector is out, I use a quote, noting that the coach "claimed" such-and-such, warning my readers to be a bit skeptical about what the source has said.

End with a thank-you. Even if a source has been arrogant, or not been particularly helpful, or hasn't bothered to keep current in the field (it happens frequently!), when the questioning is over, I offer thanks and then promise to phone to check any facts I use in my article or book. If the source has put on a dazzling show of knowledge, I offer appropriate kudos without fawning. Knowing they are busy people, I thank them for their time, give them my phone and fax number in case they wish to contact me for any reason (perhaps to add or qualify a statement, or send me documents)—then leave them be.

When you're through speaking to a source, keep in mind that a time may come when you'll want to be in touch again for another piece or book. Unless you maintain a file of sources, you are going to have to start from scratch every time you begin a new article or book. So, you'll want to keep their names in a file that you can access at any time. If you're already up to snuff with a computer, keep your source information in convenient "folders" that you can bring up easily to consult or update. If you're not, you may wish to do what I did until the mid-eighties and keep multiple address books. Be aware, however, that keeping address books is a messy and inefficient way to work, and the time you'll spend frequently revising them could be better used in a low-cost computer instruction course.

Suggestion. Keep a notebook or file in your computer of all expert sources who have asked you to send a photocopy of your published article. As someone who gets interviewed about twice a week, I can assure you that most writers who promise to send copies are terrible at following up. If you promise to send something and don't do so, you've broken the trust you've established with a source.

I make a point of transcribing my tapes right away—before interviewing the next expert if at all possible. Otherwise, I run the danger of asking too similar questions and not absorbing all that a source discussed in the interview. Each interview builds upon the one before, and it is this layering of detail upon detail that will give your article or book both readability and credibility. If I transcribe an interview and conclude that a source has not been truthful, has an axe to grind, carries a hidden agenda, or has manipulated me, I then decide whether to publish the quotations in a context that alerts readers that they should take what has been said with the proverbial salt grain—or, in flagrant cases, whether to simply discard the interview. Just because you've conducted an interview does not mean you have to print word one from somebody.

If, on the other hand, someone expresses original ideas or brilliant theories and I use the material, I feel that I have an ethical obligation to make sure that the source gets full credit for what has been said. I was burned by a *Washington Post* reporter who grilled me on my chapter on predominately African-American fraternities before the publication of *Broken Pledges*. In his article, the reporter attributed my original research to "hazing experts"—not to me. I've attributed his lack of professional courtesy to inexperience, but it left me understandably wary when other reporters phoned. A similar lack of proper attribution occurred in a biography of Louis L'Amour, in which the biographer took quotation after quotation from an interview I had conducted with the late author and attributed them to an unnamed reporter. As a result, I am careful to give sources credit for the work and ideas I cite.

Writers should not be lazy and use the same sources too often, however. Once you've gone through other articles like yours on a subject, you'll see certain names of experts that reoccur. Use them if they are the only expert in an area. Otherwise, do some digging and find new sources who can put a fresh spin on materials for you.

STAYING ORGANIZED

Always keep a short record of calls you make to experts and all the operator information calls and dead-end calls you make until you finally reach the expert. If a publication reimburses you for calls, they may want an itemized account as we require at *Arts Indiana*. If you're not reimbursed, and writing is a business for you as it is for me, you'll want to deduct these calls, whenever it is legal and appropriate, on Schedule C of your Internal Revenue Service returns. These calls add up, and you need to be able to identify whom you called in the event of an audit.

If you do interviews in person, keep track of mileage, parking tolls, plane fare, taxi fares, overnight meals and hotel expenses. Whenever legal and applicable, get magazines to reimburse you or claim legitimate expenses on your returns as you do with long-distance phone calls.

Because it's quite possible that you'll accumulate hundreds or thousands of pieces of paper while researching your piece, it's important that you keep a tight, logical filing system. Not only do I make use of file cabinets, but I make a point of organizing files on my personal computer as well. If you have trouble organizing, any reputable computer store can direct you to software that helps you organize, sort and locate materials. Don't simply dump everything into one big box as did an *Arts Indiana* writer I visited at home last week, who was understandably frozen on a big project. Your story will reflect that disorganization.

GETTING ALL THE FACTS YOU CAN

The public has the right to learn about information that is in the possession of any federal agency with the exception of some sensitive materials such as income tax returns and classified materials that may jeopardize the country's defense. Public officials like to stonewall reporters and writers because they know that few people have the time or energy to persevere in going after them. Don't give up. Be firm and businesslike, but never threaten or break the law to get what you need. Leaping over a guardrail to yank open a file cabinet might look good in a movie, but in real life the next sound you're likely to hear is that of a cell door slamming shut.

Seeking information in person is always best, but often impractical. The next best thing is to use the phone. And only when phone calls fail to produce information should you resort to filing a request citing the Freedom of Information Act.

When you write for information, use proper protocol and keep a copy of all correspondence. Save time by writing to the correct public agency to get your information. When in doubt, call that agency to get the name of a specific person (usually the one directly in charge of freedom of information requests) to whom to send your letter—and to verify that you're writing the right agency. Otherwise, your inquiry may fall through cracks in the bureaucracy. If it is a state (or District of Columbia) agency you're investigating, you can purchase guidelines for getting information from agencies within a specific state from the Reporters Committee for Freedom of the Press, Suite 504, 1735 I St., NW, Washington, DC 20006.

Always specify precisely what information you need in a brief one-page letter that has your signature on the request. To get attention in a hurry, the first paragraph of my letter says that I am respectfully writing to obtain information guaranteed by the Freedom of Information Act (5 U.S. Congress 552).

Some reporters state why they want some information. Some do not. I prefer to keep my letters short and to the point. I'm the one requesting information, not the recipient of my letter. Why should I say what I'm going to do with the information when the law doesn't ask me to do so? I do say that I am willing to pay the search and copying costs necessitated by my request up to say twenty-five or fifty dollars—but ask to be informed ahead of time if my request is going to cost much more than that. I am, however, willing to state the exact nature of the article I am writing if the agency is willing to waive its request for copying costs in the interest of the public's right to know.

To prevent stonewalling, I recommend that you ask the agency to send you the information within a reasonable time. Reporters usually ask for the information in ten (working) days, citing deadline pressures, but it's likely in the case of requests of a sensitive or political nature that it will be two, three or four months before the agency will comply.

In addition, you would be well advised to state in your letter that you see no reason why this information would be exempt from the public's right to know. Your letter also should make it clear that if for some reason your reasonable request is denied, you demand to know specifically what statute the agency is invoking, so you can appeal.

Often the various experts you contact—or the public information officers representing them—will ask that you put your request in writing. Some writers doom themselves to failure because they write several pages where only a paragraph is desirable. They are like the boss you once had who handed out five-page memorandums when a one-paragraph memo would have done the job just as well. Such writers literally cram their requests with repetitive and unnecessary information that the experts will find tedious and frustrating.

The best thing to do is to keep your request short and precise. If the experts have questions, they'll ask them. Keep your responses very brief and to the point lest you strain the relationship. I never try to mistake an expert's cordiality for an invitation to become a friend, nor as a journalist do I wish to cloud my objectivity by becoming too close to a source. If you have clippings in publications, or reviews of any books you've done, send them along with your request to assist your credibility.

HOW MANY EXPERTS DO YOU NEED?

This answer depends on your subject, how much of an expert you already are (if you are one, you may need very few experts, or none), and the length of your piece. As a rule of thumb—and only as a rule of thumb—try to interview four to six experts per book chapter or full-length magazine piece.

If you have original research to contribute, go right ahead, but be sure it is original. No writer wants to be embarrassed by claiming to have an original idea, only to find out that the same idea was expressed earlier and maybe better by another expert.

Although you want to be thorough and you want to properly attribute information, don't simply pile on quotation after quotation from experts without some analysis and discussion of what has been said. Otherwise, readers will feel overwhelmed with information, and your prose will sound as dry and lifeless as a doctoral dissertation.

Remember, too, it is important to have a healthy balance between experts who are primary interviewees and other sources who have had practical experiences that readers identify with. A sense of creativity is all-important here. Any library clerk can pull a couple cartons' worth of research out of databases. It takes ingenuity to go beyond the obvious. For an article on using all one's brainpower in a crisis, Rodale Press health writer Russ Wild not only interviewed psychologists and brain specialists, but he also talked to an airline pilot who had safely landed a burning airplane without losing a single passenger.

CHAPTER FOUR

Analysis Without Paralysis

Today's magazines are as sophisticated as professional editors, design experts and market packagers can make them, but they are only as good as the writers who supply the material they print month after month. Editorial staffs, like mine at *Arts Indiana*, are lean, meaning that more often than not, the same editor is expected to have the knack of conceiving, assigning and line editing copy from freelance writers. An editor must perform dozens of duties that big magazine houses of years past would put into the hands of three or four people.

Consequently, as a freelancer, you can take advantage of the fact that editors do not have extra time on their hands by becoming known as a writer whose copy is error-free ("clean" in the world of publishing's vernacular), one who always turns in approximately the same number of words assigned, and who possesses a crisp style with a punch and some humor. Magazines increasingly employ staff writers or editors who "save" assigned articles that need rewriting—but they also do one more thing that affects you. Magazines today rely more and more on a "stable" of dependable writers. Hence, you either please consistently, time after time, or fail in this business. Publications are positioned for success or failure, and editors whose freelance writers don't come through will soon be at home scanning the classified ads for a new gig.

"Conception is much more fun than delivery," goes the cliché. But if you're to succeed as a writer, you've got to deliver, realizing that the "fun" is in the checks you earn.

What I recommend is that you position yourself as one of the minority of writers able to analyze everything you write, separating you from the majority of writers who feel their way through most pieces relying on instinct.

Being able to analyze what you do does not mean you will paralyze yourself as a writer. It means you will be able to discuss your writing calmly and rationally with the copy and line editors assigned to your pieces. When they suggest changes, you will give cogent reasons for keeping what you've written, or you will see the logic in their suggestions and accept them. Not only will this improve the quality of your work, it will also improve your relationship with editors. And that means more assignments for you.

Want to win an argument with an editor? Be able to defend your choice of every word, sentence and paragraph? Know why every element in your article works—and be willing to listen to an editor who tells you why something has failed to click.

Don't send a piece with clunky constructions or information gaps and ask editors to fix things for you. Even if they can, it's a black mark against your judgment.

Make every sentence as vivid as you can. Just writing sentences that have no grammatical problems is not enough. A sentence that sits on the page and does no good is a detriment to the article. Be sure that every sentence has a purpose, such as working as a transition between sections of a piece, or revealing the character of an interviewee, or blending description with action—whatever. The point is that every sentence must have a purpose. Every article must be as good as you can make it. You must ask yourself the same question your editors ask themselves: what effect is all this having upon the reader?

Let me provide an example. If I write this self-description: "The author is a sports lover of medium height who wears glasses," there isn't anything much you can condemn, but neither is there anything in it to praise. Let's try to make it vivid:

> *Although nearing fifty the author plays basketball against twenty-year-olds. The exercise forces him to change the nose flaps on his spectacles twice a year because perspiration turns them green. His receding hairline collided with his bald spot long ago, and he wears baseball caps to the office to look a decade younger. He consents to wear suits on occasion, but deep down he remains the kid in tattered*

jeans who loved playing at his grandfather's farm. Yester-
day, when he fed his tropical fish, he dipped six inches of
silk tie into his aquarium.

Readers can take something from the second example, getting
an impression and forming an opinion about my character.

THE IMPORTANCE OF MODELS

I've always thought it important for writers who wish to be
thought of as experts to study the prose of experts who already
write prose that sings. A few examples of professionals in diverse
areas who happen to be brilliant writers are biologist Lewis
Thomas (*The Lives of a Cell*), paleontologist Stephen Jay Gould
(*The Panda's Thumb*) and scientist Paul Davies (*The Edge of
Infinity*).

These writer/experts have learned what all successful writers
learn: the secret of presenting complex material in a fresh way
that delights, thrills and challenges their readers. Put another
way, they have developed styles of writing that please their audience's sensibilities even as their prose performs the primary job
of conveying information.

If there is one thing all these wonderful experts have in common, it is their ability to observe the world about them and describe what they see in a way that makes readers feel they are
seated at the feet of a wise master teacher. Witness this passage
from *Arctic Village* (University of Alaska Press), a portrait of life in
the Alaskan village of Wiseman in the thirties, by the late Robert
Marshall, a professional forester who earned his Ph.D. at Johns
Hopkins Laboratory of Plant Physiology.

> *My typical day started around seven, when I arose, dur-*
> *ing much of the time before daylight, started my fire,*
> *crawled back into bed while the cabin warmed and then*
> *breakfasted with [villager] Martin Slisco. After breakfast,*
> *while we waited for the dawn, he would regale me with the*
> *latest details of his contemporary love affair, or we would*
> *play the phonograph to drive away the last vestiges of drows-*
> *iness. I would spend most of the mornings in my cabin,*
> *reading, writing, fixing up my notes, and talking with visi-*
> *tors. After cooking my lunch I might spend the afternoon*
> *visiting around town, working at home, or going for a walk.*

I recall a number of evenings when I walked out along the trail, while the far below freezing weather made my nose tingle. The southern sky would be brilliant with sunset colors, the snow all around would change from a strange purple to a dark gray, and diminutive Wiseman when I returned would be twinkling with lights. Then I would repair to the roadhouse, which was at the same time a shelter from the trail and a social center for the community. Supper would be a loquacious meal, with those who were eating there, and those who merely came to chat, talking back and forth without intermission. After supper I would sometimes remain at the roadhouse until bedtime, either listening to the conversation or dancing, sometimes receive visitors and play the phonograph in my own home, but most often drop around from one cabin or igloo to the other, talking with different friends until far into the night. Then I would walk home through the freezing air, while the northern lights rolled brightly across the heavens, and feel that life could not possibly be more splendid. While I was undressing I might play the Hungarian Rhapsody, *the* Gymnopedie, *or perhaps Schubert's* Unfinished Symphony. *The last record for the evening I always put on just before turning out the gasoline lantern, and then I listened to it comfortable from bed. When the final note was over and the automatic stop had clicked, it generally took me about thirty seconds to fall asleep.*

NICHE PUBLICATIONS

To paraphrase old song lyrics by the Rolling Stones: You can't always sell editors what you want, but you can always sell them what they need. What they need is to excel at their jobs. They do this by pleasing their readers. You swell your bank account by providing them with articles that their readers want.

That's a shorthand introduction to the publishing law of supply and demand.

The job of selling to consumer magazines begins with careful analysis of what those publications already have been selling to their readers. Break it down into its simplest terms. If you want to sell to *Playboy*, send queries on sex, celebrities, sports and personal finance. To sell to *Redbook*, send queries on women who've overcome adversity, as well as surefire ways to shed weight, save money, improve one's sex life.

How do you know all this? It doesn't take a private detective to look at a magazine's cover blurbs, its advertisements, its editor's (or publisher's) column, and its table of contents to find out what that publication has to sell. As a fulltime freelancer starting out, I used to go with a stack of three-by-five cards to my library's stacks and go issue by issue through every magazine article. Always I asked myself how I could tweak an article just enough to give it a fresh slant. For example, *Esquire* had a piece on America's most livable towns, and since I was living on the road out of my pickup truck anyway, I began querying magazines about an idea I had to do "Towns Without Pity: America's Ten Toughest Towns." It didn't sell to *Esquire*, but a smaller national magazine ended up liking the idea. The lead to my query letter turned out to be almost word-for-word the lead in my story:

> *Everyone talks about the quality of life. Daily exits from New York and Rizzodelphia (a play on the name of the controversial former mayor, Frank Rizzo) are made by residents searching for brave new whirls in Santa Fe and Reno. But just because a town is small doesn't necessarily mean that it's nice. We've all seen* Easy Rider, *after all. As a public service, we checked out the terrain in America's 50 states, and what we've found may convince you that Detroit really isn't so bad.*
>
> *So, without further ado, here are ten towns through which not even Charles Bronson would dare walk alone at night.*

Ten copy blocks, each devoted to a different tough town, followed the introduction. The article infuriated small-town America, getting the piece press coverage in dozens of newspapers.

As an editor and freelance writer, I still go back to past issues of magazines to look for ideas. Remember, the trick isn't to simply regurgitate what's in those issues. The trick is to put a twist on what you find and present the piece in a fresh way that hasn't been done before. If you don't get that distinction, you'll be berated by editors for plagiarism. Don't be afraid to find new slants to old stories—they can be found.

But just having the right topic isn't enough. Packaging your query is all important. When I take a briefcase filled with manuscripts home with me on a weekend, I want to get away from reading them so that I can play baseball with my son. So, I give writers one or two pages to convince me that this is an article worth reading to the end. If I love the lead and next paragraph or two, I'm hooked. If I don't buy the piece outright, I'll pass it along to a junior editor to see if the piece affects another human being as it did me.

If a manuscript passes my first test, and one of the other editors likes it too, I'll give it one more reading. Usually what I'll be looking for then is how much editing will be required to put the piece into the magazine. I don't care how fresh a concept someone has if the piece they've turned in requires too much time and attention to edit. Therefore, every unnecessary word or phrase you can excise is to your advantage. If the structure of every paragraph is tight and if each paragraph flows smoothly into the next, chances are such a piece will take me no more than a day to edit. That much time I can spare, and you'd have a sale. (Once in a while, if I like the idea and think the writer is worth developing, I'll invest forty or fifty hours in someone to take that person step by step through a piece. But I'd be out of a job fast if I did that with every writer.)

LAYERS OF MEANING

The job of the writer is to layer detail upon detail. The craft of a writer comes into play with the *selection* of details used. You don't want to cram everything you find into a story. You choose those details that will evoke a response in the reader. Let's say you're doing a profile of someone. You choose details that reveal the character, personality, economic conditions, and in general, the human nature of the person you're writing about. Here is how I layered details into a mini-portrait of female novelist Michael Lee West for a national magazine.

[Michael Lee West] is a jumble of walking contradictions, a rebellious baby boomer "raised right" by Southern parents. She wears a "Cowgirls Looking for Trouble" tee shirt to give neighbors gossip fodder, yet serves snacks on linen

napkins displaying two inches of tatted lace. "Just as Mela-nie Wilkes could not conceive of dishonor in anyone she loved, Michael Lee West cannot conceive of serving on paper napkins," she says.

The West family lives in a house right out of a Southern gothic novel, its beveled glass clotted with cobwebs and wasp nests. She and husband Mahlon raise vegetables for ritual canning in a fertile dirt patch she calls "Mrs. Frankenstein's Garden." The name will be on the title page of a future novel. "I've got novels-in-progress stacked up like airplanes at O'Hare," she cracks.

The author writes early drafts on legal pads, then loads them into her computer to give them editorial legitimacy. Just as Tennessean Davy Crockett personalized his rifle with a nickname, West has baptized her computer, a Goldstar '286. "Miss Hattie talks to me in a sweet, soothing voice," she says. "She takes my hand and pulls me forward."

Don't be misled by the author's glamorous publicity photographs. West says she works best who works at her grubbiest. She writes daily from 8:30 A.M. until 2:20 P.M.—the time her younger son is in elementary school—clad in a torn tee shirt atop pink sweats patched with electrical tape. Occasionally, she flails the computer keys while wearing a flannel nightie when inspiration won't wait.

Can't you just see West? Can you visualize this woman who is determined to be the best novelist she can be and is somehow creating top-notch work while making room in her life for her child as well? If all worked well in my passage, West charmed you with her sophistication and love for the finer things in life that stop short of being pretentious because she hides her beauty in skanky clothes and loves her computer enough to name it.

Since my academic training is in literature, I never hesitate to critique a piece of fiction or a play—even selecting what I see to be a literary creation's theme and what makes it work or fail. But at the same time, I like to balance that with quotations from the true experts in analyzing literature—professional literary critics. Here is how I did that in the West profile:

Novelist Michael Lee West has many admirers, but none who climb trestles to serenade her. In 1990, when Longstreet

Press launched her first novel, Crazy Ladies, *reviewers repeatedly hailed it as a distinguished addition to the canon of American literature. "There is a wealth of humanity here, a depth of understanding of character that has been equaled by few first novelists—ever," wrote one critic.*

The novel's structure is unusual. Each chapter is an extended monologue delivered variously by six women, members of the same Tennessee family. West cleverly binds the chapters together with a single theme: one violent act, no matter that it be done out of necessity, has far-reaching, destructive consequences.

The use of multiple voices with Southern accents is reminiscent of William Faulkner in As I Lay Dying. *"She writes like the Mormon Tabernacle Choir—a thousand voices, all different, all together," says novelist Diana Gabaldon.*

LEADS THAT MEAN BUSINESS

Writing to a particular length starts with the lead. If you have been assigned a piece that is 1,200 or 1,500 words, you write a brisk, snappy lead that is no more than two paragraphs and lets you get into the piece right away. For example, a computer magazine recently carried my 1,000-word feature "Class Act," describing how teachers are upgrading education with the help of computers and enlightening uses of online access.

My writing style in such relatively short pieces is always terse and direct and information-packed. Thus, the purpose of my lead was to get readers into the story quickly so that I could deliver example after example of the innovative way teachers work computers into their classrooms.

> *While many teachers are content to keep their students in line, some extraordinary educators quietly and effectively accomplish that task and more by keeping their students online.*
>
> *Online technology in the classroom can bring the educational process to life. Instead of passive recipients of information, students become active pursuers of knowledge with the aid of technology they come to know and (often) love.*

A lead for the short "openers" articles that are a staple of many specialty magazines must not only inform readers what these 250- to 1,000-word pieces are about, it must engage readers to make them want to know more. The headline and the lead must draw them into your piece, or they'll go on to the next item. Writing tight, concise prose is hard work and time-consuming, because snipping extraneous words isn't easy for those of us in love with the sound of our own writing voices.

Here is an example of the lead from an environmental news brief that I wrote for *Equinox*, the Canadian natural history magazine. My article, "Sturgeon Survival," explains how a 300-million-year-old fish is fighting extinction by adjusting to the fact of life that it must swim through troubled waters.

> *The white sturgeon, an armor-plated ichthyological Methuselah that has teetered on the brink of extinction for 150 years, appears to be staging a comeback.*

What is going on in that sentence? First, I informed the reader what the center of attention would be in the piece, namely the white sturgeon. Second, I described the creature, choosing to do so metaphorically by comparing it with Methuselah, the biblical patriarch who Genesis 5:27 says lived 969 years. Third, I stated that the white sturgeon has been in deep trouble for some time and that something is happening to reverse that awful trend. In short, this was a feel-good story in an era when most environmental stories leave readers feeling discouraged and hopeless. It was a most satisfactory lead for *Equinox*, because it gave readers a preview of what would be covered in more detail later in the piece.

Another effective way to write a lead is to use an anecdote, particularly in pieces longer than 2,000 words where brevity in a lead isn't as essential as it is in a shorter article. The anecdote may be inspiring, humorous, dramatic or whimsical. It supplies information, but best of all, it gets readers into the mood to hear a good story, predisposing them to like the rest of what you have to say. This is the lead to a story I co-wrote with opera expert Gian-Carlo Bertelli for *Westways* on Ted Puffer, who founded opera companies all over America.

> *In two minutes the tenor was due on stage at Reno's Pioneer Theater to announce the arrival of Figaro in the finale*

of The Barber of Seville. *But the singer was in his jockey shorts trying desperately to get into a pair of pink pants that were six sizes too small. The right pair of pants was locked up, and the costume crew, confident all was in order, had gone home. In panic the tenor was about to ram his shoulder into the costume door, when a wardrobe mistress who had forgotten a book arrived to rescue him. The tenor slipped into his pants, raced past the stage wings on cue, and with his last lungful of breath wheezed out his aria.*

Ted Puffer, the man who nearly gave new meaning to the term "opera buff," has had many comic experiences during his otherwise serious career.

Another way to draw readers into your articles is to set a scene. On occasion I will lead with a scene and use the next paragraph to create a second scene that contrasts dramatically with the first. Here are the first two paragraphs in my *Arts Indiana* profile of Margaret McMullan, a former *Glamour* magazine editor who in 1994 published her first novel, *When Warhol Was Still Alive*.

If author Margaret McMullan runs out of imaginary characters, she can look out her window for inspiration. From her farmhouse near Evansville [IN], she sees the house of her nearest neighbor. Desperate for privacy, he's blocked his windows with Styrofoam. Next to it is a pseudo-Victorian manse complete with cupola and widow's walk. Its owners watch crops, instead of their ship, come in.

What a difference from the sixth-floor New York walkup McMullan inhabited in the early 1980s. Then, as an assistant entertainment editor at Glamour, *her gawking consisted of celebrity watching. Now and then she spotted Andy Warhol, dressed toe-to-scarf in leather 'n' lycra, shepherding pretty young men to the current ace of clubs.*

DIVIDING THE BODY INTO SMALLER ELEMENTS

Whatever lead you write, be sure it flows naturally into the body of your piece. The best way to keep from being overwhelmed by the task of writing the main part of an article is to break the body into small, manageable sections.

My technique for breaking the body down in profiles differs

slightly from what I do when writing features.

With profiles, after I type the lead, I break the body of the piece into scenes. In a 2,000-word piece I might have five scenes; in a 3,000-word piece I might have seven or eight scenes. Each successive scene adds more layered details, impressions of the profile subject from multiple viewpoints and more information that gives the readers insight on how one person gets through life. By the end of the piece, readers should feel that they know the person intimately, and they do. After all, they've been literally on the scene with him or her.

In a service piece (such as a "how to" or a self-help article), I break the body into sections instead of scenes. If it isn't against the magazine's format, I write a subhead to introduce each segment just as I've used all through this book. I make subheads as informative as I can, making them witty or catchy as a bonus.

Each section of the body serves as a building block. Right after the lead, for example, I position an informational paragraph that gives readers a better idea of what lies ahead of them. Essentially, I make a promise that if they stay with me to the end, they will learn this, this and that. Whatever idea I am trying to introduce in this article should be clear in the section following the lead. I then take considerable care in the way I arrange the remaining sections, working in pertinent quotations and essential information. Every article has a pace all its own, and each section must be in harmony with that pace. Be certain that you anticipate every question that your readers will have and supply the answers so they leave your article feeling satisfied.

The body of each feature contains the information I've gleaned from the three to seven (or more) experts (with a capsule of their qualifications) I've interviewed, using paraphrased material and powerful quotations to bolster any points I wish to make.

Today's nonfiction articles are loaded with tips, practical hints and solid information. You as the writer must be prepared to define any terms that are likely unfamiliar to your audience. The Rodale Press method was to break up the copy with frequent subheads (or A-heads as we referred to them). Here is a small portion of a section on "Knee Injuries" from my "Joints and Bones" chapter in Rodale's *The Prevention Pain Relief System.*

The vast majority of all knee injuries can be classified as "overuse" injuries, says James G. Garrick, M.D., director of the Center for Sports Medicine at St. Francis Memorial Hospital in San Francisco. "Overuse injuries to the front of the knee are the single most common injury that we deal with," he says. "More often than not they are the result of knees not being strong enough for the level of activities people are pursuing."

Another common acute problem is torn cartilage in the knee, says James M. Fox, M.D., director of the Southern California Orthopedic Institute in Van Nuys, noting that some people prefer to use the term cartilage instead of meniscus. In this acute condition the injury involves "two small cushions between the bone's surfaces," he says.

MEET THE DEADLINE AND ASSIGNED WORD COUNT

If there is something akin to malpractice in the world of magazines it is when a writer misses a deadline. Always strive to make your deadline, and if you're going to be late for any reason, phone immediately with a warning so that an editor can replace your piece if necessary. This is particularly important with timely pieces that must run immediately or be hopelessly out of date if they're run a month or more past the scheduled issue.

Some writers also frustrate their editors because they continually undershoot or overshoot their word count. If an editor asks you for 1,000 words, you can get away with being a few words short or long, but don't miss the mark either way by twenty percent or more. The word count is given for a reason. Your editor needs to plan an entire issue, and your failure to keep to a word count will disrupt that plan.

However, just as bad as undershooting or overshooting a word count is the writer who pads a piece with repetitive and unnecessary verbiage just to make the agreed-upon total. As an editor, if I have to slash whole sections out of a piece and ask the writer to supply more material, I find the experience as frustrating as if the word count had been missed in the first place.

A writer who consistently hands in pieces that are on time and within the right word-count range has a disciplined attitude that every editor appreciates and insists on.

THE END

Some magazine articles may have "the end" as a tag after the final words, but the conclusion fails to satisfy readers. If readers have stayed with your article this long, you owe it to them to provide a conclusion that impresses them as the perfect way to say goodbye. A good ending provides a feeling of closure that is in sync with all that came before. The ending is the bow that makes the whole editorial package appealing.

How long should a conclusion be? In general, the overall length of your piece dictates what you write. If a piece is under 1,500 words, I usually strive to wrap things up in a single paragraph. If my assignment is 3,000 words or more, I might allow myself the luxury of concluding my piece in two or three paragraphs, rarely more.

One common device for ending an article is to conclude with a powerful quotation from a source. In a piece I wrote on a young screenplay writer named Garry Williams, I introduced his successes only after chronicling his years of failure as an actor and his long apprenticeship as a writer. In my conclusion I left the reader with a very human reaction from Williams's wife, Julie:

> *"I was never afraid you wouldn't make it," Julie Williams admitted after the sale of his script to MGM, "but I didn't want it to be when we were sixty."*

During the eighties I profiled rodeo clown Leon Coffee in an article called "Send in the Clowns," which describes his job as one of the world's deadliest professions. Aging and near retirement, Coffee stressed that he didn't want his career to end with him skewered by the horns of an angry bull. I ended with a quotation that emphasized the punishing nature of his business, telling the reader what it's like to be gored:

> *"Stand two feet away from Reggie Jackson and let him hit a home run right through you," says Coffee. "That's basically what it feels like."*

Sometimes a conclusion simply sums up all that has gone before it. That was my aim as I ended an editorial for *The Nation* on a Minnesota power co-op that had refused to listen to the fears of farmers who cited studies indicating that a proposed power line could possibly pose a health risk for people living close to electromagnetic lines. I closed the editorial with a terse two-sentence summation.

*The function of a public utility is to serve its customers.
From all available evidence, Minnesota's utilities have done
their rural customers a great disservice.*

If it seems natural, using humor and/or hyperbole is an effective way to end a piece. I wrote a *Men's Fitness* piece on mentors
in which I talked about my failure to find a mentor in the Catholic
junior seminary I had attended. I was lost without adult guidance
and eventually left the seminary. The article then detailed the
experiences of businesspeople who credit their successes to
company mentoring programs. I came back to the first-person
in the conclusion of my article in a mildly humorous way.

*Had I found a mentor at that junior seminary nearly 30
years ago, my life would have been much different. I had
loved the priests played by Bing Crosby and Spencer Tracy
in* Going My Way *and* Boy's Town. *I was disillusioned to
discover that there were none like them at the seminary.
Jeez, had I found a priestly mentor back then, by now I
might be Pope.*

Readers find it satisfying if a piece seems to end naturally by
making a reference to something in the lead or ends with the
same tone that the piece led off with. Such pieces satisfy the
reader's desire for completion. In a piece I wrote for a satellite
television magazine on Gene Autry, the singing cowboy turned
business mogul and baseball team owner, I began and ended
with humor. Here's the lead:

*Gene Autry tells this: "My friend Pat Buttram once said,
'Autry used to ride off into the sunset; now he owns it.'"*

Twelve hundred words later I finished with a humorous
glimpse of a young boy from Oklahoma who still lurked inside
the aging cowboy.

*Autry's sense of the past is wrapped up in humor. When
he was in Tennessee taping* Melody Ranch Theater *(a collection of his shows), he ran into ex-Angels catcher Ed Bailey,
who now lives in Knoxville. Bailey asked him if he would
send him a souvenir of Champion the Wonder Horse. Soon
after, a brightly-wrapped package arrived from Gene Autry.
Inside was a pile of horse manure.*

Another way to end is with your voice intruding on the piece to express your viewpoint. This is editorializing, but in a direct way—nothing hidden about it. I gave my opinion at the end of a sad, inspirational story for *Boston Magazine* about three blue-collar men from a working-class neighborhood who took their race horse against all odds to the Kentucky Derby, only to have it come down in the stall with a near-fatal intestinal disorder. In spite of their disappointment and misery, the three expressed concern for the horse, nothing about their lost chance for glory. Here's my conclusion:

> *Thus, two butchers and a used-car dealer were thwarted in their effort to show the world what they had all along— a winner. But they showed something else a damn sight more meaningful: true class.*

Sometimes you can close a story with a prediction. That's a common way to end a sports story. However, I also used a prediction to conclude a somber 1978 *Human Behavior* piece on hell-night hazing deaths in fraternities and college drinking clubs. The prediction was a dire warning that unfortunately was not heeded since at least one hazing or pledge-related death has occurred every year since the piece appeared.

> *Until a limit is self-imposed by all fraternities and social groups, there is no question that more fraternity deaths must necessarily follow.*

SIDEBARS

Everyone loves a sidebar—the tiny mini-feature stitched into a magazine article like a sidecar on a motorcycle. As an editor I love them because I have a better chance of drawing readers into a feature, keeping them with my magazine a little longer. As a writer I love sidebars because they allow me to use some snappy, fascinating, often service-oriented tidbits that would be lost in the old-fashioned features that had only subheads to break up text. And art directors love them because they can use color, shading techniques and illustrations to spruce up a layout.

Sidebars will demand close attention. So short that even a single wasted word jumps off the page, they must by snappy, witty and concise. You must put all your powers of concentration into writing them. There is no room for digression, no room for long, meandering anecdotes either. Sidebars have all the action of a first-round knockout.

Standard writing advice about "studying a market" is very important when you write sidebars. Magazines have a particular style, and if you go off the path, you can expect to get your piece back for a rewrite or (if the changes must be made too close to the issue's deadline) find it completely rewritten by an in-house editor.

It's a good idea to think about sidebars from the moment you first wish to write about a subject. As an editor, I prefer to read queries that include two or three thoughtful ideas for sidebars. If you include these with your proposal for the main piece, you'll come across as a savvy professional. Be sure to take sidebars and features into consideration when you negotiate with your editors. Almost always I get one amount for a piece even if there are two or three sidebars included. Once in a while, I'll find a publication such as *CompuServe* magazine that pays by the word count, meaning that your check is a little heftier when the editor wants sidebars.

Looking at Sidebars from All Sides

There are many kinds of sidebars that editors like to see, but they must be as well-researched as longer features and equally conform to the rules of good journalism. Don't knock them out as a side thought. Careful thought and accuracy are essential. Someone can sue you for libel over a sidebar as easily as they can over a ten-thousand word feature. Here are some of the sidebars I have written or have assigned as an editor:

Service with a smile. Whenever you write a feature on people who are doing something of consequence—be it volunteering, rock climbing after fifty, or going back to normal activities after major surgery—you can take advantage of the reader involvement you have created by doing a sidebar that tells readers how they can do similar sorts of things.

Lists of lists. Maybe it's the influence of David Letterman—so universal that President Bill Clinton referred to him in his 1995 State of the Union Speech—but many magazines are including "best and worst" lists, as well as suggestions in list form. For example, an article I assigned on landscape architecture for *Arts*

Indiana included the Top Ten examples of landscaped public places in the Hoosier State. A piece for a sports magazine like *Inside Sports,* on the baseball trend to have better-fielding first basemen, would shine if it contained a ranking of the best and worst glove men in the major leagues.

The first-person account. One of the standard forms of sidebars I wrote for *Satellite Orbit* was a first-person account by an athlete to accompany a profile of that athlete. This was always a section from my interview in which I asked the player how a fan at home could enjoy the game or activity more while watching television. In another sidebar, I had African-American rodeo clown Leon Coffee give pointers on what to watch for when clowns race into the arena after a bull throws a rider. People love to hear celebrities and ordinary people talk about what it's like to do something.

As another example, if you wrote a piece on alcohol abuse in colleges and high schools, the sidebar could be a first-person account from a young person who nearly died from an overdose of alcohol. These can be very powerful for your readers.

Finally, one variation I use frequently as editor at *Arts Indiana* is to include an interviewees's responses in a question-and-answer (Q&A) format. This is an edited slice of the interview with a subject that contains your exact words and those of your subject. A few magazines, including ours, will even run Q&A-format interviews as full-length features.

Find out all about it. Your readers may appreciate the names of books, CD-ROMs and other valuable information. A profile about an actor or actress in *Parade* often has a sidebar with that person's stage credits. Some magazines run certain sidebars as a regular part of their format. *CompuServe* magazine, for example, runs "Read All About It" sidebars with features that inform readers where they can go online to get additional reading materials. An article on battered women could have a sidebar containing the names of places that readers can turn to for help.

"What do *you* know about it?" Sometimes sidebars draw readers into the article by revealing their ignorance on a subject they feel they should know something about. An article on the average guy's ignorance of what women want from their partners could have a sidebar quiz to show readers that there are many things they themselves don't know. A piece on personal finance could have a quiz that convinces readers they aren't as financially secure as they need to be.

Be aware as a writer, however, that such quizzes are tricky. They must not insult or demean the readers, only challenge them.

Examples. You've been enjoying sidebars all your life even if you didn't know they were called that. Articles on cooking low-fat meals always are accompanied by recipes in boxes. Fitness articles on ways to reduce stomach flab or tighten buttocks and pectorals may have boxes with specific exercises, often accompanied by photographs or illustrations depicting people doing what is described.

You may want to put definitions and technical explanations in boxes. I once wrote a piece about quarter-horse racing for a national magazine, and when my article was published, I was surprised to see it accompanied by a sidebar explaining the difference between quarter-horses and Arabians, defining both. I wished I would have thought of doing that.

CHAPTER FIVE

Make Your Writing Sing

Your voice on paper is likely to age nicely—maybe better than the rest of you. The advantage we writers have in coping with advancing age is that we can see our skills improve, unlike people in many other professions who must endure their disintegration. Unlike baseball players, we're not over the hill at thirty or forty; we're still learning vocabulary words and new writing techniques at sixty or ninety. As long as we can thump a computer key, there's always the hope that our next manuscript will be a best-seller, and there's the almost certainty that the voice we have on paper will get better with each passing year.

The voice I used in the sixties and seventies was unpolished like I was then—cocky, swaggering and uncompromising. I cringe when I reread those pieces, the way people feel uneasy looking at photographs of themselves in high school, cigarettes dangling from their lips, clothing too flashy for street wear. I started out writing humor, and had an image of myself as a humorist. However, much of what I wrote doesn't seem very funny to me now.

Although I published professionally in my teens, it was not until my mid-thirties that my voice on paper matured. I began to think of myself as a journalist who used storytelling techniques to please an audience. Never having taken a writing class, the growth I had at that time was the result of input from my editors and my voracious appetite for reading—especially creative nonfiction, magazines and quality newspaper journalism.

SOME LESSONS LEARNED

What can you learn from my early mistakes to help you whack years off your own learning process? Plenty.

Above all, avoid cheap tricks to get attention as a writer and—unless it's your dream to be a tabloid journalist—anything that smacks of sensationalism. Instead, concentrate on creating vivid word pictures that give readers a sense of being on the scene with you, the teller of stories.

Always select worthy models, but don't parrot their styles. Growing up my writing idol was Hunter S. Thompson, and I should have stopped with admiring his prose, but I didn't. For about two years I tried to write like Thompson, and that was time that should have been spent perfecting my own voice. Not only did I lack Thompson's crazed edge and habits, my attempts at creating a hyperbolic style read precisely like what they were—bad parody. Needless to say, those were largely unproductive years, marked only by one or two pieces worth saving in a portfolio. The fact that I published enough unworthy pieces back then to support myself as a writer was good, however, because these small victories kept me from giving up altogether.

Fortunately for my writing career, by the early eighties I began reading and, on my own, analyzing the work of authors John McPhee, Tom Wolfe and Garry Wills. Abandoning humor and farfetched travel stories, I began writing polished prose. I worked hard at learning to set effective scenes, at using minimal direct quotation in favor of paraphrasing, at emphasizing characterization over mere summation, and in general, using the devices of a short story writer to create well-crafted nonfiction pieces.

One piece of good fortune I had in 1981 was to write an article for Bob Wallace for a regional publication called *Rocky Mountain*. Wallace, a one-time *Newsweek* editor who was destined to become an important editor at *Rolling Stone*, edited my piece about an Idaho backcountry pilot who took me with him on his dangerous sojourns into River-of-No-Return country. The piece, "Life on the Wing," was the best thing I had done to that point, and I learned much from Wallace about the importance of selecting only those details that grab readers, culling anything that was dull.

Learning From a Good Editor

I'd recommend that you keep alert when you find yourself writing for an editor who has sensitivity and skill. Learn from that person. Compare your last draft with the final edit, studying every improvement the editor makes in your piece and making darn sure you understand why the changes were made. If you don't know why something in your copy was added or altered—ask, don't stew. Working with a top editor on a single piece can be more valuable than any writing course you'll ever take.

Have realistic expectations of what it will be like working with an editor. Don't think you have to form tight relationships with your best editors. Rejoice if you have a common passion for good writing and don't fret because you aren't becoming soulmates. As a writer, I never formed a friendship with Wallace (who eventually quit magazines to become a television executive), partly because I missed him on my one visit to the offices of *Rocky Mountain* in Denver and therefore dealt with him exclusively by phone.

Sure, it would be wonderful if you received the kind of attention from one or more editors that novelist Thomas Wolfe, author of *Look Homeward, Angel,* received from Maxwell Perkins, the famous Scribner editor, but you cannot count on such attention. Most magazine and book editors today are swamped with more work and pressures than editors had in the thirties and forties. They have less leisure time to drape a comradely arm around your shoulders and pull every last bit of talent out of you the way Perkins used to do with Wolfe, Ernest Hemingway and F. Scott Fitzgerald. Until it happens that a single great editor recognizes your special genius, it's much more likely that you, like most contemporary writers, will acquire professional insights from your collective dealings with many editors, one blunt suggestion at a time.

Recognizing Flaws in Your Editors

Also understand that there are occasions when you will work with a truly awful editor. For example, you may end up with an editor who acts more like a writer and destroys your voice in the editing process. It may be an editor who wants only one style and edits every submission to sound as bland as a label on canned corn. There are many other editing faults: insensitivity, sentimentality, too much or too little guidance, unclear ideas when making assignments, failure to guide a writer through the use of complex writing skills (such as getting a handle on point of view), or inability to diagnose precisely where a manuscript went off track. Whatever.

If an editor at a magazine or publishing house is someone you absolutely cannot work with, contact that editor's superior and tactfully say you'd prefer to work with someone else. If that fails, or if you have little faith in a publication or publisher because the editor in charge is a destroyer instead of enhancer, go elsewhere. There comes a point when it's best for all concerned if you make a difficult decision and cease the relationship. I should emphasize that I don't jump ship for any little disagreement. I've done it only three times in my writing career: in 1982 when a longtime editor of mine told me that my query was great but that he had assigned the piece to another writer who didn't require expenses or as big a fee as I required; in 1983 when an editor failed to get back to me about an idea, and I later saw he'd used my idea—with my title—as a cover story (but I didn't sever the relationship until I chewed out that editor and got him to give me a replacement assignment); and in 1994, when an editor's flighty behavior in too many editorial decisions made me certain that I never wanted to work with the magazine again.

GETTING OVER OVERWRITING

On the other hand, I've found that extraordinary editors are as rare as the truly hopeless ones. Bob Wallace might not have been a genius, but he was the right editor for me at that point in my career. As a result of working with him, my prose became leaner and I stopped using abstractions, relying instead on hard nouns and verbs that barked and hissed at the reader. I found that if I gave my readers a concrete image, there was no need to use adverbs and qualifiers to make them see what I saw in my mind's eye.

What I wrote instead were pictures in words. I couldn't begin to include in my prose every human complexity of the people I wrote about, as I had once tried to do. Instead, I emphasized a few traits and tried to find keys to meaning in what those people said—and, more importantly, what they tried to keep from me. Here is the lead to "Life on the Wing":

> *Backcountry pilot Jim Searles keeps a map of the Idaho wilderness pinned to a trap door in his Air Unlimited terminal in Challis, Idaho. When passengers appear the map vanishes as the trap door becomes part of the ceiling. The*

map is dotted with red markers, grim reminders that the skies punish a pilot for even the slightest lapse in judgment. Each marker signifies a fatal crash.

"These are all something we've had something to do with or people we've been close to," says Searles, running a finger from red marker to red marker. His sapphire eyes scan the map of the territory he knows so well. Although he is only of average height, his erect bearing makes him seem tall. His windburned face and blond beard give Searles a mariner's countenance—the look of a man more accustomed to boats than planes. He wears jeans, a checked wool shirt, and a hat he changes almost hourly. When Searles removes his hat, thick wiry hair flecked with gray swoops back from a smooth forehead that belies the fact that the man is in his mid-forties. "The accidents occurred in the same type of place," Searles says in a flat, hushed voice, "in small canyons."

The land outlined on the map is as foreboding as it is magnificent. Much of it has not changed in the century that has passed since the Shoshone-Bannock Indians inhabited the territory they called Idaho, gem of the mountains." The Indians hunted to survive. The trappers who swarmed to the region nicknamed them "the sheepeaters" because the bighorns that roamed the high country constituted an essential part of their diet. The land is broken by peak upon rugged peak, glacial lakes, and mountain valleys. There are only three ways to travel here, even in the kinder summer months: on foot, on horseback, and in a snug, single-engine plane that touches down on strips, little longer than a stretch of putting green, carved from the land.

In winter, pilots serve the few ranchers, miners, outfitters and hermits who brave the outback year-round. Only four air taxi services and a monthly government mail plane even attempt to supply goods and emergency services in Idaho during winter. About 75 percent of the work is charted in advance; the rest, rescue work or emergency pickups and deliveries of parts, means that Searles and pilots like him are on call 24 hours a day. Searles is the senior member of the elite group of Idaho's winter pilots. Many of the rest have retired or are now red pins on a map.

Searles points to a rounded red marker. "This is a 210 with six people in it who were killed," he says. "The guy should've never been back there; he wasn't experienced enough." Searles, like the Idaho wilderness he patrols, has no use for careless pilots or mistakes in flight. "He figured he was turning up Pistol Creek or the river, but the mountain climbed faster than he could." He eyes the map, perhaps envisioning a gutted fuselage, a broken body, a stretch of pink snow at each red marker. "This one came out of Cascade and snuck along the bottom of this creek. He couldn't turn around."

Searles turns and pushes back his cap. His voice changes. "One thing you can never do is get yourself in a position that you can't change your mind at any time to turn around. . . . Go somewhere else! Do something different! Never commit yourself to a one-way shot at something." He could be talking about his own life.

AVOIDING INERTIA AND OVERINVOLVEMENT

If you take one lesson from this book, let it be that it is important to keep the conviction that one day you will make your writing sing. It is a bonus when an editor has faith in your potential as a contributor and praises the qualities in your writing and gently points out what is obtrusive and deadening as well. But from my viewpoint as an editor, I believe too many writers fail at that critical stage when they began to publish regularly. They lose the benefits of inertia and so they stall, satisfied that their bylines go often on tables of contents, straining only now and then to perfect their word choices and selection of layered details. If a rock climber put a similar half-hearted energy into scaling a sheer-walled cliff, that person would eventually fall into an abyss. So too it is with writers. As an editor and college writing teacher, I've seen too many talented young writers falter while more aggressive and persistent writers with half their peers' obvious skills go on to achieve prominence.

The best writers communicate something akin to spiritedness or playfulness that readers easily sense. Even if the subject is tragic, like Shakespeare they use comic elements to heighten the dark moments they're presenting.

That spirit of fun can't die even if you, like many writers, are trying to produce a manuscript under less than ideal conditions, or with less than ideal cooperation and support from your loved ones. Yes, writing can be laborious, and it can require you to keep brutal hours, but it's a mistake to work so intensely that you lose your spirit of fun.

What fun I had in the early eighties as I wrote story after story—selling an average of one freelance magazine article per week for years. One of my favorite pieces was an article I wrote in the first person while playing minor league baseball for the Montreal Expos' organization in spring training, communicating what it was like for those I played with to get a shot at life in the big leagues and what it was like for those who failed.

What was particularly fun, and challenging, about this assignment was that I had to be completely involved in trying to play a game where pitchers and infielders fired 90 mile-per-hour balls at me—even as I kept detached enough to whip a tiny notebook out of my uniform back pocket now and then to capture what was happening.

Not until I became an editor did I realize how many writers fail because they cannot—or will not—keep a certain amount of distance from their subjects. I had one writer develop a passionate fixation on a man she interviewed, handing in copy so dripping with unrestrained fawning that it embarrassed me and enraged my managing editor. I had a writer—a would be fiction writer—spend his time with a nationally known novelist on a profile assignment telling her all about *his* prose, and coming away with almost nothing of value about her. And I had a writer get so involved in an arts cause that her entire piece fell apart into a sort of ardent editorial for that cause, failing to objectively get the viewpoints of the opposition.

Don't fall into that trap. If the day ever comes that you find yourself unable to keep a professional distance from someone or something, do your editor and readers a favor by handing back the assignment. If you're in this business to party with celebrities, to get access to contacts you couldn't ordinarily meet, or to advance a hidden agenda, you're badly in need of a course on publishing ethics. Keep your professional distance.

This is not to say, however, that you cannot write books and articles that help change the world for the better. Far from it.

What I'm condemning here are writers who have been assigned to write objective pieces and then lose all objectivity.

WRITING THAT MAKES A DIFFERENCE

In the late eighties, influenced by the nonfiction books of Tracy Kidder, I began asking people I interviewed to reveal their inner thoughts at times of tragedies and triumphs. The idea was to go beyond the surface lives of the people I wrote about, probing their emotions and revealing what it was truly like to be human. The writing was very much like fiction, except that every scene, every word, was true. What I wanted to do was to take one final step from being a journalist/storyteller to being a journalist who reflected upon the meaning of the events I observed.

After years of research, in 1990 I told the tragic story of a family nearly destroyed by the death of their son during a fraternity initiation. I spent untold hours in the company of Eileen Stevens, an ordinary housewife who became an anti-hazing activist after her son died following a night of drinking sponsored by a local fraternity. The young men had hoped to show they were willing to do whatever it took to become members of the organization. On more than one occasion, she shared what it was like to lose her beloved son (by a former marriage), Chuck Stenzel. Here is the opening of *Broken Pledges: The Deadly Rite of Hazing*; I set the passage in italics as a device to capture the reader's attention even prior to chapter one:

> *The call came in the middle of the night. Eileen Stevens's son was dead. She was alert and numb at once, her flesh no longer part of her. She wanted to hang up. She wanted the caller to stay on the line forever. She wanted to know what had happened and how. But most of all she wanted the call to be a dream, a very bad dream.*
>
> *The pain in the caller's voice, the small break in his professional manner, revealed the truth, told her the worst had happened. She was ready to bargain with God. The devil. The caller himself: Take my life, my soul—take me. I've lived. But make it untrue. Take me, not Chuck.*
>
> *But Chuck was dead.*
>
> *She wandered through the house. A gong vibrated between her ears. She eyed the refrigerator. The freezer held*

the ingredients for chili. Chuck alone in her family loved it. Parents Weekend at Alfred University was approaching, and she had planned on taking him a special meal.

She went into his room. In the closet were the boots and skis she'd given him not two months earlier. He'd used them only once. She was glad she exceeded the budget to buy them. She could still hear his squeal of joy on Christmas morning. Twenty, he'd acted like a four-year-old. His joy was infectious; his hugs, genuine. If only she had kept hugging him forever, never let him go.

The caller's words roared like a waterfall in her mind. Chuck's "probable cause" of death was an overdose of alcohol, "at a party," the dean of students had said. He had also repeated that explanation to her husband, Roy, in a later call. But how was that possible? Sure, Chuck drank a few beers with his buddies, his fellow clammers on nearby Great South Bay, but he'd never had too many, to the best of her knowledge.

She wanted to leave immediately. But a winter storm had intensified, adding 3.4 inches of snow to the twenty-two already on the ground in Alfred. Flying into a commercial airport within a ninety-minute drive of New York's Southern Tier was going to be impossible until snowplows could do their work. She contemplated going by car, but Roy convinced her she would have to wait out the night.

A staunch Catholic, she spent the long night cradling her husband in her arms, taking comfort in her religion. Then the thought struck her. She'd have to ask if someone had summoned a priest to administer Extreme Unction, the sacrament her faith promised would permit her son straightways into heaven.

Little did she know that her boy's spiritual welfare was the last thing on the minds of those who shared his last hours. To the ghastly end, fraternity rites prevailed over last rites. And human rights.

THE SUBJECT'S THOUGHTS AND INSIGHTS

The preceding scene took a great deal of time to get precisely the way it is now. The method I used was to take a scene of high drama—the worst moment of a mother's life—and through selection of details, give the perceptive reader insights into her character.

I began with something unspecific—a phone call in the middle of the night—that was calculated to have an emotional effect on readers. You have had a ringing phone chill you after midnight, no doubt, and you can identify with a mother's terror whether or not your worst fears ever have been realized in that call.

In the second sentence I used very simple words to convey the enormity of the situation and to introduce the name of the woman taking that devastating call. Right after that I went through the mixed thoughts that raced in Eileen Stevens's head as she accepted the news and fought it simultaneously.

At this point I chose to keep the caller's identity from the reader for a second. The reader learns first that the caller is someone in authority who is in emotional pain as he breaks the news, and a few sentences later, as Eileen learns her son's supposed cause of death, it is revealed at last that the man on the phone is dean of students at Alfred University. The dean—a decent man who responds in less-than-ideal ways to Chuck's death as a result of his own prior involvement with a fraternity—is to play a very important part in the book. My intent in that opening page was to create some reader interest in him before he is introduced in person a few pages later. Because I introduced three people by name on the opening page—and I wanted readers to unconsciously absorb the identity of the trio—I chose to withhold the dean's name at that point.

One of the biggest problems I had was to keep the reader from viewing Eileen in a stereotypical way. I needed to get across that she was an ordinary housewife so that her transformation in the book is all the more dramatic and impressive, but I didn't want her to be such a stock figure that the reader takes no notice of her. I did that by giving the reader insights such as her willingness to die for her son (*Take my life, my soul—take me. I've lived*), the self-incrimination she is experiencing (*If only she had held him forever, never let him go.*), and her unselfish concern for her boy's welfare even in death, hoping that he's received the last rites to ease his entry into heaven.

Significantly, what else I tried to do in that scene was to cause the reader to bond with Eileen by following her thought patterns and seeing how she used her husband's love and her religion to get her through the terrors of a long night that must pass before she can reunite with the lifeless body of her son the next day. The reader also has the same question the mother had that night which would motivate her to charge pell-mell into the all-male system of fraternities to demand answers: If Chuck was a light drinker, how then did he die from an overdose of alcohol?

Finally, the theme of the book went into the final sentence of the passage. Namely, barbaric fraternity hazing practices have superseded the bounds of proper behavior and have trampled on human rights.

All that in nine paragraphs that is, for most readers, nothing more than a simple story that seems to be occurring as they read, horrified, as I was when I interviewed Eileen. If you and I do our jobs, all the many bits of business we agonize over as we work to rework a passage will never be noticed by the general reader, leaving the illusion that the passage has been written without effort.

Hint: Get readers emotionally involved in your nonfiction from the first sentence and keep them that way until the last sentence. If the content has zing, the prose sings and sometimes stings.

PURE INFORMATION MAKES FOR DULL READING

These same techniques used in creative nonfiction also can serve you well when writing how-to and informational articles/books—known in the business as service journalism. Readers turn to service journalism for ideas, believing that your article or book will benefit them. Whether the topic is something of as major consequence as living with AIDS or as relatively minor as some tips to improve one's tennis game, readers are willing to pay a certain amount of money because they place a certain worth on acquiring new ideas. This is a pact that you as a writer cannot break. Don't disappoint readers by writing a lead that fails to deliver in the rest of your text. Give them what they want and they'll read you again and again.

Always keep in mind that readers are busy people who want to be entertained while they learn. Moreover, since readers now have visual media to turn to for ideas that used to be the province of magazines and books, it is more important than ever that what you write must grab the reader from word one. Recent studies indicate that most magazines keep a reader's interest for no more than one hour per issue, meaning that many articles go unread.

One of the best ways to dispense ideas is through the words of successful people. One format is to get the reader personally involved in someone's story, then have that someone dispense advice as if speaking directly to the reader.

One of my favorite examples is an article I wrote on super salesman George V. Smith of Houston in 1983, showing how he'd used common-sense sales techniques to go from broke to being a millionaire in less than seven years. Watch how easy it is to give your reader sales tips just by integrating tips into the story of Smith himself. See how you can pack many ideas and a great deal of information in story form. This is especially easy to do if the advice of the person you are quoting is given in a conversation, not a sermon.

> *Serving himself a $42 million chunk of the annual sales pie is George V. Smith of Houston, very likely the most successful black salesman in America. Back in 1975, the dynamic Smith grew tired of earning money for others as a pipe supervisor in the oil fields and put his $4,000 life savings into an enterprise he named Smith Pipe Companies, Inc., selling oil-field supplies and equipment.*
>
> *"I was broke, black-skinned and uneducated," says Smith with a smile, recalling his start. "A man can't have more strikes against him than that."*
>
> *Working twelve-hour days six days a week with a Sunday break to fish, Smith built a sales empire from scratch. A believer in hard work and setting strict personal goals, the Texas millionaire's determination comes through when he discusses his philosophy of success.*
>
> *"The difference between winners and losers," he says, running a hand over his balding dome, "is that losers do what they want to do while winners do what they have to do. I don't make up excuses why I can't do something; I just find a way I can do it."*
>
> *Consequently, Smith has earned a reputation as a man who refuses to give up on a sale. To snag a reluctant client, he paid 18 visits—each requiring a 2,000-mile plane trip. The final trip won a $250,000 order. Today, Smith Pipe*

does in excess of $4 million with that client's firm.

When George Smith talks sales, people listen. He has a few rules based on common sense and long experience. One he never violates is to see clients at their convenience, never phoning them to set up appointments in the early morning because that's when they're most likely distracted by work that cannot be delayed.

"I don't care if you make a blank trip," he says. "Don't see a man until he has time to see you. If you force your way inside when he doesn't have time, you're not going to have his attention. You're talking to him, but that's all you're doing because he's not listening. When I see a man, he gives me his undivided time and attention, because I've given him the time and respect to get what he needs to do done."

At *Arts Indiana*, when I need an article on a particular dance performance, I prefer that the writer refrain from getting too pre-occupied with the technical aspects of a performance. A writer brings individual dancers to life by getting performers to reveal what a performance means to them. Rather than give a laundry list of every technique the dancer must do in a particular dance, the successful writer gets the performers to describe those tech-niques that are most difficult for them. Once again, the key is getting readers to relate to someone else by giving examples that create empathy.

Cluttering a piece with too many technical expressions turns off most readers. A little jargon sprinkled lightly as parsley in a dish, however, pleases readers, giving them the pleasant feeling of learning something new, but stopping short of boring or over-whelming them.

Thus, in a service piece when you use technical terms or jar-gon, it's best to immediately provide definitions for those words. For example, in a piece I wrote for *GQ* on how to buy handmade craft goods, I gave a nontechnical definition of macrame and then gave tips for buying macrame that used the same terms I'd put into that definition:

Macrame is best described as a creative exercise in knot-making. Two basic knots, the half-knot and half-hitch, are used in endless variations to make an infinite number of patterns. The knots eventually go into useful items such as hanging planters, tote bags, clothes, purses, bracelets, room dividers, rugs and wall hangings.

The beauty of a piece of macrame is in the movement of the knots and the way the artisan combines selected yarns into a matrix of designs. Craftspeople may elect to use a single color in a complex pattern or two or more colors to create depth and perspective. Beads and feathers are often added for variety and contrast.

Examine macrame items for some particular problem areas. Occasionally, knots are tied too tightly, or a design is irregular. Be sure that the artist has selected yarn that doesn't detract from the textural quality of the knots. Since the knotting procedure involves considerable rubbing and friction, be sure none of the knots are frayed. Finally, if the creation is to hang in natural light, make certain that the yarn is color proof. Certain materials—jute, for example—fade over time.

Use Humor

You can write a manuscript that is well researched and that is on a topic of interest to readers, but still get rejected. Why? Too many pieces lack a breezy style and assume far too serious a tone for the subject matter, succumbing to dullness.

One solution is to inject humor into your manuscripts, and you don't have to be Roy Blount or Dave Barry to succeed. The object isn't to get your readers to roll on the floor laughing at every page; the object is to get them to crack a smile, to nod approvingly from time to time, and in short, to get them in sync with what you are saying.

For example, one time I was asked to write a piece on phero- mones, showing how fragrances and odors cause a strong re- sponse in human beings, insects and animals. This article for *Men's Fitness* was a rather strange assignment for me. I don't wear cologne or aftershave, and I get migraines in elevators when someone reeks of cheap perfume. But an assignment was an assignment and the way I made this one informative and fun was to set a devilish tone and to inject a healthy dose of hyperbole into the piece for would-be lotharios.

On another occasion I collaborated on a fashion and grooming book for large women with Carole Shaw, the publisher of *BBW* magazine, which I discussed in chapter two. Although I needed to write the book with sensitivity and empathy—which I truly felt for my readers whose lives often have been besieged by mental cruelty over the issue of their weight—I needed to lighten up the tone to make the readers feel lighthearted as they read the book from 200-pound Carole's point of view. Here's my lead to chapter four—"Sex and the BBW":

"Is it different making love to a large-size woman?" talk-show host Tom Snyder asked Carole.

"How would I know?" she replied. "I've never made love to a large-size woman."

Your job in trying to write humor is to remember always to create a series of fast-shifting pictures in the reader's mind. The reader sees one conventional picture of a man and woman together when Snyder is speaking, and then sees quite a different picture in Carole's witty retort. The contrast in images creates laughter.

As always, remember your audience when you create humor. Know what experiences and knowledge they possess when you shoot for a laugh. What is funny to the readers of *Soldier of Fortune* might be confusing or offensive to the readers of *Ms.*

In particular, remember that something is even funnier to readers if they can see themselves in a situation. My lead paragraph for a piece on a whale-watching excursion counted on readers having experienced at least one bout with seasickness:

> *Twenty passengers aboard the Oceanic Society's whale watch vessel are in determined competition. Everyone wants to be the first to spot a gray whale, and no one wants to be the first to throw up.*

Use Anecdotes

In addition to humor, you can always please readers by satisfying their craving for meaty anecdotes. These are mini-stories within your larger story that readers can retell at the office water cooler. One of my favorite ways to tell a story and grab readers is to open an article with a mini-story, particularly if it contains humor like the following lead I wrote for my *Inside Sports* profile of basketball star Wayman Tisdale:

Put yourself in young Wayman Tisdale's place. You're the tallest kid in your class—by far the tallest—and you're self-conscious enough about the fact. And you didn't even want to come to school today, but here you are. Now the nun is getting all excited about putting on her Christmas play for the parents. She's got someone to play Santa Claus, and a couple guys to be the reindeer, and now she needs an elf. "Someone who's really going to stand out," she says.

You sink way down in your seat and try to ignore the pain shooting through your knees as they go through the desktop, but it's no use. It's your way she's looking, and in your little boy heart of hearts, you know you're doomed.

"It was the most embarrassing moment in my life," says Tisdale, the hottest-shooting, 245-pound, 6' 9" elf in college basketball. "I had on black leotards with a green elf suit on top. I hated it."

And Wayman's mom, bless her soul, manages to stifle a grin and look hurt over Wayman's words. "I had to drive all over town looking for those leotards," she says. "I thought I was going to have to dye a pair."

Use Restraint

Always consider your reader when contemplating what to include and what to leave out of an article. Readers who frequent the pages of *Scientific American* expect far more detail and more complicated scientific data and explanations than do readers who purchase *Popular Mechanics* or *Omni*. None of these magazines would buy manuscripts that sounded as though they were written strictly for professionals.

This goes back to what you've heard many times about studying your markets. While every magazine is going to demand that you be accurate, some permit more complex explanations than do others. Most prefer simple prose, clear explanations, and, as I said earlier, only a small number of technical terms. Most also stress human interest angles. If you can find a person who not only is knowledgeable but personally engaging, you have a far easier time making your story readable because readers will have someone with whom they can identify.

Here is an example. In 1989 I wrote an article for a general interest magazine on the attempts of an 86-year-old scientist named Dr. Charles Burnham to bring back the nearly extinct American chestnut, a victim of a terrible blight that occurred earlier this century. Here's how—in the simplest of terms—I explained a genetic disaster after immersing myself in scientific prose that was all but unreadable to the layperson.

Burnham prefers to be called Charles, because he says that every old horse in the country is called Charlie. Most of his colleagues under 50 are too awed to refer to him except as "Dr. Burnham."

Once Burnham became convinced that the chestnut could be saved, he immersed himself in research, learning that information about the American chestnut—a member of the beech family (Fagacae)—filled many journal articles and dissertations. Scientists knew nearly everything about the blight that had attacked the species—everything, that is, but how to overcome it.

Paleontologists believed that many millions of years ago, before radical changes in climate split the geographic makeup of the world into continents, the chestnut trees of North America and Asia had a common ancestry. If so, like ancient human beings who underwent changes in their genetic character when they became widely separated, the American chestnut may have gradually lost an important trait for fungus resistance that Asian trees maintained.

What is known for certain is that during the Great Ice Age of the Pleistocene period, the various ice advances in the world affected the range of the chestnut tree and other plant life. Because the main American mountain ranges (save the Great Smokies) extend north and south, unlike the Alps and Pyrenees of Europe, which mainly have an east-west axis, the chestnut and other tree life managed to "escape" the approach of glaciers. Where once the chestnut was found naturally in what is today Alaska and Colorado, gradually the tree found a home in North America in a range that extended from Maine down the Eastern Seaboard into such Deep South states as Mississippi, Arkansas, Georgia, and Alabama. To the West the natural range of the chestnut ended in Michigan and Indiana. Because settlers who abandoned homes in these states to settle elsewhere

brought chestnuts with them to plant, that range eventually
extended to include present-day Iowa, Wisconsin, Illinois,
Minnesota, and California.

The challenge in the previous passage was to use everyday conversational language to explain what had occurred. The task required me to pare down the explanation to its simplest form, leaving out details that readers didn't need or want to know.

Give Useful Advice

Most popular-market science and health writing targets very specific audiences. What you need to do to reach any of these markets is the same, however. You must absorb tremendous amounts of data and put your findings into a form that pleases the readers of your target audience. Rodale Press, in particular, stressed the importance of giving personal advice in candy-coated terms.

For example, I once contributed multiple items about "curative options" to *The Prevention How-To Dictionary of Healing Remedies and Techniques*. This book not only explained therapeutic theories, surgical procedures and home remedies, but also used chatty, easy-to-absorb prose to tell readers how they can be applied. To write a single item required one or multiple interviews with healthcare experts and the reading of a dozen or more reference articles culled from top journals. Here is a small section from my entry on sclerotherapy—the obliteration and removal of varicose veins.

Women with small vein disease are particularly good
candidates for sclerotherapy, says D. Brian McDonagh,
M.D., a phlebologist (vein specialist) in Schaumburg,
Illinois, and founder of the Vein Clinics of America. Unlike
surgery, which would require too many incisions to be a
practical solution, sclerotherapy can be an effective treat-
ment to eradicate this problem, he says. Proper physician
training and experience are critical.

With this method, which was developed in Europe, the
doctor injects a special solution (such as sodium tetradecyl
sulfate) into the offending vein. "The goal is to eradicate
existing vein disease without damaging the surrounding
tissue," Dr. McDonagh says.

The term sclerotherapy—*which comes from the Greek word for "to harden"—is actually a poor choice of words. After the vein is injected, it only temporarily hardens, says Dr. McDonagh. The real good of the procedure comes when the inflammation and hardening subside, leaving a minuscule band of scar tissue in its place, he says. In effect, the useless vein dries up and withers away to nothing.*

Voila! Your legs no longer resemble a topographical map of Minnesota's 1,001 lakes—and because there is no surgery, there is absolutely no scarring, says Dr. McDonagh.

CULTIVATING SOURCES

Your articles and books can be only as good as your research can make them. An important attribute that separates brilliant authors from the commonplace ones is the former's ability to find and cultivate expert sources. The John McPhees and Tracy Kidders realized early in their careers that the best reporting techniques only mine fool's gold if primary sources are anything less than the best in their areas. In addition, where a less-than-stellar writer looks for people who are ultra-colorful to make a piece lively, authors such as McPhee and Kidder have such incomparable powers of observation that they can make almost any human being come alive on the page.

Sometimes it isn't easy to find subjects when you're dealing with a topic that hasn't already been covered in detail. That's when it is important for you to be creative and to find experts in areas similar to the area that you wish to cover.

For example, my work on hazing was begun at a time when very few people had paid any attention to the behavior of fraternity men and sorority women. Researchers had not yet awakened to the fact that they had a veritable laboratory of curious human behavior right in their midst. I managed to find a professor of education who had stayed in a fraternity house to observe the dynamics of group behavior, a renowned anthropologist named Lionel Tiger who had written about the way men act in groups, and a handful of people who had done some work on initiations as part of their doctoral research. These were all helpful, but I still needed more insights, more focus. These came only after I had contacted Irving Janis, now deceased, a Yale University psychology professor who had never written a word about hazing, but who generously shared with me his expertise in group psychology that was crucial in helping me get a fix on why individuals haze and why others let themselves be so abused.

Your interactions with sources does not have to be parasitic. When you question your sources, don't be surprised when they in turn question you to benefit from your insights and your perspective. Both Janis and Tiger had several questions for me, and it was a learning experience to see how quickly they acquired facts and were able to get an instant handle on new material. Tiger, for example, who co-wrote *The Imperial Animal* and wrote *Men in Groups*, picked my brain for my research into the tendency of some females in some sororities to physically and mentally abuse new pledges in ways that mimicked what fraternity men had traditionally done.

From my experiences I hope you can learn that cultivating the very best sources is an essential skill you must develop to write the best books and articles that are in you. If you do nothing but read like a scholar, you can go only so far as a writer yourself. To be truly successful, you must communicate your ideas to impartial experts who can criticize, suggest areas you need to explore, and recommend additional experts you need to contact. Then, once you have these names and have read all that you can on what they have written, you contact them as well.

Do not compromise by using lesser experts if you can help it. You cannot make fine wine from inferior grapes. Spare no labor or expense to reach the best sources.

The experts will pick apart deficiencies in your research and ideas, but don't be downcast. You will be able to repair cracks and leaks that otherwise could cause your work to be turned down by an editor or destroyed after publication by critics.

And, on those occasions when learned men and women become excited about some aspect of your research, take pride in knowing your work is worthwhile and is adding to the world's storehouse of knowledge.

As an example of how I worked my interview with anthropologist Lionel Tiger into *Broken Pledges*, here is a brief excerpt from a section treating a hazing death due to an alcohol overdose at Rutgers University. Note how I have worked in a minimum of short, essential quotations from him, a quotation from a newspaper article, a reference to one of Tiger's books, and facts that I have compiled such as the statistic that fraternities essentially have a 100-percent membership turnover in four years. Observe the way I've cut some extraneous material in the *Washington Star* quote by putting in four periods (an ellipsis) to let readers know where something is missing. (Clarification: Use three periods if you are referring to excised material at the beginning or in the middle of a sentence; use four periods if the last part of a sentence is omitted as it was in my excerpt from the *Star.*) See also how I have taken what could have been a string of quotations from Tiger that would have bored the reader, making them highly readable by paraphrasing them instead and using them in context in this passage:

> *Coincidentally, one of the most respected authorities on male behavior, anthropologist Lionel Tiger, teaches at Rutgers. Tiger believes that male hazing rituals stem from basic competitive drives that include sexual competition for desirable women and a need to find a comfortable niche in a group. One Howard University member of Omega Psi Phi, for example, told the* Washington Star *that he joined his fraternity "because Omegas always have the most athletes and the prettiest women. . . . When you tell some college girls that you're an Omega, you've got instant respectability."*
>
> *Tiger occasionally lectures to college groups to discuss a chapter on fraternity behavior in his 1969 book* Men in Groups, *which Greek leaders routinely cite as the best available interpretation of why men haze.*
>
> *He believes that hazing often reflects "in pathological ways" what might be normal relations between young males and slightly older males in fraternities and other organizations. Hazing allows males to see themselves as powerful. Other variations would be the ancient knight-squire connection or today's relationships between mentors and the young people they take under their wing. "I think the hazing situation is a kind of acting out or working out of that general process," says Tiger, "but with a very practical and often punishing kind of reality. To have a taboo against hazing per se would involve a kind of level of self-consciousness that I don't think young males are likely to have. After all, these are the most volatile and complicated people*

in a society to discipline."

Nonetheless, Tiger says, those who deal with young males must find institutional solutions to deal with hazing and alcohol-related abuses because the problems are "not going to go away." He thinks it is foolish for fraternal leaders to make an announcement that hazing has stopped, then expect young men to comply, particularly in fraternal groups that lose and replace approximately a quarter of their membership every year. Hazing cannot be dealt with by raising consciousness—that presumes a higher aware- ness than most teenage males possess—and therefore the Greek elders must try to solve the problems by highly struc- tured means, says Tiger. He points out that recent innova- tions such as dry rush can help stop hazing deaths. "But there is something intrinsic to the relationship between older and younger males in this kind of semi-secret or secret envi- ronment that can get out of hand," warns the anthropolo- gist. He adds that males at this age are far more likely to be susceptible to peer group pressure than to moral qualms, a fact that college and fraternal authorities must keep in mind when they attempt to eradicate hazing.

Sometimes it happens with a quote that you need to change a word slightly without altering its meaning. For example, per- haps the sentence you're quoting would have a tense problem if you didn't change the tense; or perhaps the writer uses the pronoun "he" instead of a man's last name. If the presence of the original word makes a sentence unclear, put in a more spe- cific word (or a couple words) enclosed in brackets. If you quote someone who says something inaccurate, and the inaccuracy itself is worth noting, put the Latin word *sic* in brackets to alert the reader.

VERIFICATION

When you interview experts it is essential not only that every nuance of what you write be correct, but that you verify every- thing that you plan to use in print.

There are many mortal sins in the business of writing, but the sin of inaccuracy is rarely forgiven. If you would endear yourself to editors, show them you can produce accurate copy. Even if you really know your subject, you cannot prove it to an editor if your copy is riddled with misspelled names, out-of-date titles, and other problems that force the magazine to run a correction box.

Always double-check names of organizations and the titles of the people you interview. One consistent problem that I've noticed as an editor is that many arts organizations refer to themselves in a shorthand version of their incorporated names for the sake of brevity. But in print, they rightly expect to see their organizations referred to by their correct (and legal) names. That's why I like writers to attach to their manuscript some photocopied evidence (business cards, company brochures) of organizational corporate names and the titles of sources.

Prior to handing in your final draft, make a point of methodically going through a manuscript point by point the way a fact-checker will do, making certain that every last detail is correct. By way of example, in the past year, articles about me have listed my title in print as editor, executive editor, managing editor and editor in chief. The last one is correct. All the other reporters had a key fact wrong in their stories. Some of these writers have approached me about writing for *Arts Indiana*, but they would have to convince me that they had abandoned their sloppy ways before I would assign them anything.

Get in the habit of finishing a piece at least four days before it is due on your editor's desk. Leaving just one day to check your facts is not good enough. Sources don't always return calls right away. It is important to allow yourself time to proofread and to look at all facts with a critical, unweary eye.

This last chance to check facts gives you an opportunity to probe your sources one last time. If you spot some inconsistencies in the information they gave you, chances are they may have spoken to you without double-checking figures themselves. Even if sources make the mistake, writers and editors end up looking foolish. Whenever possible, make sources document everything they say. If you have any doubt on any piece of information, confide in your editor when you send the piece in. You'll gain trust in a hurry that way. It's better than phoning a week later and asking an editor to correct some misinformation. Writers who do that make me nervous. In such instances I always wonder what else a writer may have neglected to check.

If you assume something is right and it's not, the next thing you and the publication will assume is responsibility for your error. That's flirting with professional suicide for you and your editor.

ORIGINAL IDEAS

The most exciting part of publishing for me is the opportunity to express original ideas that have some effect on society, whether it be changing public policy or altering someone's behavior for the better in some way. For example, my *Broken Pledges* has been used by lawmakers in Illinois who were examining a state anti-hazing statute to see whether or not it violated the constitutional rights of defendants. The most original (and often-quoted) idea expressed in *Broken Pledges* was that there were links between initiations that got out of hand whether hazing occurred in Greek-letter groups, adult secret societies, military institutions, high school clubs, athletic groups, bands, honorary societies and so on. Another important idea was that, ironically, educational institutions had not used scholarly research to eradicate the problem of hazing deaths in their midst that had been occurring since the nineteenth century.

Having original ideas like these is important. Your ideas are what will give you a reputation as a thinker. Writers that merely take the ideas of others and collect them piecemeal in a volume or article may be doing someone a service, I suppose, but there is no possibility such works will have any permanence. They read no better than the vast majority of term papers written by undergraduate and graduate students that merely stack chunks of copy taken from books and publications without any attempt to display original thinking.

In your writing it is important that you improve upon the ideas of others, just as many inventors take established products and make them better. Or, if you have the evidence to back what you say, it is important to disagree with the ideas of others, showing where their arguments or conclusions have been flawed.

You also must make certain that your articles and books acknowledge the source of all ideas expressed in your writing other than your own. Not only must you always mention books and articles that you've drawn from, but also the interviews and letters you've cited as well.

CITING SOURCES

If you use material that has been published in a book or periodical, you must cite the source of the material in your own work. In general publishers allow short passages of 500 words or less to be used without permission so long as the source is cited, and exceptions to the rule usually are contained on the copyright page. Because interpretations of fair use of copyrighted materials have differed when such matters have gone to court, there are only two ways to be certain you are not violating copyright: Obey the restrictions on a book's copyright page and write the publisher for permission to use a specific passage or passages.

The publishers of song lyrics are less forgiving of fair use. Be sure to obtain permission from copyright holders each time you use two or more lines of song lyrics. Likewise, if you are quoting from a movie screenplay or television script, you need to obtain permission from the copyright holder of the work.

Regarding letters, journals and similar unpublished materials, you need to become aware that fairly recent untoward changes in the law have now forced writers (including biographers) to obtain permission from the copyright holders—the writers or legal heirs. This rule also applies even if the letters can be read in the special collections of a university, or private or public library. In my opinion, the law is unfair and is a hindrance to scholarship and the public's right to know, but I nonetheless recommend that you obey the law to the letter in light of some notorious lawsuits against biographers by their subjects—such as author J.D. Salinger's court actions against Ian Hamilton, his biographer, that have made all authors and publishers understandably cautious.

Source Notes

You probably already know that you don't want footnotes—with a few exceptions—in your nonfiction book for a popular audience. It is far better to incorporate documentation naturally into your text. The footnotes signify a dry-as-dust style that is death on sales.

However, sometimes it is impossible to insert documentation without injury to readability. The alternative is to use citations for sources at the end of the chapter or (as I prefer) the end of the book. Be sure to start each chapter's notes with #1. Be sure to include a bibliography at the end of your book to allow you to use the shortest possible source notes, abbreviating everything you can. Or, if you (or the editor) do not wish to include a bibliography, run a full source entry the first time you have a reference to a book or periodical and then run an abbreviated version in subsequent references.

CHAPTER SIX

Be Your Own (and Maybe Your Best) Editor

When editors receive the published samples of writing that writers usually send along with article proposals, they wonder who *really* wrote these "clips." They know too well that other editors, faced with losing an article otherwise, often will rework pieces to save them.

If unprofessional writers get the benefit of several "saves" like these, they can and do use them to get a foot in other publishing doors to get more assignments. Such writers last on the fringe of publishing for a few years, but most of them eventually surrender and try other fields. Before they leave, they manage to raise the general anxiety level of more than a few editors.

If you are serious about your writing, it is important that you gain the trust of editors the first time you work with them. Repeat work means everything to you as someone who submits on a freelance basis. Although minimal editing changes are expected in a manuscript, you should not feel good about an acceptance if your editor drastically rewrites your piece. Even worse, if a magazine assigns you a piece and kills it after you've submitted it, you've closed a connection to the publishing world forever unless the failure was no fault of your own.

PLAN TO SUCCEED BY HAVING A PLAN

There are many reasons that writers fail to deliver, but after working with so many writers as an editor on a one-on-one basis, I've concluded that the reason for a great many failures—if not most or all of them—is that writers don't think a piece through at the beginning.

If you start a piece without a plan and some sort of written or unwritten outline, you tend to find yourself stymied along the way. Working without a blueprint, you start tinkering with rewriting pieces of your article before the entire assignment is completed, because you don't have any sort of point of reference from which to make judgments.

Remember, every sentence and every paragraph you write is "good" or "bad" only in its relationship to the piece as a whole. Your editor (and readers) get their impressions by starting at line one and going to the end. If you keep forgetting the Big Picture and overhaul and oust whole sections of your uncompleted manuscript, or if you find yourself frozen and unable to start at all, you have failed to read as an editor reads.

This jumping back and forth in an unfinished manuscript to make changes is especially dangerous on a Mac or PC. If you edit before you have a finished article or chapter, you can and will destroy some fine work that would have needed only minor reworking had you edited it with the whole piece in front of you.

Even though I always wait until I have a draft in hand to make big changes, I occasionally err in deleting copy blocks that aren't quite right but have some gold dust here or there that should have been saved. Once erased, the gold's gone.

Hence, like I do, you should print all drafts. If you X out a paragraph or sentence on the printed drafts, you can always reverse your decision later. To keep paper from clogging your desk, staple the pages of each draft together, mark "Second Draft" or "Third Draft" on the top page, and put these into a single file folder. Pitch these drafts after a manuscript has been accepted, because you want your files to be free from clutter, but before doing so, see if there is any unused material that is worth keeping in a clipbook to spark future ideas.

THE CREATIVE AND THE CRITICAL

Resist the urge to edit unfinished copy. Tell yourself that the changes you make without the benefit of having a whole draft before you are too often going to be the wrong alterations. Remember, if you're always blotting lines and reconstructing them, you cannot get a sense of a piece as a whole.

What's the solution?

Instead of *editing* as you go, continue the *writing* process to its natural conclusion. Working from an outline, always get some sort of draft completed, letting the individual sections of your piece sit untouched so you can look at them with some perspective. Don't destroy the parts without reading them in the context of a finished work. If you work in piecemeal fashion, you'll tend never to *finish* an article or chapter—you'll more likely just abandon it. You'll find yourself continually, in the patter of the workplace—stressed out—until the day of deadline falls; then you'll whip a piece out of your printer to deposit the imperfect baby on the doorstep of your publisher, hoping that some kind editor will make everything all right.

If you are an academic or have attended graduate school, be sure that you avoid writing prose that reads like a research paper. "You have to wipe the stink of academia off your prose," a writer and historian named Richard Etulain advised me when I quit graduate school to pursue a full-time career as a writer. He was right. Academic writing is a contradiction in terms. It may be academic. It isn't writing—not good writing anyway.

As Clemson University writer-in-residence Mark Steadman, author of well-crafted novels such as *A Lion's Share* and *Angel Child*, noted in my *Rendezvousing With Contemporary Writers*, professional writers put chunks of prose together, while academic writers of scholarly criticism take the prose of others apart. The big problem with critics when they write is that they haven't put in enough hard work to learn how to put their own pieces together. Conversely, too many writers take a perverse (and ultimately destructive) pride in being unable to put their work together and then take it apart again. Maybe, as Yogi Berra said, a baseball batter can't think and hit. But when writers write without thinking, they can't hit the mark. It is not only helpful, but ultimately essential, that you be able to break the writing process into a series of manageable steps.

Working purely by inspiration may work for some isolated geniuses, but I doubt it. I think it helps your work to see it from a sort of distance the way a critic does, so that you can shift from the task of writing to that of editing.

Here's a suggestion: When you edit your own copy, put your creative self away and let the critical side of you become dominant. Here are some ways you can do this.

- Edit your work in manuscript form, not on the computer. In that way, you'll be a little closer to seeing your words the way an objective third party—your editor or reader—will see them.

• Edit your finished drafts in the kitchen or someplace cozy and quiet away from your writing space. When I was on the road writing, I'd sometimes leave my motel room with a completed draft to read it over in a nearby coffee shop. Anything you can do to get yourself out of writer mode into editor mode is a help.

• Phone a friend and read the piece aloud. You'll hear the mistakes and detect places in need of revision. Don't read it to people in your presence. In that case they'll have the benefit of your body language and vocal inflections to help them understand what you've written. By the way, be interested in how they *react* to your draft, but don't rely on them for suggestions for changes. Keep control of your manuscript.

• Always finish your work well ahead of deadline. You're too emotionally involved in your manuscript when you edit scant minutes or hours after writing it. The longer you wait to edit a piece you've written, the greater the possibility that you can read it with some objectivity.

• Have another editor read your manuscript. After you've been in the business for a while, you may form a friendship with an editor or writer who doesn't mind reading your pieces and who bounces his or her in-progress work off you. Take suggestions from a professional, but think twice before taking them from people who know less about the editing process than you do. Not being a writer, they'll be impressed just that you've strung ten or twelve coherent pages together.

LINE EDITING

There is no secret to line editing—editing your piece word by word, line by line, paragraph by paragraph—it only requires hard work and a passionate belief in the need for correct grammar and proper usage.

While it is more important to get words down on paper during the writing process, you must focus on getting every detail right during the editing process. When I read the work of students at writers conferences and in the classroom I comment on both content and mechanics. At the risk of oversimplifying, it is the *writer* in a student that I evaluate when I look at *content*; it is the *editor* in the student that I evaluate when I look at *mechanics*.

To edit your work successfully and impartially, you must acquire the ability to bring out the critic in yourself, forcing the writer in you to sit, preferably gagged and bound, as far away as possible as you take apart what you put together.

Unless you teach yourself to gain some distance from a manuscript, you'll read right past glaring errors. Get in the habit of comparing your original sentences and sentences your editors revise for you. Be able to say specifically what makes the revision better.

On your first reading, the job is to read for style—for "mechanics" as copyeditors say—and not for content. Doing this accomplishes two things. First, it gets you out of writer mode and into the role of editor. Second, it makes a game of ensuring that your manuscript conforms to whatever style manual a magazine uses.

Many publications use *The Chicago Manual of Style*—a reference book that seems to have gone into more revised and expanded editions than the bible; it has been published by the University of Chicago Press since 1906. Some editors, including me at *Arts Indiana*, use the stylebook but make some slight changes (we call these improvements) to fit our needs. This is another reason editors are always telling you to study the publication. Mild deviations from our magazine's style never bother me, but writers who show absolute disregard for style always (no exceptions!) have other sloppy writing and research-gathering habits that put me on guard like a fencer when I work with them. We try very hard to be consistent in our usage, and other editors (as a rule) are equally as manic as I am about maintaining consistency in their various publications. Don't ease your conscience by rationalizing that it's an editor's job to set these things right— remember what I said about leaving a baby on the publisher's doorstep?—it's your responsibility first.

How can you know what style manual a publication uses? For us, as with many publications, it's simple. Just write for our guidelines (attach a stamped return envelope to your request) and buy a sample issue to study. I'd suggest buying *The Chicago Manual of Style*, too, and getting familiar with other stylebooks as well.

The "Mechanics" of Style

Go through your manuscript with a copy of your target magazine (or a book by your target publisher) close at hand to check style variations and options. Here is a checklist of things to look for in your manuscript. Compare them with the way they're used in your target publication or book and the proper style manual.

- Spelling and Word Options. Does the publisher use *advisor* or *adviser*, *O.K.* or *OK* or *okay*, *archaeology* or *archeology*, *dialog* or *dialogue*, *theater* or *theatre*, *installment* or *instalment?*
- Capitalization. Does the publisher use capitals with titles and offices? Have you correctly used capitals in reference to such things as seasons, place names and historical, religious and cultural terms?
- Abbreviations and use of titles, academic degrees and so on. Know when publishers use an abbreviated term and when they use terms without shortening them. This includes the use of months, states, measurements, eras, and the names of people.
- Use of underlining, italics and quotation marks. Know when to use them, and be aware of the proper form for presenting titles of books, short stories, books, movies, operas, paintings, songs and other creative works; the names of vessels, foreign words, words you wish to emphasize, genus and species, legal cases, and so forth.
- Citations, editor's notes, and headings within your text.
- Use of plurals. Be consistent with a publisher's style for plural abbreviations, letters, numbers, proper names and titles of works. Be certain that you have used apostrophes correctly with plural forms.
- Numbers. Know when to use numerals and when to spell numbers out (for example, "a half" or "½"; eleven or 11).

If you are reading properly for mechanics you should have little or no sense of content. If you find yourself changing the content of your manuscript at this point, it means that you've lost concentration. Go back to the place in the manuscript where you stopped editing for mechanics and start over.

Above all, be ruthless. Writers tend to be defensive. Professional copyeditors become inured to being bullied by writers who turn into frothing psychopaths when confronted with questions about their prose.

TRIMMING QUOTATIONS

One of the most important things I do during the line editing of my manuscripts and those of writers who publish their work in

Arts Indiana is to make certain the prose isn't top-heavy with direct quotations.

Like a lot of writing faults, a tendency to use too many direct quotations in a piece isn't necessarily a sign of laziness in a writer. More often it's a problem some writers have because they are properly concerned with being accurate and fair. "We're taught to try to quote exactly and maybe we're a little too diligent sometimes," notes Ron Rudolph, senior editor at *Snow Country.*

He cited a piece he once edited written by an overly careful writer whose personality profile of athlete Greg LeMond ended up sounding like one long monologue. The writer conscientiously had spent hour after hour taping his interviews with LeMond, and then had structured the piece as one long quote after another. "LeMond had many good and interesting things to say," recalls Rudolph, "but after a while it gets a little boring for the reader even though it is Greg LeMond."

The solution is to paraphrase, taking straight quotations from your subjects and putting their thoughts into your voice.

For example, in a piece for an in-flight magazine on poet and novelist Jim Harrison, he told me that he'd had a fairly stable and happy childhood. "We were always a close, larger family. In my family it was easier because nobody in it had ever made any money. If you were making even a living as a writer, that was incredible. My father was a college graduate. He thought it was wonderful that I wanted to go off to New York and be a writer because he read a great deal. He liked Faulkner and Erskine Caldwell and Hemingway."

Paraphrased, this is how that section of interview appeared in print:

> He came from a big, close-knit family. His father, Winfield, was a farmer who liked to read Faulkner and the classics.

There is no rule of thumb about how often you should put down a direct quote. So if your high school journalism teacher once told you to use a quotation every three or four paragraphs, strike that advice from your consciousness. Susan Ager, a syndicated columnist for the *Detroit Free Press*, finds that some writers err in thinking that stories have to possess some magic minimum of direct quotes.

If you throw in a quote for the sake of throwing one in, chances are you've included something that is gratuitous, states the obvious, or detracts from the pace and flow you worked so hard to establish in your lead. Or, perhaps you're putting in quotes out of insecurity. Insecure writers put in weak quotations from people for the worst reasons—because they've spent time and money going out to see someone, or because they think sources will be offended if they were interviewed and not included in the piece. (Never mind that what they had to say was of little consequence!)

Remember, quotations go in when quotations have a reason for going in. Once in a while I'll use one because I feel certain that at some point the reader is going to get tired of too many paragraphs of exposition, but mostly I use a quote to specifically coax the same reaction out of a reader that it pulled out of me. Or, perhaps someone has said something far better and more pithily than I could—or I need to attribute a point directly to the speaker's subject of expertise. For example, in *Broken Pledges*, it is far more convincing for readers to hear a pathologist call a hazing death a case of "manslaughter" and a "white-collar crime" than it would have been had I done the same thing in exposition.

The fact is that it's harder to write a piece that uses your best writing techniques—instead of piling one quote-heavy paragraph atop another—to advance the story from point A to B and beyond. Inappropriate quotations muddy truth. They make factual information redundant, robbing a story of all grace and subtlety. Such "strung-together" quotations are tedious, giving editors and readers no incentive to stay with your piece to the conclusion. Unlike a good question-and-answer format interview that is broken up naturally by an interviewer's questions, the article that depends on strung quotes is the equivalent of a boring sermon.

Useful quotations serve all the best functions in a story. Of utmost importance, they tell someone's version of truth in the person's own words. For example, in *Rendezvousing With Contemporary Writers*, author Harry Crews told me why he has gotten no satisfaction from publishing critically acclaimed novels that sell very few copies: "If you're going to spend a . . . year writing a book that two thousand people read, what kind of business is that? If you had a chainsaw and you had some timber, you wouldn't cut down nine thousand trees just to sell five of them, would you? You'd just think, hell, I'm in the wrong business. If the shoe business were handled like the publishing business, we'd all be barefoot."

Sometimes quotations reinforce factual information. Suppose I wanted to get across to the reader that the late author Louis L'Amour's prodigious outpouring of novels and short stories was done for something other than commercial reasons. In that case, I could use an inspiring quotation from his poolside interview with me that was published in my book, *Rendezvousing with Contemporary Writers*, from Idaho State University Press. Said L'Amour, "I love to write; I will always write. I could not live without writing."

Quotations have other specific purposes. Sometimes they expand on a theme, hammer a point home, or give readers someone's voice so clearly that they almost swear they're listening to that person.

For example, I once wrote a piece on James Dickey, the poet from Columbia, South Carolina, who told me he hated playing safe with his work, changing his techniques and experimenting constantly to make his work always fresh and new. In so doing he ran the risk that unappreciative critics might say he had failed. Rather than quote him exactly in the lead to that piece, I did a bit of experimenting myself. I tried to introduce a voice that was as down-home as the poet's, then cemented the lead with a hard-hitting quotation from Dickey:

> Before y'all read a James Dickey poem, you'd best pop some vitamin pills and conserve your strength. You gotta be prepared to rassle that man's poems when you come to him. Each line increases tension. Your forehead creases like a collapsed accordion, and sweat leaks from your pits. Reading Dickey's latest verse takes commitment. Critics say that indulging in his poems is a visceral experience which, in plain English, means his carefully crafted images turn your gut over.
>
> America's unofficial poet laureate rejects assemblyline creativity. He takes creative chances, believing that a fall after a gigantic leap beats successful running in place. "I'm

a natural-born gambler," he maintains. "I want to try something new—to see if it works or to see if I can work something out that I haven't done before."

TURNING SHALE INTO GOLD

In addition to paraphrasing the information you get from interviews, you must always improve your skills at condensing numerous interviews into a single chapter or article. It is not unusual for me to talk to twenty or thirty people in the course of researching a feature, and I realize full well that if I dump quotations from all of them into one piece I'll make my reader's head spin.

You must limit the number of people you introduce in your nonfiction, and you also must extract only the most essential information and ideas out of interviews—even those that might have taken you two, three or four days of work.

Expert writers understand they can't use everything they uncover. When collaborator and ghostwriter Ed Claflin was writing *The Art of Winning* for America's Cup winner Dennis Conner, he wanted to interview people in a multitude of fields who exhibited qualities that made them winners in Conner's eyes. "I asked him to list the people *he* admired for their perseverance, accomplishments and so forth," said the Philadelphia-based Claflin. "Then, armed with a list of phone numbers, I sat down to do interviews. The idea was, if I could talk to those people and find out what made *them* successful, I would find out more about what Conner considered to be 'winning' qualities."

One of the qualities Conner admired was the ability to shift objectives when necessary. Claflin went through his long list of potential interviewees and decided on millionaire Charles Bird (CB) Vaughan, Jr., head of a well-known sports apparel company. In 1963 Vaughan had earned world acclaim by setting a world's speed record in downhill skiing of 106 miles per hour. He, the press and his fans expected him to win an Olympic medal the next year. However, he failed to even make the Olympic team. He was a downcast downhill racer indeed.

Thirty years ago Vaughan made a hard decision. He had wanted the thrill of being on top again, but four more indifferent years in Europe as a professional racer told him that he already had gone as far as he could go. His new dream, he told Claflin, had been to start his own skiwear company but there were minor obstacles—he knew zilch about the industry and had no money to start a business.

"Vaughan was hard to get hold of—but a first-class interview," recalled Claflin. "He talked a blue streak about the incredible success of his company, about determination, and about what a great guy Dennis Conner was. He promised that he'd send me a load of clippings and information about his company CB Sports. FedEx, the next morning, it arrived."

Claflin's major problem was that Vaughan had indeed sent him a ton of information—eighty pages of company promotional materials to go with ten pages of interview notes. Unless Claflin could distill all this down to a few essential facts, the information was superfluous and counterproductive. He needed to create a snapshot of Vaughan and his enterprises that would fit into a single topic—"shifting objectives."

Claflin decided he had to find a quotation from his source that showed his readers that Vaughan had to stand firm when the sporting world questioned his decision to switch from a racer to an entrepreneur. Here is the quotation he selected: "They looked at me like I was really bizarre," Vaughan had said, adding that he wasn't surprised people found it strange that he'd gone from wearing ski pants to reading books about how to make them from patterns.

Claflin also wanted to emphasize that anyone who wished to start again after a career defeat could use that defeat to jumpstart a new career. He found this quotation from Vaughan: "When you are successful at the majority of things you've done, you begin to take things for granted. The lesson I learned as an athlete was that the reality of defeat could become a motivating factor."

Bingo. Claflin knew that readers could substitute any profession for "athlete" and find the seeds of renewal in defeat. He wrote an excellent snapshot that captured Vaughan's start with just $5,000 and his willingness to sell clothing out of his car trunk all over New England. "I thought it really highlighted the spirit of start-over-againism," said Claflin. Besides, the resonance with Dennis Conner's experience in 1983 of being the first American skipper to lose the America's Cup was perfect. Conner had used the defeat to motivate himself and his crew to win the rematch in 1987.

Claflin had to mine ninety pages of material to extract two

quotations that were gold. Rarely do professional writers get to put all their research into a book or article. It takes a good eye, a better ear, and fine sensibilities to distinguish truly compelling material from the mundane and ordinary.

As a writer you need to develop all three to qualify as an expert. And developing a little of Charles Bird (CB) Vaughan's determination—and Ed Claflin's—wouldn't hurt you, either.

DOES IT ALL HANG TOGETHER?

I am a magazine junkie. I visit musty stores that sell used books, and like to sift through boxes of old commercial and literary magazines to find useful articles. When I taught at Ball State, I once foraged through old magazines that the Department of Journalism had decided to pitch. I found a *Saturday Review* from 1958 which probably wouldn't fetch more than a quarter in a bookstore, but an article in it gave me advice that changed my writing career for the better.

The article, by a veteran author and magazine writer named Catherine Drinker Bowen, was titled, "The Editor: Midwife or Meddler?" Now prior to reading this piece I had always been a careful wordsmith in that I followed dictums from those giants Edgar Allan Poe and Ezra Pound to pay attention to every *word* I wrote.

What I hadn't been doing was seeing the *paragraphs* I constructed in relation to everything else in a particular article, chapter or book. Bowen pictured an editor bold and blunt enough to demand of a writer: *"What does this paragraph mean, and where is it headed, philosophically or dramatically?"*

After committing those words to memory and, in fact, putting them on a notecard on the wall above my word processor, I now look at what I write in an important new way.

Try it some time. Pick anything you've written and picture yourself defending it to the toughest editor your imagination can produce. If you were critical of your prose before, vow to become three and four times as hard on yourself. Can you honestly answer these questions?

- What does this paragraph mean?
- Why did you put it in?
- Where is it coming from and where is it headed?

- Does the mini-picture you're putting into the corner of the canvas somehow support the Big Picture you're painting?
- Does your selection of details tell readers something they don't already know and must know?

If you can't answer those questions, you have another draft or a couple of drafts to write before your piece is ready to submit for publication.

KILLING YOUR BABIES

The only thing that irritates editors more than getting a manuscript that is thousands of words longer than they assigned is getting an article that is the correct word length—but has been padded so much that cutting superfluous material makes the piece fall far short of the assigned word count. Sometimes the problem is that the writer hasn't padded the manuscript but has fallen in love with her own brilliant prose, making it impossible for her to make cuts. When newspaper people say it's necessary to "kill your babies," they mean that you need to delete the cute phrases and philosophical ramblings that you wrote to please yourself—not your readers.

As an editor I've had writers ask me for a bigger word count when they were on deadline. What I usually do is ask them to fax me what they have at the moment. More often than not, since I'm not as close to the piece as they are, I can find numerous things to snip without hurting the piece at all.

Rarely do I get a manuscript that isn't better for the pruning. There often are phrases that add nothing to the text but make editors think—often with justification—that the writer has done a rush job. Every editor has pet peeves; these repetitious phrases bother me:

- almost never: Say "seldom" instead.
- temporarily suspended: Skip the adverb.
- totally unnecessary: Why the qualifier?
- true facts: They wouldn't be facts if they were untrue.

As a contributing writer with *Inside Sports* for seven years, I learned to avoid what I called *sportswriterese.*

Some of the redundant expressions that irritated my sensibilities were "teammate of his," "huge/small in size," "totally destroyed," "really good/bad/strong/whatever," "rate of speed," "all-time record," "city of Buffalo," "rules and regulations" and "gathered together."

WORD PICTURES

James Thurber used to say that his first drafts read as though a sixth-grader had penned them. I'm not certain what level your first drafts attain, but I'll bet they read nothing like the final versions you send to editors.

First drafts tend to be wordy and abstract. By the final draft, if you have done your job, your prose should evoke a visual and emotional response from readers because you have provided concrete images they can visualize.

Another $3'' \times 5''$ card on my wall above my PC admonishes me to "Make It Vivid," a message that I first saw above the writing desk of author Jim Harrison.

In the first rush of creativity it's more important to me to get words down on paper than it is to polish them. I'm never going to be one of those writers like the late mystery novelist Rex Stout. He told me during an interview in the late sixties that his first drafts were so perfect that he rarely needed to revise.

During the revision process you should read a hard copy of your work, marking places where you've used abstract words and expressions. The trick is to scratch what you have written and to replace the abstract with a concrete image. Readers respond to word pictures on several levels. Here is a single paragraph from my *Broken Pledges* that depicts the night that Alfred University student Greg Belanger had to drive home the bold blue truck of his friend and lookalike, Chuck Stenzel, who had died following a traditional night of drinking sponsored by Klan Alpine fraternity. Stenzel had loved that truck, keeping it painted, polished and in tiptop running condition.

> *Something about driving Chuck's truck had Greg Belanger's emotions sanded down to the nerves. He had been in it dozens of times, but always in the passenger seat. Belanger thought nothing of borrowing ten bucks from his friend, but he had never considered asking Chuck to use the Ford. The vehicle was just too special. It symbolized more than Belanger could bear. The tears came. He drove down Route*

17, his head thrown slightly back, shrieking as if his dead twin were in his hands instead of a steering wheel.

GOOD AND BAD WRITING

Put someone else's prose to the same word picture test. Pick up the daily paper. Circle all the words that are abstract and vague. Ask yourself how the writer might have improved passages by making those words concrete.

Now locate one of your own drafts. Be brutally honest as you go line by line through your copy. Mark the abstract words with one color and concrete words with another color. Chances are that if your prose is riddled with abstract words, you'll decide that your work needs a rewrite—fast.

Pay particular attention to the nouns and verbs you write. If your nouns and verbs are strong and give concrete details, you can eliminate the story-killing adjectives and adverbs. This makes the writing tight, engaging readers instead of making them plod through more verbiage than is necessary. Be vigilant against overusing "to be" forms and words like *was, is, were, are.* Too many auxiliary verbs indicate that your story lacks movement—in other words, it drags.

As an editor, I don't often have run-ins with writers, but one I won't forget is the academic who told me that he wasn't going to do one more draft. Thomas Wolfe had Maxwell Perkins to make his prose sing for him, the writer told me.

The PG version of my response is that I, too, might spend my evenings and Saturdays editing a genius like Wolfe, but I'd be darned if I'd stay late doing this professor's job for him.

One warning flag telling me a writer hasn't spent enough time revising is the use of a great many prepositional phrases, which kill the rhythm of the prose. Just by going through the manuscript and deleting the unnecessary phrases, I can greatly improve the rhythm of an article.

In addition to prepositional phrases, I also go on guard when a writer stuffs a piece full of qualifiers that add nothing but flab to the writing. For example, "He was indeed the person for the job" reads as well without the "indeed."

Some writers use qualifiers to make their prose wishy-washy because they are reluctant to take a stand. Here is an example:

"Fran appeared to be annoyed, as if she wanted to throttle her boss." Far better to say, "Fran was annoyed. She wanted to throttle her boss."

As a rule of thumb, describe only the unusual. "He coughed for three minutes" says something specific. "He coughed for a moment" needs the last three words deleted.

Watch out for obvious crutch words like "very," the most overused word in the dictionary. Your protagonist is angry; there's no need to describe her as very angry.

Or sometimes writers will say that someone "appeared to be almost glamorous." Such prose annoys me and I'll edit those five words into one or two words and improve both the sense and rhythm of the line. "Might be" and "may be" also offend, and it might be and may be I won't buy the piece if too many constructions like those interrupt the flow.

One of the marks of professional writers is that, busy as they are, they take the time to revise. Getting their words exactly right is a joy for pros. The more an editor can help them improve a piece, the better they feel about it. When editors return a manuscript to them with blue pencil marks, they are grateful that these professionals care as much about the integrity of a piece as they do. The best writers take the time to study their pieces when they appear in print, comparing them with their own final drafts.

Here is some advice that I have always heeded. Try to learn one new thing about writing from each editor you work with. Too many writers learn nothing from their editors' marks on their copy. If you never repeat a mistake, eventually you will be one of the best writers in the business.

Although today's overworked editors cannot always get the final version of your edited manuscript back to you, many do strive to do so. The best editors want to make certain that changes in your copy have not altered your meaning. They want to hear from you if changes result in making something inaccurate, ungrammatical or unclear.

You have to be somewhat understanding if your editor has to trim a piece to fit the art director's designed pages. Pros understand that cuts occur even if their copy isn't at fault. On the other hand, if you find your copy has been cut to the detriment of the piece, let your editor know how you feel. A good relationship with your editor begins with good communication.

CHAPTER SEVEN

Other Opportunities for Experts

W ill it be your good fortune to have your first book become a best-seller? Will a Hollywood production company adapt it? Will your writing income alone afford you the leisure time to do precisely what you want to do in life and to write only what you want to write? If so, you will be the exception to the rule, and I will cheer as loudly as anyone.

I have always loved Jack London's eloquent explanation of why some writers achieve publishing success. "The great writers arrived by achieving the impossible," wrote London in his *Martin Eden*, a novel with many episodes drawn from his own struggles to get recognition. "They did such blazing, glorious work as to burn to ashes those who opposed them. They arrived by course of miracle, by winning a thousand-to-one wager against them. They arrived because they were Carlyle's battle-scarred giants who will not be kept down."

My dreams no doubt are as big as yours, but over time I have had to face the reality that my annual income from my books and magazine articles has been comparable to what I would have made had I become the high school English teacher I studied to be in college. Nonetheless, I *have* earned enough income to support my family, help my older son pay for five years of college, and buy a home and several new vehicles. How? By taking advantage of additional financial opportunities available to me as a writer who has attained the status of being known as an expert in multiple areas.

If you are a talented writer with the courage to go after your dreams as a writer, and the intensity and dedication to overcome all the setbacks you no doubt will encounter, you can have a long career and many, many successes. If the breaks come your way, and you keep your health and sanity, you may acquire great financial wealth and fame. Other than "the check for your book has been approved," the nicest thing I hear when I meet someone new is, "I know your byline."

If the future finds your books and articles earning you a reasonable living, and you're able to find satisfaction from a career that many envious nonwriters would love to have, perhaps some of the opportunities I've found to boost my income may interest you.

PURSUING OPPORTUNITIES TO TEACH

Ordinarily college writing teachers must possess doctorate degrees. If you possess one (even if it is in a nonjournalism area such as political science), you should make an attractive candidate for many academic positions—in English, journalism, communications—if you have published clips as well.

Yet, there are ways to get around a lack of a doctorate. Although I lack a Ph.D., I taught in tenure-track positions at Clemson University and Ball State University for five years, and I have taught continuing education classes at a Temple University branch campus in Pennsylvania and at UCLA. I now teach an elective in writing about the arts at IUPUI (Indiana University-Purdue University at Indianapolis).

Nor is it particularly unusual that I have gotten such opportunities with only an M.A. in English. Although many universities discourage journalism and English departments from hiring "practitioners" for tenure-track jobs, other schools allow the hirings; their students learn from writers and editors with extensive real-world experience. Most institutions that waive the Ph.D. do require an M.A. degree in English, mass communications or journalism, or an M.F.A. in creative writing. Occasionally, colleges hire someone with considerable professional expertise and only a B.A. or B.S. degree. For example, the Department of Mass Communications at Quinnipiac College in Connecticut recently advertised for a working journalist with either a bachelor's or a master's degree. In nontenure track positions, if writers are willing to teach part time, they find many universities employ practitioners with only B.A. or B.S. degrees. My wife, for example, had only her bachelor's when she taught copyediting classes at Ball State University.

One trend I have spotted is the occasional openings in some journalism departments for professionals-in-residence. These are usually one-year contracts (often renewable up to three years) that require significant media experience. For example, a professional-in-residence opening for the fall of 1995 in the department of journalism at California State University, Chico, required someone to teach one media course and advise the student newspaper.

Another opportunity for published writers is to advise student publications. One of my duties at Ball State University was to advise the student magazine. I was thrilled when BSU's low-budget magazine won prestigious national publications awards, and I won the College Media Advisers' award for student magazine adviser of the year (1988-1989). I enjoyed working directly with young people on a publication, giving them the experience to embark on careers in the magazine industry.

There are two types of advisers for student publications. The first, similar to mine at Ball State works in a department, usually journalism, or under the umbrella of mass communications as an adviser or publisher. The second type works as a director of an independent company serving a university and responsible for publications such as the student newspaper, magazine, yearbook and directory.

JOBS IN MEDIA

I have found that the best way to track positions at universities is to subscribe to two publications, the *Chronicle of Higher Education* (1255 Twenty-Third Street, N.W., Washington, DC 20037) and *Editor & Publisher* (11 W. 19th Street, New York, NY 10011). Both contain advertising sections which list tenure-track, nontenure-track, and adviser positions at universities and the private companies serving specific universities.

You also may wish to join professional organizations that list job openings in their own periodicals. For writer-in-residence and journalism positions in English Departments, write to the Modern Language Association (MLA) for membership and job listings. For information specifically on advising, write the College Media Advisers (CMA) for membership information and a newsletter that lists advising vacancies. For membership information and a newsletter listing job vacancies in journalism and mass communications, contact the Association for Education in Journalism and Mass Communication (AEJMC). Consult the *Encyclopedia of Associations* for current addresses for these three organizations.

Remember to start your search one full year prior to the academic year in which you want to teach. Positions for the fall almost always have been filled by the previous May, but occasionally some late openings and mid-year openings occur.

OPPORTUNITIES AS A CRITIC AND/OR REVIEWER

If you become an expert in such fields as theater, media, books, food and music, there are numerous local and national publications that will allow you to display your expertise. My magazine, *Arts Indiana*, publishes two to five reviews every month. While I rely on local writers to cover theater, opera and symphony concerts, I also have a stable of national writers who review books, poetry chapbooks, music CDs and occasional independent films. All of the latter reviews must have some sort of connection to Indiana. In addition, because I edit a state publication, I use numerous correspondents to report on the arts in South Bend, Gary, Fort Wayne, Evansville and other Hoosier cities.

Most daily and weekly newspapers are open to hearing ideas for reviews of cultural activities from nonstaffers with some expertise. So are many specialty and trade publications. *Publishers Weekly*, for example, assigns short book reviews and author interviews to freelancers. Always contact the publication to get the name and title of the person assigning reviews, or if there is no specific person, get the name of the managing editor. When you write to them, send three writing samples with your letter. Be prepared for some turndowns, but this is one area where persistence likely will pay off for you.

Some newspapers will assign nonstaffers a regular column once reviewers have proved themselves reliable and knowledgeable. An Indianapolis professor of art, Steve Mannheimer, is a critic and reviewer who writes arts and restaurant columns for the *Indianapolis Star*. An Anderson University publications editor, Jack Williams, writes a regular column for runners in the *Anderson (IN) Herald-Bulletin*. Early in my career I wrote a freelance newspaper column for tropical fish hobbyists that brought me an assignment for *The Aquarium*, and also a book review column which led me to believe that someday I would write them, too.

Quite often if you have expertise in one area, a periodical will allow you some time to develop expertise in other areas. For example, if you already consider yourself an expert in classical music, an arts editor may ask you to branch out to cover rock concerts, opera and jazz. Getting a start with small publications and newspapers is an effective way to polish your writing, gain expertise, and acquire clippings that will enable you to write for mass-market magazines. You also likely will get an opportunity to expand your horizons from reviewing to writing criticism. If you have had experience in some area as a performer or participant, you may have somewhat of an edge over potential reviewers and critics who lack practical credentials. I have observed that many of the arts reviewers and critics I rely upon have advanced academic degrees, but I also have worked with college dropouts who know some particular area such as jazz or blues.

In short, while there is no single sure way to get into reviewing and criticism, opportunities in these areas are numerous. The same creativity that goes into your reviews or column will serve you well as you approach various publications.

Writing reviews and criticism requires honesty, a flair for language, and good powers of observation. Avoid hyperbole. Use superlatives and scathing commentary only where these are truly appropriate. Writers who use strong nouns and verbs always have an edge over those who merely string adjectives and adverbs together. I prefer to obtain quotations from the performers and writers when I write reviews. Other reviewers prefer to write about the work without speaking to those who create it.

Here is an example of a book review headlined "Love in the Time of the 'Gay Plague' " that I wrote for *Arts Indiana*. Although this first novel by former *Glamour* assistant entertainment editor Margaret McMullan had flaws, it had enough qualities to make me want to read more of her work.

When Warhol Was Still Alive *by Margaret McMullan,*
The Crossing Press, 1994, $18.95, 199 pages.
Margaret McMullan's When Warhol Was Still Alive *works*
the theme of the inability of protagonist Catherine Clemons
to find a home. Catherine works in New York as an editor-

on-the-rise for fictitious Women *magazine. She knows not where home is, nor where to find it. "In America everyone is from someplace else," says McMullan, interviewed in Evansville (IN). "Doesn't everyone feel homeless at one point?"*

By book's end the heroine becomes citified, losing her innocence but not her faith in herself. New York might be the pits, but it had become her pits. "Because that is what Catherine would have," McMullan writes. "She would have a home."

Much of the plot revolves around who's having sex with whom. Life at Women *offers frequent opportunities for sexual encounters, but rarely do these 1980s human beings connect.*

Her novel is set in a time before AIDS awareness scared sexually active people into donning condoms and choosing fewer partners—particularly heterosexuals smugly blissful in the misconception that this disease was the gay man's plague.

In Warhol *Catherine's diet of men lacks the right nutrients. Her longtime lover (Daniel), an older man with prissy habits and tastes, heads to Rome, paving Catherine's way for a series of sexual encounters.*

*She has sex with Lewis, a comic not long for this life (*Warhol *is dedicated to deceased comedian Andy Kaufman), and with Michael, the lover of Fran, entertainment editor at* Women.

Michael, in turn, buggers Catherine's best friend, Joey, art director of Women *and a flamboyant homosexual who is destined to die of AIDS. (Catherine comes into the room during the act of betrayal—fictive justice since Fran previously had observed her assistant in a fight with Michael, finding out that the two were lovers.)*

These 1980s characters lie easily and well. Being nice is not a priority for New York guerillas (Michael sells junk bonds) on the make. To be envied is a big goal, to be a trendsetter is better. To be famous—even if only for a Warholian fifteen minutes—is best. To get to the top, to stay there, people sacrifice friends, lovers, careers.

"It's interesting when people do the wrong thing," says McMullan. "That's what fiction is."

Life is never the same for the betrayed and betrayer. Neither can undo the act; neither can look at each other as they once did. Yet forgiveness, if bestowed, adds another dimension to a relationship. Even a heel needs to heal.

Catherine and Joey reconcile while the art director is on his deathbed. Catherine and Michael (father of Catherine's aborted fetus) become friendly acquaintances, although something less than friends.

Catherine elects to make the most out of the world in which she lives. She transfers from the hip entertainment section to write how-to pieces that will not only make Women *better, but presumably enrich the lives of millions of women who read it. True, it is still a version of Dante's hell, but the pitchfork she carries is of her own choosing.*

In an ending that races uncomfortably to completion, losing the unhurried pacing of the book's beginning, Catherine comes to terms with her father's death and reaches an uneasy truce with the mother who's been waving a white flag all the novel. Joey dies of AIDS complications as abruptly as if he's been felled by a stroke; the pacing here also is off.

The reconciliation comes almost too late. Abandoned and lonely, the mother plans to marry an old gentleman with Alzheimer's. Unlike Catherine, such a husband not only won't carry a grudge—he can't even remember slights. The daughter realizes that her mother needs to be needed and to connect.

Unfortunately, McMullan as yet has not mastered Anne Tyler's skill at presenting a fully realized minor character. The mother in Warhol *is lifeless and unconvincing. The author, in trying to change the autobiographical characteristics of her own mother on whom she says the fictional mother is based, fails to breathe life into the character. McMullan acknowledges* Warhol's *birth defects. "All first books are pink and ugly," she says.*

This novel about life in the unreal world of women's magazines is an exercise in self-examination by McMullan. She writes bravely and well. One character, Joey, realizes that it would have been better to have never loved at all, than to have loved and lost his life. McMullan's novel may answer the twentieth-century question of what's this world coming to. The answer is that we humans are all we have.

At novel's end, Catherine learns she can find a home only if her definition of "home" changes.

Home, with apologies to Robert Frost, isn't where they have to take you in. It's where you take your stand.

LOCAL PUBLISHING OPPORTUNITIES

Far more often than you might think, there are opportunities to write books for organizations and institutions. Corporations and universities frequently hire freelancers to write their histories. As I mentioned previously, I once accepted a position to research and write a history of a women's college. For me the decision proved unwise, because the amount of time the project demanded failed to come anywhere near a fair hourly rate even halfway through the writing. Yet I enjoyed the research on women's education, and I liked the people on the editorial board I worked with, so the project was not as torturous as it might have been.

You may decide that such projects are worth your time as you try to build credentials as an expert and writer. If so, keep an eye on the classified section of various papers and subscribe to the city edition of the *New York Times*, which advertises such opportunities under "Writer" in its Help Wanted section. Other ways to learn about such opportunities are to join a local writers organization and also let your local arts and humanities council know that you are available for writing projects.

Almost always you will be asked to sign a contract. Read it carefully and know what you are promising to deliver. The downside to these projects is that you're sometimes working with people who do not have a clear idea of what they really want. Therefore, you may find yourself doing needless additional drafts until those who have hired you find the right focus.

In short, these local publishing opportunities are always worth looking into, but be somewhat wary, negotiate for compensation and expenses, and have a qualified attorney go over a contract with you before you sign an agreement.

COLLABORATION

I'll never meet the likes of Tiny Boyles again. A giant who weighed 389 pounds, his appearance intimidated both friend and foe. A tangled black mat of beard hung down to his massive chest, and savage tattoos adorned his stovepipe arms—testaments to his younger days as president of a motorcycle club. A chain belt circumnavigated his enormous midsection, and he wore a skull ring with movable jaws that bit on impact. If all that didn't impress you, he kept a .357 magnum strapped to his right side and a .45 to his left, and twirled a .410 heavy-load shotgun in his paws as if it were a Tonka toy.

Boyles worked as a skip tracer for several bail-bond outfits. He operated under the protection of an 1873 Supreme Court decision (Taylor vs. Tainter) that essentially gave carte blanche to bounty hunters in pursuit of escaped prisoners.

He and I co-wrote four novels in the "Bounty Hunter" series imprint under some good editors like Bob Gleason and Mel Parker, the latter considered one of the best in the business at marketing paperback books. Boyles, a throwback to the tall tale spinners of American folklore, could neither read nor write, but that never hindered his ability to work with me on character development and plot. The books attracted a fairly wide readership and were twice optioned by a Hollywood producer, although no movie was made.

However, I grew to be very uncomfortable with the relationship with my co-author. Our publisher sent him alone on talk shows and newspaper interviews, and he decided to color his already colorful career by falsely claiming to have tangled with real-life people who were the prototypes of the made-up villains in our novels. He was angry, confused and hurt by my coldness to him, and by my insistence on telling some reporters that these stories of Tiny's were fiction. We were barely speaking at the time of his death in 1984.

As I discuss elsewhere in this book, I also collaborated on a book with a lovely person named Carole Shaw, the publisher of *BBW*, but that project fell apart when our editor was fired. We could have stayed with our publishing house, but the new editor—who now is a well-known book agent—wanted Shaw to go against nearly everything she was espousing in her magazine. For example, Shaw's philosophy is that a large woman should wear whatever she wants and not be a victim of the Madison Avenue "thin is good, anorexic is better" way of thinking.

I was on the phone in a three-way conversation with Shaw and the editor when he demanded that she put into her fashion chapter a section on how stripes can "camouflage" fat. Shaw kept her cool, but she told him that what he wanted was unacceptable. When the editor hung up the phone, I no longer had a book contract (although Shaw did get me a small amount of money by publishing the book under the imprint of American R.R. Publishing Company). Nonetheless, I admired her for sticking to her guns and having the courage of her convictions. I lost my shirt, but I profited as a person from the experience.

I also had a chance a few years ago to collaborate with Ferguson Jenkins, the Hall of Fame pitcher, but was of the opinion after meeting him that he wanted to avoid delving into some of the more unpleasant aspects of his life. Moreover, while I liked his agent, I did not trust his live-in girlfriend who kept wanting him to end his conversation with me so that they could go shopping. I respectfully said that I was the wrong person to write the book. A few months later, I read in the newspaper that the girlfriend had committed suicide in Jenkins's recreational vehicle, compounding the tragedy by having the athlete's young daughter die with her.

My experiences as a collaborator have been both positive and negative. I would do another book with someone if the circumstances were right. If collaboration interests you, perhaps you can learn something from my experiences good and bad.

Be Patient and Flexible

The first thing you must know in advance is that you and your collaborator will be working in circumstances closer than those of some married couples. You can anticipate some of the joys and anguish you'll experience while working together, but more likely Fate has some surprises in store that you could never imagine beforehand.

My experience in collaborating with Tiny Boyles was different from collaborating with Carole Shaw. Boyles, in spite of his biker appearance, thought like a businessman. He valued our relationship in direct proportion to the amount of income and fame he was getting from our book series. Shaw, on the other hand, welcomed me into her family, and has stayed in touch to this day. She seemed to appreciate my show of support when she ended the contract with the first publisher, and while we were working, she would ask from time to time if I had any disagreements or lack of comfort with anything I was writing.

My advice would be that you team up with someone who seems to care about you as well as the book or books you write together. There are friction points in any relationship, and if you can't stand to be in close contact with each other at the beginning, you may not be speaking by the time you've written the final chapter and are ready to hit the road to promote your creation. In a *Men's Fitness* interview I once did with Peter Wylie, Ph.D., head of a counseling service for troubled partnerships, he told me that every business relationship had to have trust, respect, affection and confidence. It was necessary for both partners to be able to listen as well as to talk things out. While I always was able to clear the air with Shaw, whenever I tried to do so with Boyles he felt threatened, partially because he was a high school dropout and both feared and was intrigued by people such as myself who possessed graduate degrees.

One advantage when I worked with both Boyles and Shaw was that they respected my abilities as a writer, and deferred to my judgment in matters of style and structure. I, on the other hand, saw each of them as true personalities—real American originals—and I tried hard to faithfully record *their* individual voices—while losing my own.

Wylie said that all partnerships needed that intangible quality we call chemistry for a collaboration to work.

Ask yourself, *Are the two of us in sync?* If you are, there is a good chance that you're headed for the best-seller lists. If you're not, you could be headed to court to let a judge divide your assets when the partnership dissolves.

Ghostwriting

In my career I consciously have decided to bypass one of the more lucrative—if frustrating—ways to make money in the writing business. I'm a lone wolf by nature, and an alpha wolf at that. Ghostwriters must possess a personality that allows them to function on the outside, even when seething on the inside, and that just isn't me. As a freelancer I have interviewed dozens of celebrities—many of the interviews have been as hard for me as they were for them as I pumped penetrating questions into them like bullets—but no amount of poverty or praise could get me to co-exist with a celebrity for the time it would take to establish his or her manufactured life on tape.

But ghostwriting may be right for you. Certainly it has worked for dozens of ghostwriters like Charles Leerhsen and William Novak who have written best-selling autobiographies—I use the term loosely—respectively on business dynamo Donald Trump and former Chrysler executive Lee Iacocca. Whenever a publisher announces that it is looking for an author to write a book for a famous politician, athlete or businessperson, there is no shortage of candidates, including reporters for prestigious news organizations like the *New York Times*.

One of the advantages of ghostwriting is that for about a year's work, you get a fee that can amount to what you'd probably make as a full professor in a mid-sized or large college. In other words, at least you know that you and your family will eat and you'll get the house payment to the bank on time.

The disadvantages of ghostwriting are many. Unless you have a really cagey agent and you're a name that an editor just has to have for a particular celebrity's book, you won't receive a dime in royalties. William Novak's ghostwritten *Iacocca: An Autobiography* sold more copies than any other nonfiction book ever published save the Bible and a cookbook by Betty Crocker, but he received only $40,000—although he did get onto the college lecture circuit. Another best-seller, Leerhsen's' *Trump: Surviving at the Top*, also failed to net that ghostwriter one dime in royalties.

But for me, an even bigger disadvantage is that you're probably going to have to fudge, perhaps prevaricate, and leave out uncomplimentary anecdotes about your celebrity's life. The last thing most celebrities want is a tell-all autobiography, and they will not hesitate to fire you from a project if what you write displeases them. Sonny Bono, the singing caveman turned politician, canned his first ghostwriter. So did comedian Henny Youngman, because his ghostwriter wasn't spending enough time with him, he told the *Wall Street Journal*. Others who got rid of writers who displeased them were T. Boone Pickens, Zsa Zsa Gabor (who has had nearly as many ex-writers as ex-husbands), and singers Peter, Paul & Mary.

I make no judgments about writers who are able to compromise and write a sanitized version of their subjects' lives. Let me just say that as a writer who tries to tell the hard truth in books like *Broken Pledges*, no matter how many people I make angry, it is clearly ethically and professionally unacceptable for me to write a "puff" autobiography. The *Wall Street Journal* has alleged that a conflict of interest may have existed for several writers who were being considered to write computer tycoon Bill Gates's biography. They allegedly had written profiles of Gates for their respective publications that smacked of favoritism and were clearly unbalanced pieces of journalism.

But I have no doubt that some ghostwriters are able to get the confidence of those they portray and may even write a book that is close to the truth.

There are two main ways to get a contract to write such a book. The first is to have sufficient freelance credits or a job with a reputable publication and most likely a book or two that has been written under your own name. The second is to have written a story about your subject, who may warm to you and invite you to write his book.

THE LECTURE CIRCUIT

Although I have elected not to pursue ghostwriting possibilities, I have succumbed to the lure of the lecture circuit. While I have given a few talks for money on steroids and a couple on bounty hunting, these seem inconsequential compared with the demand that I found for me to speak on college campuses on the subject of hazing following the publication of *Broken Pledges*. From 1989 to 1995, I became a part of the talk show circuit and appeared on programs such as *Joan Rivers*, *CNN Sonya Live* and *ABC Home Show*. I have had the opportunity to speak at schools as prestigious as Cornell University and the University of Pennsylvania, as large as Indiana University and the University of Colorado, and as small as Dickinson College and Lafayette College, both in Pennsylvania.

Should you let a large speaker's bureau represent you, or should you represent yourself? I have tried both ways. Both have their advantages and disadvantages that I'll talk about here.

I approached one of the larger and better-known speaker's bureaus, K&S of Boston, and after months of negotiation they agreed to take me on. They are efficient, take care of all details, and make sure you're paid the day you speak or shortly thereafter. On the other hand, you do have to split part of your fee with them. But for me the biggest disadvantage was that, because they had so many big-name clients I felt I got lost in the shuffle; I went on my own in 1992 as a result.

Representing Yourself

If you want to represent yourself and speak on the college circuit, I suggest that you join the National Association for Campus Activities, which allows you to list your lecture topic with hundreds of member colleges and universities. You can attend NACA regional and national conventions and run a booth if you so desire. In addition, you can advertise in publications such as their annual directory. In turn, NACA will send you a list of member schools and the names of key contacts (such as the head of the lecture board or the head of campus activities) to whom you can send your materials.

You will need to develop a publicity packet. Mine has a one-page bio sheet, a business card, a description of my talk and book, a current head-shot photograph, press clippings (*New York Times, Chicago Tribune, Denver Post, Boston Globe, USA Today*), reviews of *Broken Pledges* run in magazines such as *Entertainment Weekly* and scholarly journals, information on ordering *Broken Pledges* and a contract. I send these out twice a year, in August and December, finding that my talks are usually scheduled at the start of the fall and spring semesters.

Each school usually will send you a contract to sign. It is customary to have the school pick up your airfare, transportation from airport to the college, accommodations, and one or two meals. Insist that a check be given you the night you speak. Billing takes time and is frustrating. Bring a box of your books with you to sell and autograph after the talk. I have never had a student's check bounce.

Writing a Speech

Unlike many people who worry about what they are going to lecture about, you—as an expert on one or more topics—shouldn't have that problem. Likely the biggest problem you'll have is getting so much information into a sixty-minute presentation. My recommendation is that you narrow your focus and cover only what reasonably can be covered in an hour. Try to raise questions in your audience's mind, then answer them. You will leave out much that is in your head. You must or lose the audience. Get your talk as tight as you can make it. Leave them wanting more.

My first talks were not nearly as good as the ones I give now. Because I was afraid that I might step in front of a microphone and go brain dead, I typed out every word of my speech. Consequently, the early talks ran about thirty minutes overtime, and they lacked all spontaneity. Before long, however, I reached a point where I was confident enough to simply write keywords on notecards to direct me through my talk.

Notecards should also work well for you. Not only will they make you confident that you will remember all your key points, but soon you will feel comfortable enough with an audience that you can even ad-lib. Concentrate on the faces of several people in the room. Their posture and facial expressions will guide whether you need to change your inflections, pace and tone.

Preparing for the Talk

No two audiences are alike. Prior to your talk you should have at least two or three conversations with the people bringing you to campus to speak. Ask them to describe your probable audience and to give you any information on local tie-ins to your topic that you can bring naturally into your talk. Ask how many people will be in the audience and whether the facility has any limitations you need to consider.

The more prepared you are, the better you can visualize your audience. The better you visualize it, the more comfortable you will be on stage.

I've heard that some speakers find success talking to just one person in the audience. If that works for you, fine. I try to look over my entire audience. After all, if I please just one person, I'm going to bomb this day. I work hard to make every member of the audience feel that I've said something that could change their attitude and possibly their life.

Why Give a Speech?

First of all, you may have to. My first speeches connected to my writing were on the legalities of bounty hunting; I spoke at a Mystery Writers of America convention when my co-author, Tiny Boyles, and I were on the road on a book tour. After your book or article comes out, you may be asked by your publisher or the magazine to do some promoting. Speaking to large groups is a good way of making sales and getting additional offers to speak.

GIVING EXPERT TESTIMONY

Depending on the expertise you develop, one possible scenario you might not have expected is that you may be asked, for a fee you set ranging from $70 to $200 per hour, to be an expert witness in a trial. My own particular expertise—the fact that I'm one of only a handful of hazing experts in this country, and at this writing the only person ever to write a book on the subject—has put me in this position. I am an expert, not only in the viewpoint of my readers, but in the eyes of the law of the land.

Thus far I have been asked to be a witness for the prosecution in four civil suits involving hazing-related deaths or injuries. I have accepted only one because my full-time editing job does not give me the flexibility to adjust to delays in scheduling appearances for depositions—a fact of life in all civil suits. If you are a freelancer, you won't have a problem adjusting or changing your schedule at the last minute, but if you have a day job, you'll need the understanding of your superior before saying yes when asked to testify.

The case I agreed to get involved in as an expert witness was that of Bertha Thomas, mother of the deceased Harold Thomas, who brought suit against Omega Psi Phi's national office after her son died on the track of Lamar University. The case was brought to the district court of Jefferson County, Texas, in the 136th judicial district. The firm that retained me was that of Umphrey, Swearingen, Eddins & Carver. The case was settled out of court to the satisfaction of both parties.

Should you be retained as an expert witness by either the prosecution or the defense, what should you expect?

You will receive many boxes of documents and depositions to read that have a bearing on the case. The attorney retaining you will ask you to give your honest expert opinion on what has been sent. In my case, I had to determine whether or not the incident was a hazing in Texas, and what the usual responsibility of a national fraternity is in similar circumstances. I also had to give an opinion as to what was a reasonable amount of education that a national organization needed to provide to its members in order to try to keep hazing out of its initiations.

After I rendered my opinion, the attorney retaining me as an expert witness required me to give a deposition in New York City, paying my expenses to get there. I was questioned first by that attorney and then by the defense attorney for the prosecution. I answered all questions honestly and happened to respect the professional demeanor of both attorneys, even though it was the job of the prosecution to try to tear my testimony apart. Weeks later, the case was settled at the eleventh hour. Had it not been, I would have testified before a judge and jury in Texas.

The experience was a positive one. I learned a tremendous amount about how an attorney prepares a case and am using that information to become an even better researcher. It also has made me glad that I have kept current on hazing issues—something I do because I believe I have the knowledge and power to work toward eradicating these senseless deaths and injuries that are due to peer pressure.

CHAPTER EIGHT

Attitude Adjustment

Back in 1982, my wife-to-be from Indiana and I drove to Los Angeles to tidy up loose ends on a book project of mine that was to be published later that year. The trip was a homecoming for me since I lived in L.A. for a couple years in the seventies. Jenine insisted that I meet Garry Williams, a Hoosier friend of hers, a struggling actor and neophyte screenplay writer living with two other actors in a tiny Hollywood dung-a-low. Jenine and Williams had worked together in community theater productions in Indianapolis, he as an actor, she in production.

After introductions the three of us visited the Larry Edmonds Bookstore, a Hollywood shop that carries plays and books on screenwriting. My reluctance to meet this wannabe dissipated as Williams and I discussed mutual dreams, the terrors of creativity, and the difficulties of living in a world peopled with agents, producers and publishers.

Abandoning the bookstore Williams and I walked along Hollywood Boulevard to visit my favorite cheap burrito emporium. We stopped when a frustrated shout came from behind us. We'd forgotten Jenine, a stranger in the city, and she wasn't happy.

KINDRED SPIRITS AT WORK

This wasn't the first time that I'd met a writer and recognized a kindred spirit that I wanted to keep for a friend. There is something inside writers—something struggling or successful—that I see time and again in the people I interview or run into at various conferences where we teach. Maybe it's self-confidence. Maybe it's those inner demons taunting the homunculus inside every one of us. Maybe it's the shared experience of confronting a new challenge every day of our writing lives.

Better yet, call it an attitude. Writers—just like the best magazines—cop an attitude, and it's visible to one another and outsiders alike.

This story of one writer meeting another is on my mind because at a recent conference sponsored by a writers' group in central Indiana, I happened to compare Garry Williams with David Harrison, a Hollywood friend and fellow writer I'd met in the mid-seventies. Their fates could not have been any more different. One has hit the big time. The other is dead, a victim of his own inability to see that writing success comes from having a carefully executed lifelong career plan.

David Harrison, as had I, had been homeless for a time in California until his writing and editing skills, like mine, had begun to earn money. He—in his silk shirts and flamboyant shoes—was quite a contrast to me, in my jeans and pre-grunge era grungery, but we were each other's boosters as well as friends. He never seemed embarrassed when I showed up in my grubbies at the parties of his hip friends like British rocker John Mayall, parking my '58 Buick alongside their Prussian roadsters.

When I had a birthday, Harrison invited his buddies from Tom Petty's Heartbreakers to liven up the party he threw for me. When I played softball for Rhino Records' team and hit a home run to defeat the *Happy Days* cast led by Richie and the Fonz, Harrison led the cheers. When I took a plane to Florida to play minor league baseball for the Montreal Expos' organization on a Plimpton-like magazine assignment, he drove me to the airport. On the day my first wife left for good with my older son, he stuck with me until my despair became mere sorrow.

I introduced Williams to Harrison, having invited them to join Jenine and me one evening. I often see that evening in my mind's eye. It's a special occasion when you introduce one writer to another and all things click. We talked about theater, novels, movies and school horror stories. Both men, it turned out, had quit college. I, however, had overcome expulsion from high school to get bachelors and masters degrees in English—fearful back then of not having something to fall back on should my dreams of writing success vaporize.

To a lesser degree, Williams and I have achieved some of the ambitious dreams we shared that night. Williams supports himself entirely as a screenwriter, writing and fixing scripts for MGM and independent production companies from his farmhouse in Logansport, Indiana. I've been a paid consultant for an NBC-TV movie, *Moment of Truth: Broken Pledges*, with Barry Bonds and Linda Gray, and have had my novels twice optioned by Hollywood producers.

But David Harrison failed to achieve his dreams of writing success. His suicide on an L.A. beach in the late eighties left friends and family with memories and grief. He also left a foot-high pile of unproduced screenplays.

When I talked about my friends Harrison and Williams at the conference, hands flew up all around. I could read the same question in everyone's eyes. Why do some creative spirits earn their keep—some making millions of dollars and gaining personal fame—while some who may be better writers and harder workers fail to even earn a living? Given the fact that all three of us were dedicated, had at least a measure of writing talent, and were willing to live in poverty for a time to polish our work, how was it that two of us succeeded and one failed?

"Was it luck?" demanded one person. I acknowledged that luck had to play a part. Bad luck as well as good luck, I said. But it would be too simplistic to blame luck for what happened to David Harrison. More to the point, I said that the Harrison tragedy had a lot to do with the fact that he had failed to cultivate a proper perspective. He had given himself a deadline to achieve a certain amount of fame and fortune in a specific window of time, and when in his opinion one major project too many fell through (the specifics of which I'll discuss in a moment), he saw his life as meaningless and killed himself.

KEEPING THINGS IN PERSPECTIVE

Thirty-two years after cashing my first check for writing, I honestly believe that having a realistic, but generally positive attitude has not only helped me attain longevity in the writing business, but also kept me from choosing the way out my friend David chose. Just as you never know when you'll make—or lose—a friend, you don't always know which story you're working on will lead to your big break. Therefore, even in the midst of your worst defeats, you must stay focused, hopeful that the project in front of you is the one that's going to help you break through. "If you're in trouble, you write your way out of it," former *Esquire* associate editor Pen Pesta once advised me. I've always followed that one piece of advice.

Every magazine article assignment is a possible opportunity to use my findings to write a proposal that earns me a book contract. While most of the time that won't occur, it has happened that way once in a while. A magazine article on latter-day bounty hunter Tiny Boyles led to a four-book fiction series. A couple of interviews with major league managers for *Inside Sports* inspired my agent to get me contracts for my *Strategies of the Great Baseball Managers* and *Strategies of the Great Football Coaches*. An article on fraternity hazing for *Human Behavior* in the late seventies led to my receiving a grant from the Gannett Foundation to further study the subject; that research went into writing a book proposal that convinced Longstreet Press to give me an advance to finish that book.

You can never lose your fighting spirit, never give in to depression. When things aren't going as well as they should, I find it healthier to see what's good about the work I am doing—indeed to keep seeing the best in myself as a person, not the worst. What, in my opinion, sent Harrison into a brutal depression was the fact that a Hollywood producer (a former TV series actor) reneged on a verbal commitment to produce one of Harrison's scripts. Harrison went deeper and deeper into himself. What he should have done was to pour his frustration into writing another script. He had the talent; the opportunity would have come.

In addition to developing your writing talent, my advice is that you need to develop resilience. Setbacks happen in the business of writing to the majority of us. You have to almost perversely love those setbacks—tell yourself that in some way yet unforeseen they are enriching your work and will only lend spice to your future best-selling autobiography—and move on to yet another challenge, and another, and another so long as the business still excites and satisfies you. When the day comes that the act of writing itself fails to satisfy you internally, or is detrimental to your health or spiritual well-being, it's time to leave the business. That's as true of writing as it is of teaching, practicing medicine, or being a tennis pro.

Garry Williams, for example, could have given up when

twelve years spent off and on in Hollywood pursuing his Muse failed to pay off. He found himself in his thirties—lonely—and with his own leading lady, a nurse named Julie Jackson, back in Logansport, Indiana, wondering how long she could put her own life on hold while her man battled for success. In the mid-eighties he packed his typewriter and sparse belongings into his beater of a car and headed to Indiana to marry Julie and live in an equally ramshackle farmhouse that she had inherited.

CREATING A NEW SCENARIO FOR YOUR LIFE

"Coming here was a real risk," Williams admitted in my interview for *Arts Indiana* that I conducted with him at the now-refurbished farmhouse." You asked me if I thought I'd failed or had given up—I didn't feel that, because I knew I was coming back to write and plug away. I had a sense that I was opening a new chapter. What I had decided consciously was that I was going to become as good a writer as I am an actor; so I knew for whatever amount of time, no matter how long it was going to be, I was coming back to write."

And write he did, hunkered down at his kitchen table by night and hammering the farmhouse into shape by day—getting a few dollars here and there by acting in several Indianapolis and Muncie TV commercials. In short he did what he had to do to attain a revised dream, using every spare hour he could to demystify the writing process, concentrating on the nuts and bolts of producing quality work. "The best way to learn to write anything is to read what you can about it, [as well as] read the plays and screenplays of others—and just do it and do it and do it," Williams told me.

In short, Williams had gone to Hollywood and it hadn't worked out; now Hollywood, dammit, would come to him. *I'm not giving up*, he reassured himself, *just going to a tranquil place to work*. "Sure a lot of that probably was self-justification and self-protection and things like that," admitted Williams. "But I've always had an odd kind of knowledge that I wouldn't quit trying until I was dead."

If people truly want to see their byline in print, they find some way to overcome all obstacles to succeed. Because I was a less-than-stellar student in high school, ultimately getting expelled from the first one I attended, I had to teach myself grammar as an adult. We all have something to overcome.

And although I have not yet written the Great American Young Adult Novel, I haven't given up that I may some day do just that. In the meantime, I try to be the best nonfiction writer in Indiana and one of the best in the nation. I've changed goalposts, in other words, but they're still the same height. Joe Paterno, a legendary college football coach I interviewed for *Inside Sports*, told me that when a player is permanently injured and unable to play any longer, Penn State's coaching staff tells the kid to write a new scenario for himself. If the player insists upon keeping football in his life, Paterno and his assistants give him advice about opportunities in coaching.

GOALS

You have to follow your dreams, but sometimes you need to be flexible. David Harrison loved screenwriting to death. Garry Williams loves screenwriting, but had the perspective to always know that his personal life was important too. At different times in my life I have been as manic about my career as Harrison and as philosophic about it as Williams is and was. The happiest time in my life has been when I've struck a balance between being devoted to my craft and being loyal to my family. I'm not saying it's the only way to do things. It's just the way I function best.

For an increasing number of people seeking a balance between family and career, working out of the home as a freelance writer has become The American Dream. In traveling on assignment to forty-nine states plus Mexico and Canada, and teaching at writing workshops sponsored by universities as large as the University of Southern California and as small as the University of Southern Indiana, I have found people everywhere who'd really rather be freelancers. They have a dream of interviewing celebrities like athlete Deion Sanders or actress Susan Lucci (as I have) and sitting in front of a personal computer to fashion manuscripts that earn respectable checks from respected publications. They are, in short, like you.

The fact is that anyone who starts any home-based business does so with trepidation. To be sure, the road to becoming a freelance writer is fraught with warnings that can kill the adventurer in anyone: 1) you must reside in New York City, 2) new and even venerable magazines go belly-up every day, 3) editors are only looking for "name" writers. You've heard all the clichés and there's no need to repeat them all. Especially because they're not necessarily true: 1) I've made a decent living as a freelancer in New Mexico, Indiana and Idaho. 2) While it's true that many magazines are folding, there are more magazines with million-plus circulation figures than there have ever been in the history of publishing. 3) Few magazines have the budgets to hire only name writers. Most depend on no-name pros like myself who keep churning out good, clean, accurate copy.

That's not to say that freelancing is a sure way to attain success—it's not. Because freelance writers are independent businesspeople, they tend to assess their self-worth by the bottom line in their savings accounts. Naturally they are preoccupied with success and failure. But that's true in any small business, not just freelance writing. According to statistics kept by the Small Business Administration, most small businesses fold in five years or less.

Don't let those figures depress you, though. The old saying— "the odds are bad but the opportunities are good"—applies to freelancing no less that it does to other operations that people run out of their home offices.

YOU CAN GO IT ALONE
Two highly successful freelancers, Sarah and Paul Edwards, say that Small Business Administration statistics should not discourage you. The California-based Edwardses, a married couple who have written top-selling books like *Working From Home* and *Making It On Your Own*, have been called in print "the gurus of the work-at-home movement." They cite a comforting survey by American Express and the National Federation of Independent Business that found a 70 percent success rate among some three thousand businesses that were tracked.

So even if you've tried freelancing (or some other business) on some prior occasion without success, you should still take heart. The Edwardses say you just may be one of the many people who get better with hands-on experience in the writing trade. "People now understand that there is a learning curve," says Sarah Edwards. "A lot of people fail several times before they get going."

If you do start a freelance writing business as a full-time enterprise or sideline and it falters, my advice is to take a what-of-it attitude. If one article falls through the cracks, try to focus on those that went well for you. Take pride in what you've achieved, rather than indulge in the no-win practice of self-loathing or beating yourself mentally to death.

Thomas Edison tried thousands of times to get the right filament for his light bulb without success, telling himself with each attempt that it was just one less thing he'd have to try in the future. Best-selling author William Least Heat Moon was unemployed and about out of prospects after *Blue Highways*, his manuscript about life on the road, had been rejected by ten publishers. Heat Moon submitted it to editor Peter Davison of Atlantic Monthly Press who found merit in the unsolicited manuscript and published it to international acclaim.

Significantly, after *Blue Highways* was published, I interviewed Heat Moon. He had recently received a letter from a woman in Washington, DC who had been reading his book on a plane and was deeply touched by a quotation in it uttered by a farmer from Nameless, Tennessee. The farmer said, "A man becomes what he does." The letter writer's life was at a low point at the time, and she wrote the author that upon reading that sentence she went to the back of the plane and started to cry. At that time, Heat Moon told me, "she didn't know what to do with her life, but she knew very definitely there was something wrong with it."

Even more exciting for me was that Heat Moon, at our meeting, told me that he was acquainted with my own on-the-road experiences. He had read about them in my "Tales of the Freelancer" in 1979 *Writer's Market.*

My own impetus in 1976 to abandon doctoral studies in English at the University of Nevada at Reno and enter the world of publishing full time came about because I wanted to write articles and books that people would read and care about—not term papers that my profs might or might not pore over before I shoved the work, forgotten, into a file cabinet. At that point I had invested five years in graduate school, and worried I had wasted all that time. I since have come to realize that the research skills I learned in graduate school have been valuable: Nonetheless, there is no way in the world I would ever trade the fifteen books I have published for the dissertation I never finished.

Don't Let Loved Ones Stop You

If you decide to leave a job to freelance, know in advance that you cannot let your co-workers, parents or friends make you feel like a failure—especially if their standards on what constitutes success or failure are based solely on the pay you used to bring home. For example, before work-at-home guru Sarah Edwards and her husband/co-author hit it big, her mother—with good intentions—practically detonated Sarah's self-image whenever the writer called home. "I'd get on the phone and tell her all kinds of good stuff happening to us and she'd say, 'Well, are you making any money?' " recalls Sarah. "It feeds right into your doubts."

Painful as it may be, Sarah Edwards recommends limiting or even discontinuing relations with people who undermine you and judge your accomplishments a failure even when those efforts are still in progress. Her alternative was to communicate with other home-based writers and other professionals on a computer network like America Online, Prodigy or CompuServe to get the emotional support she craved. Those computer networks all offer forums for writers who share your value system and your enthusiasm for the writing you're doing.

"Just being online with a bunch of other people who are doing it, believe in it, and know that it happens and that *you* can do it makes a difference," says Sarah Edwards. As the systems operators on CompuServe's Working-From-Home forum, she and her husband Paul often cheer writers and others who have suffered setbacks, supplying them with what they term an "emotional road-map" to lead them away from temporary depression and destructive emotions. (They do not, however, attempt to cure people with true diseases such as anxiety and panic disorders which require professional counseling.)

I myself have a valuable online network of writing peers, but I also decided in 1993 to join a group of Indianapolis professional writers who meet at a once-monthly lunch to swap stories and practical advice. I was hesitant about joining any group of writers and had resisted doing so for more than thirty years. But the group that invited me to join was made up of people like author William H.A. Carr (*The duPonts of Delaware*) with healthy egos and enough collective publishing successes to let one another be individuals. We learn from one another, never drain each other and on occasion share a professional opinion or contact. In my opinion, that's what any writers' club should do. If your writer's group becomes a mutual sniveling society, or if one member dominates or berates the rest of you, it's time to form a one-person club with you as president.

THE FEAR OF FAILURE NEVER GOES AWAY

I suspect that all writers at some time succumb to doubts and fears that their best work is behind them and that failure is around the bend. It's just that most of us who stay in this business permanently develop coping mechanisms for getting past the times when insecurities flail us. In addition to labor and time, going on your own as a freelancer means you have to put your professional pride and self-esteem on the line. And yes, occasionally there are failures—but you have to pick yourself up and start a new project. On a couple occasions it's been the welcome encouragement of a sympathetic editor that's kept me going through the dark days of a book project that I just couldn't seem to jumpstart. Mostly, however, I've listened to my inner voice that has made me acknowledge my fears, shove them to some cobwebbed back of my brain and focus on the work at hand. It's that simple—and that complex.

It's neither helpful nor healthy to expect that the next book you write has to be a best-seller. Too many variables are beyond a writer's control. Sure, when a snafu occurs I fume and lament my fate like anyone else, but I keep some sort of equilibrium by looking at my past successes and promising myself that there will be others, as big or bigger, in the not-too-distant future.

Fighting Back

Whenever I suffer feelings of worthlessness due to some publishing-related trauma, I do one or all of three things to perk up. One, I exercise—lifting weights or mixing it up on the nearest basketball court. Two, I do something that gets me away from my computer like making a sackful of sandwiches and going fishing, or swapping my usual jeans and tee shirt for a suit to attend an opera or symphony with my wife. Or, three, I pull out my portfolio. Paging through clipping after clipping helps me relive all the fun and satisfaction I had on various assignments, like playing minor league baseball, or riding in a plane with a back-country pilot a few feet above Idaho's "River of No Return," or visiting a leper colony. These published reminders are always enough to restore my equilibrium and send me back to my word processor to crank out article queries for more great assignments.

When I was younger I loved the novels of Jack London in which someone overcame all odds and the elements to come through some trying experience. Freelance writing gives its practitioners the heady feeling of succeeding on their own. I learned how to write by studying the work of my peers and my betters, listening to established writers, and reading books such as this one on every imaginable writing topic.

TAKING CHARGE OF YOUR WRITING CAREER

One of my strengths when I taught writing courses to college students was that I cared about their work almost as much as they did. I take pride in the fact that as students, or shortly after graduation, my pupils placed stories in national and regional publications such as *Seventeen, Ladies' Home Journal, Indianapolis Monthly, Kiwanis, Saturday Evening Post, Boys' Life* and *Sports Illustrated for Kids.*

If you decide your writing could benefit from taking classes (or even getting a graduate writing degree), my recommendation is that you talk to other writers to find someone with a reputation for drawing good writing out of students. You don't want teachers who are trying to clone students in their own image. Nor do you want someone who is going to lie to you by praising you too effusively or tearing you down because you pose a threat to their delicate egos. In my view, you would benefit most if your teachers have a track record of successes as a writer. You can learn bad habits as easily as you can good. While it's possible that unpublished teachers may be able to turn out students who turn the publishing world on its collective head, the odds are that it won't happen.

While you may not have a teacher patting your shoulder and pointing out ways that you can tighten your prose, you should know that you are not alone. I used to tell my students that they could succeed as writers as soon as they reduced the odds against their attaining success. Even the most successful and long-lived writers have a fear of failure, but those who keep from burning out are the ones who learn to manage that fear.

That doesn't mean I've stopped taking risks. You have to take them—once you've weighed all options, that is. When I quit an editing job to go into freelancing full time in the spring of 1978, friends in secure-as-Gibraltar jobs questioned my sanity. Sixteen years later, some of my friends' "secure" jobs have been anything but—and only a handful are still employed where they were then. For example, Ben Pesta, a good writer who had entered the editing profession after winning a national essay contest sponsored by *Esquire*, wanted other challenges in life and is now a successful attorney practicing criminal law.

If anything, the job world in the nineties has become even less secure. One of my editors on several health books had nearly two decades of experience at Rodale Press, but she quit the company after Robert Rodale, her mentor and company president, died in a car wreck. A neighbor and friend, a technical editor with fifteen years invested with a company producing oxygen products, got the axe at Christmas—along with dozens of other employees caught in a "downsizing." Another friend worked as a school principal, but at fifty, sick of violence in the schools and hassles with parents, he found other work in education where he felt appreciated.

Me? In addition to editing by day, I'm still freelancing nights and weekends. While my lifestyle is modest compared to the multimillionaires I've interviewed, I'm hardly on the public dole. My wife and I have bought one house, paid my older son's college tuition and purchased several vehicles. Best of all, I am free from a malady that author Robertson Davies refers to as "acedia" in an essay called "The Deadliest Sin of All." Loosely interpreted, acedia is middle-aged spread of the mind, an inability to experience great highs, or even feel great pain when we experience a loss that would have laid us low when we were young. In large part because my freelance career requires me to interview vibrant people doing exciting things, I still feel passionate about good writing—mine and anyone else's, travel, my lovely wife (who is also the best copyeditor I've worked with), two great sons, cooking, teaching, editing, working out, playing softball against athletes half my age and learning new things on computers.

Incidentally, it's not the friends who have lost their jobs, gotten ticked off at the system, and then found the resolve to put their lives back on track that worry me. It's the ones who have stayed in dead-end jobs and allowed acedia to overtake them that I worry about. Those spiritless friends have been role models in reverse for me. I've seen how their growing indifference to life, success and their families has destroyed them, their families and their dreams. If the day comes when I go belly up because I've gambled two or three years' work on a book project that fails to pay off, so be it and so what. I'll always come back. One of the most treasured things my wife Jenine ever said to me was that she hopes I'll die while on assignment—then she'll know I died happy. She's right.

That's why I never felt bad for Toby Halicki, the independent filmmaker and actor who made a small fortune with a cult film about car thieves called *Gone in Sixty Seconds*. He died accidentally when a tower fell on him during a movie shoot in western New York. Halicki—for whom I did some script-fixing work in 1978—went out doing what he loved most. He was likely sky-high with excitement about his latest project the day he died.

DEALING WITH "FAILURE"

Nothing in this life worth doing goes exactly as we had planned. I had long envisioned my name on the list of credits on a made-for-TV movie. When that dream came true, though, it was hardly as I had envisioned it. First of all, the type in the credits was tiny, and NBC had squeezed as many names as possible into each frame. My name rolled by so quickly that neither my wife nor father-in-law caught it; they had to play the tape to see it. And the worst slap of all was that the network had split the screen so Jay Leno could hawk his upcoming show in a promo. Talk about getting no respect! Nonetheless, the simple fact that I earned that credit has opened a couple professional doors for me already, and I intend to use it to open more in the future.

In the three-plus decades that have passed since I saw my first byline in print, much has gone wrong that I could not have helped. It's frustrating, for example, when an editor who has been buying your work for years decides to leave a publication or book company—or is fired. The publishing industry—with the exception of some blessed corporations—is a high-turnover industry. If you're a writer or editor, you either accept that fact or you're doomed to a life of frustration.

Sometimes there is nothing you can do when a treasured contact leaves a company. I've seen several female editors like Toy Gibson Igus at *LA Style* leave to rear their children. I've seen editors such as Anita Shreve, my editor at *Us*, quit to write one critically acclaimed novel after another. I've seen other editors give notice and have never heard from them again as they presumably turned their backs on the pressures of publishing.

But suppose you do—all right, let's say the word—F*A*I*L. You're unable to deliver a manuscript. An assignment falls apart because you can't pry information out of sources. A family member gets ill. In my opinion, the healthiest thing you can do at this point is come back from failure as quickly as you can. And one thing you can do is put down on paper all that you've learned from a setback to avoid a similar situation in the future.

The fear of failing is very real for all us self-employed types. Jessica Tandy, the late actress, used to admit that she worried almost to her dying day that no producer would ever again offer her work. Failure is a social stigma that few of us think we can bear, so too often we doom ourselves to lives that are less than we really could make them because we avoid taking chances that might put us flat on our faces a time or two. No one plans to fail, but failing to plan—that's something we all would have to admit if our left hands were atop a bible.

I've made some mistakes that have raised my stress level exceedingly. I'm still dealing with the consequences of those mistakes. The worst mistake I made was to over-research *Broken Pledges*. I was so hungry to learn about hazing incidents that I traveled all over the country to interview the families of victims, never stopping to see that what I was getting was highly repetitive. Consequently, much of the information—which was obtained at great emotional expense as I wrung interviews out of distraught parents—was never used in the final product. It remains unused, possibly forever, in my file cabinets. Not only did this take a great deal of time, but I spent far too much of my advance (and a foundation grant) on these interviews. So, when it came time to interview behavorial specialists, I had little choice but to use my credit cards for expenses and went some $20,000 in the hole. I reasoned—rationalized—that the book would be so hot I could pay off that amount within a year after publication.

That's when circumstances beyond my control occurred. The publication date of *Broken Pledges* coincided almost to the day with the outbreak of the Desert Storm conflict with Iraq. The newspapers and television media had little time for the deaths of a few young people every year when it seemed as if thousands might die in war any moment. It took some four years for the media (*New York Times, Chicago Tribune, NBC Nightly News*) to discover my book, and by then it was too late. My editor had quit the company to go into college teaching, and without her presence, my publisher decided to remainder the book. I had to swing a large loan to pay my credit card debts in order to keep my credit pristine. I can't begin to tell you how much stress my wife and I felt before we obtained that loan. We began to think that we might lose our credit and might even go bankrupt. Thanks to the loan, in a few years I'll be free of debt when the final payment is made. But you can bet any new credit card debt I incur is paid the same month the bill comes to our house.

If you make a major mistake—or a series of minor ones that begin to add up—you do what I did. You pay the penalty, you stop self-sabotaging yourself, and you go on. But you must learn from the mistake, never repeating it (or rarely repeating it in case of a relapse). And, unlike my late friend David Harrison, you must go on. In this business of writing for a living, if you don't quit there is always an opportunity to turn a defeat into victory.

Novelist Barbara Shoup, a member of my writers' group, says that I've come back from defeat more times than Rocky. I take that as a compliment.

Expertise Has Its Limits

T he best authors, journalists, essayists and feature writers by nature are thinkers, educators and doers. When you join the ranks of these writers, others will begin to perceive you as an expert in one or many areas of knowledge. Becoming an expert means being willing to lay your reputation on the line again and again. It takes far more guts and ability to write a piece in which you say what the facts *mean*, than merely to say what the facts *are*.

The names of reporters who merely pile fact on fact are unknown to you or me. Their work may have consequence, I suppose, but no one will note their passing at the end of their careers. As an editor I would prefer one writer with a wonderful gift for thinking, analyzing and articulating to one hundred human tape recorders who spew back what they've ingested. There are many wonderful writers who have processed information in such a complex way that other journalists go to them for quotations when experts are needed. Here I could single out Richard Rhodes's Pulitzer Prize-winning *The Making of the Atomic Bomb*; John McPhee's exploration into any number of topics including geology; and David Quammen's science and nature journalism.

So let me say at the outset of this chapter that I do not intend to admonish writers to confine themselves to narrow boundaries. What I mean by "Expertise Has Its Limits," is that even professionals who transcend simple reporting in their work have guidelines that all but the most freewheeling mavericks follow. Put another way even the experts must respect a higher authority. These limitations are imposed by serious writers upon themselves.

The limits of expertise are set by the ethics of a writer and the standards of the publisher. Although the *New York Times* and the *National Enquirer* might very well select the same experts to interview on a given topic, their presentation is going to be very different—although the current age of tabloid, celebrity-coverage journalism is shredding even the *Times*'s perception of what constitutes newsworthy events and people. Nonetheless, it's evident that the readers of the *New York Times* hold that publication to a very high standard in content and the quality of its reportage. Even the most devoted readers of the supermarket newspapers will tell you that they're buying them for smut and scandal and sensationalism, not for the all-round excellence of their coverage. I want readers to also hold *Arts Indiana* to the highest standards of editorial quality. On occasions when errors and confusing information creep into the publication, we do our best to print corrections and clarifications. I keep the same high standards for myself in my books and magazine articles.

OPINION ARTICLES ARE OFTEN SUBJECTIVE

One of the characteristics of magazines today—particularly as a result of the growing popularity of city magazines—is that they render critical judgments that by their nature are subjective. I am referring to comparitive articles such as "the best" drives for foliage in the fall, the best golf courses, best restaurants, and their direct opposites, "the worst" lists.

In the case of judging the best colleges, for example, a publication will poll university presidents or some other class of experts before making its list. Or, when coming up with a list of "good" and "bad" places to live or retire, the magazine may check with experts in a number of different areas, such as air quality, arts and recreational opportunities and so on. Because these lists are subjective, however, it often happens that writers and editors are the final judge of winners and sinners.

Having written and edited a number of these articles over the years, I can attest to the fact that readers take them seriously. Some of the most passionate and angry letters I've received have come as a result of such lists.

Such opinion articles by their subjective nature are different from fact-driven articles such as pieces on the pros and cons of heart bypass surgery for a consumer health publication. Nonetheless, because you genuinely want to present the best lists you can devise, it is important when you write such articles that your choices are as logical and fair as you can make them. It would be wrong for a student magazine, for instance, to include a professor in a list of "Ten Worst Professors" on the basis of information given by a single student who had failed a course and could be harboring a grudge against that professor. As an advisor to the award-winning student magazine at Ball State University in Indiana during the eighties, I managed to get students to rethink their way through similar articles that had the potential to get the publication, students—and me—sued.

STANDARDS OF ACCURACY

Informational articles are another matter entirely and you must base opinions on facts when giving the recommendations of doctors in a health article, for example. If your advice on a type of birth control medication were worded in such a way as to endanger the health of women (an event that happened in the nineties when a popular magazine for women gave some incomplete advice), not only your credibility, but the credibility of the editor and the publication would suffer. Public retractions would have to be made, and if injuries or deaths occurred, lawsuits certainly would follow. In the case of the mistake made by the national women's magazine, announcements went out in daily newspapers that pointed out the mistake and the publication by name, stressing that a misuse of the medication could be dangerous, even fatal.

Unlike lawyers and doctors, writers and journalists and editors don't have an equivalent strong professional association that condemns practitioners equivalent to ambulance chasers in law and quacks in medicine. I, for one, wish we had one, and I applaud organizations such as the American Society of Magazine Editors, Society of Professional Journalists and the National Writers Union for their collective efforts to upgrade standards. Yes, it's true that the consequences of our ineptness or malpractice normally lack the life-and-death consequences of a surgeon's mistake, but nonetheless what writers write does change other people's lives for the better or worse. With such a power comes responsibility.

It is always good to keep in mind that your readers, to varying personal degrees, are putting their trust in you. Giving them false, incorrect or incomplete information can have unpleasant consequences. Your editors and readers, consciously or unconsciously, will make critical judgments about your credibility as a writer depending upon what the accuracy of the advice you give them.

Let's take the case in 1994 in which a publication predominantly for African-American readers printed a piece that said it was theoretically possible to take forty thousand dollars off one's taxes as a deduction—citing the post Civil War proclamation that freed slaves were entitled to forty acres and a mule. Many readers took such advice to heart, but they did so at their own peril—a point the magazine failed to emphasize. The Internal Revenue Service reported that a smattering of readers did file such deductions, saying that it had informed those filers that it was not in the business of righting civil wrongs. Let's speculate for a moment. Should the IRS ever rule that those forty thousand dollar deductions constitute frivolous or fraudulent returns, wouldn't those charged have a right to feel that the magazine they trusted needed to take a little more responsibility for the consequences of what it claimed?

In my opinion, writers and their publications very well could be guilty of questionable and possibly unethical behavior if they fail to protect their readers. When you assume the role of an expert and give advice, it is essential that you have an image of any readers who may be hurt if they follow what you write too closely. It's all well and good for, say, a health magazine to have a disclaimer somewhere that keeps the publication from being sued. That's good business. But I think all publications that strive for credibility and excellence also have an ethical responsibility to warn readers of the consequences its reportage and its comments from experts might have upon readers. The aforementioned publication for African-American readers, for example, should have stressed what the penalties for taxpayers might be should the IRS ever rule that claiming the deduction constitutes a violation of law or its policies.

DECISIONS, DECISIONS

People read material in books, magazines, newspapers and newsletters and make major and minor life decisions based upon what they've read. These decisions can be as major as deciding whether to tell a spouse about an affair or whether to put an aged parent in a nursing home—to rather inconsequential decisions such as choosing a scent that's right for them.

I can think of many decisions I made after reading books, magazines and newspapers. I changed my lifestyle to lower my blood pressure after my father died of a stroke, following to the letter the advice of magazines urging me to give up alcohol and high-fat foods like meats, granola and (groan!) rich ice cream. I bought my vehicle after studying a *Consumer Reports* comparative study on pickup trucks. I analyzed some almost overwhelming feelings of jealousy I had after my wife took a sexy role in a play opposite an actor twenty-plus years younger than she, checking out several scholarly books in the behavorial sciences and a cover story on jealousy in *Psychology Today*. I've learned about using computer databases for investigative reporting, gifted education, magazine design components and proper racquetball technique from books and articles others have written.

Perhaps you can pause a moment here to make your own list of behavioral changes you've made as a result of what you've read in the so-called popular press. Take this book, for example. No doubt you've made several adjustments to the way you approach your own writing as you've read the previous chapters. We human beings take expert advice seriously. Therefore, writers must honor the pact they've made with readers when they assume the role of experts.

Superficial knowledge can be a dangerous thing. If you are assuming the role of an expert, you must check all facts with recognized authorities in the field. These authorities do no less, submitting their research findings to boards made up of their professional peers.

In the end experts can narrow down choices for readers, but they can't answer every "what if" for them. For one thing, people's lives may be similar, but no two are alike. It's possible to predict a given individual's likely behavior, but variables come into play here, of course. In fact there is even such a place as the Center for Decision Research at the University of Chicago that studies the behavioral choices people make depending on their education, life experiences, occupation and so on. If a magazine writer quotes a psychiatrist who gives one situation in which it's better to inform a spouse about an affair, it's unlikely but possible that if a reader follows such advice violence might result. As a writer I try to think of possibilities and give readers warnings where they might be appropriate.

It's important to understand, however, that the writer's job—like that of other professionals—has limitations where responsibility ends. You can't ultimately make correct choices for all readers, saying "Quit your job," "Leave the SOB" or "Sell now," with 100 percent certainty. That's the responsibility of the hundreds or millions of readers relying on what you've written. Some of them are bigger risk-takers than others, for one thing. Given the confines of word limitations and the particular audience you're addressing in a given book or article, you can only give people the best expert advice you can muster within a reasonable amount of time before a deadline arrives. That's an important consideration. If you don't have the time to do a subject justice, don't take the assignment. The amount of time I had for my own writing diminished considerably once I accepted the responsibilities of putting out a monthly magazine. As a consequence, I've determined that I can only put out a book every three years, instead of writing one or two books a year as I often had done while devoting my life entirely to freelance work.

INTERVIEWING EXPERTS

Some writers are lazy, and make an interview difficult for experts. Giving interviews takes time, but even the most time-pressed expert is cooperative as long as she gets to answer difficult, soul-searching questions that may open new gound and increase the general public's knowledge about a subject. Writers who fail to do their reading beforehand, and even fail to request information packets so that the experts must answer the most basic questions, make it difficult for future writers to obtain interviews.

At Rodale Press, prior to interviewing an expert on biofeedback techniques to reduce stress, I spent several hours phoning various biofeedback clinics asking them to send me their literature, published scientific papers and relevant data. You should make a point of doing the same thing no matter what subject you choose to write about. Sure, such materials often are slanted, but you need a feel for what's out there as you start to gather additional facts on your own. Writers who make wise use of time and resources get the best stories. Those who do not, write the dime-a-dozen rehashes that turn off editors and readers.

I can give one bit of advice gleaned from my Rodale Press

experience where I interviewed healthcare experts every day. Although the best experts have trained themselves to be dispassionate, few have succeeded completely. Most have prejudices, biases and agendas that they would vociferously deny having. I need only refer you to any trial in which expert witnesses called to the stand have experienced the discomfiture of having a crack attorney expose biases and unsupported opinions they didn't know they had.

Thus, you as a writer must serve as a sort of attorney when you interview experts, making them defend their opinions and prove their facts.

When you yourself have a thesis you are developing in an article, essay or book, don't stack the deck in your favor by publishing only the results of interviews with experts who agree with you. Your readers are intelligent. Give them both sides and let them draw conclusions. When you provide dissenting opinions you are building credibility with both readers and critics.

For a major piece on graduate writing programs for *Arts Indiana*, I am gathering research from experts who say such programs develop writers, and quotes from other experts who say that they impede the development of writers or exist mainly as a "cash-cow" source of revenue for beleaguered English departments. My piece is going to show that strong writing programs at Notre Dame, Indiana University, the University of Iowa and elsewhere do benefit writers, but that even these have drawbacks that students ought to be aware of before committing two or three years to graduate study.

Experts Are Only Human

Many authors are fabulous researchers. Many authors are deep thinkers. Then why do so few authors achieve worldwide acclaim and loyal audiences that cannot wait to purchase the first editions of their work?

The answer is that authors such as Tracy Kidder, John McPhee, Lillian Ross and Joan Didion have worked hard to get their special voices into their prose. Their readers recognize the very human tone in their different, respective writing styles. Low key to the point of being self-effacing (but not quite!), such authors have learned to take a tremendous amount of research, distill it in just the right way and serve it as prose glasses so exquisite that few readers can resist sipping the contents.

The best authors find a way to introduce real people as major and minor characters to present complex concepts that otherwise could be presented only during long, boring passages of exposition. John McPhee presents complicated environmental issues, for example, through the eyes of environmentalists and their natural human enemies. My own challenge as the author of *Broken Pledges* was to take the social problem of hazing, which plagues fraternities and many other institutions in society, and somehow humanize one death so the readers could see how individuals within an organization themselves become damaged when an initiate dies in their midst. To do so, I spent many, many hours in the company of fraternity advisors and fraternity members who had had the misfortune of being connected with a hazing death.

In the following passage, I attempted to show that the inaction of a well-meaning, but uninvolved advisor played a role to a lesser or greater extent in the death of Alfred University sophomore Chuck Stenzel, the son of Eileen Stevens, who founded the Committee to Halt Useless College Killings (CHUCK) after her son's death during an alcohol-laden initiation known as Tapping Night.

> *Steven Peterson, the new Klan Alpine advisor, was watching the late news in Buffalo the day after Chuck's death. The mention of an Alfred fraternity death alarmed him, and he rushed to the store the next morning to purchase a copy of the Buffalo* Courier Express. *The lead story was the death at Klan Alpine, accompanied by a photograph of the fraternity house.*
>
> *Klan Alpine students had asked the young professor to advise them three months prior to the fatal Tapping Night. He took on the responsibility, he says, primarily "because the Klan had always had kind of a bad name, and yet the individual students I knew from Klan always seemed so nice." Among those members he regarded as topnotch people were Scott Sullivan, the president, and Rocky LaForge, the last member to see Chuck alive. "I said, 'I'm not really comfortable with certain aspects of fraternities and so on, but this group seems like a bunch of nice individuals,' so I said, 'what the heck.' " Other Alfred faculty members had*

turned Klan down. Peterson was paid nothing for his ser-
vices. He had no special training to become a Greek advisor,
not even the minimum training session that the dean's of-
fice required all resident assistants to attend.

A self-described student of politics, Peterson admits that
his knowledge of sociology and human behavior was "not
very sophisticated." His awareness of small group social psy-
chology was limited to the concept that "Individuals start
accepting group norms when, if they were outside, they'd
probably say, 'This is kind of dumb.' . . . It's the sort of thing
where collectively you just lose your common sense when
you're in an organization." While Peterson did seek assur-
ances that no men would be discriminated against for their
religion or race, he failed to give much thought to other
aspects of the pledge program. "I just thought it's kind of
dumb to put people through Hell Week and not let them
sleep and so on. From my point of view, silly as [hazing] is,
it's not necessarily harmful as long as people understand
that they're going to be penalized in their classes and so on
. . . I hadn't even thought to ask about hazing; it just didn't
occur to me that it was an issue. I remembered that in the
[early] seventies there had been a wave of hazing deaths
and accidents. I had, foolishly in retrospect, assumed that
it was over—that standards had been tightened and that
fraternities had recognized the difficulties. Silly, silly me."

Peterson, a slender man with rumpled hair and a gentle
demeanor, says he experienced a feeling of emptiness after
reading that first newspaper article about Chuck's death.
His first thought was, "Oh, my God! Some poor kid is dead."
Although Peterson was out of town on Tapping Night, he
says that he wouldn't have attended the ceremony at Klan
Alpine had he been in Alfred . . . He would have learned
about the tragedy via a ringing phone. After the tragedy,
he attached reins to his young charges as best he could.
"What the devil will you be doing this year?" he asked Klan
members. They assured him pledging would be on "a much
lower key." But, without his knowledge, limited mental haz-
ing was still conducted in the late seventies.

The previous passage on Stephen Peterson illustrates the importance of obtaining interviews with key individuals who may not be experts in the usual sense of providing statistics and an overview, but who are the human beings that illustrate in a specific way what the experts are saying. In addition to Peterson, I interviewed many families of victims killed in hazing incidents, maimed survivors of such incidents, and people who hazed another human being and were horrified to see that person die. These people may not be "experts" in the usual sense, but they are crucial ingredients for every story you write.

Such people need to be approached in a different way from the experts you interview. The experts are experienced in interview situations, and people such as Peterson are not. But Peterson, a good man caught in a horrible situation not of his own making, illustrates full well how today's fraternity advisors must always be on their guard so that hazing deaths can be prevented. His specific experience, and those of the many other individuals I talked to for the book, illustrate the truth of what the experts say, and when you reveal the personal experiences of the interviewees, readers can identify and empathize with them.

Broken Pledges would not have been an effective book if I had interviewed only experts. It was important to find other human beings who had their lives altered forever by a hazing death to convince readers of the need of vigilance to prevent future tragedies. Such people involve readers in a way that experts cannot.

After you've done enough interviews, you begin to get a sense for how valuable a source is going to be before you're more than a few questions into the interview. Some experts are misnamed. They have some knowledge of their subject, and a lot of knowledge about how to self-promote their careers. Use extensive information only from those experts whose opinions are worth listening to, worth noting. Evaluate what's said just as you evaluate what you read. Use the minor "experts" as backgrounder material, or to illustrate only a few points in a larger piece.

Once you jump into an area you know little about, you run the risk of learning so much, so quickly that you lack distance from the material. For that reason I suggest you keep a file in your computer containing the questions you asked when you first began your piece. Looking at those questions before you write will help you organize your material and will keep you from writing over the heads of your readers.

Experts are bound by the laws of the same legal system that you are. Any negative information an expert gives you about someone must be checked out thoroughly. Libel cases in recent years have given authorities less of a right to be candid in their opinions. Some courts will allow suits to be brought forward for an opinion. Keep that in mind whenever you print the words of experts in which they denigrate someone else.

How you present the opinions of experts is as important as what they say. Readers have a right to know how you obtained the information you're putting into your article. Did Dr. Sawbones's theories on knee surgery come from papers he published in a specific medical journal? Cite the source. Did she enlarge upon those opinions in an interview with you? Make it clear in the context of your piece that you have done your homework.

As an editor I almost always ask writers to provide a bit more background on their actual interview with an expert. For example, I want readers to know what the person they are reading about looks and sounds like.

Although there are exceptions owing to space considerations and other editorial decisions, if an interview was done in person, I prefer that the reader get a glimpse of the expert in a particular setting. If the interview was done by phone, I prefer to say so. Again, this is a preference. However, if an expert renders an opinion through a spokesperson—say a superstar surgeon at a large university research hospital—I always try to give such particulars. I might write, "Dr. Sawbones said in a signed statement," or "Dr. Sawbones said through hospital publicity director Gwendolyn Carter." In such cases, information given through a spokesperson makes it more likely that facts can get muddied. My advice is that you insist that the spokesperson get the pages containing information referring to Dr. Sawbones initialed by her, signifying that everything attributed to her is correct. To do so lessens the possibility that the spokesperson will claim to have been misquoted or misinterpreted after your article appears.

PRIVACY MATTERS

Ours is an age of dastardly creative limitations imposed by courts, by the families of deceased public figures, by many public figures themselves while they are alive. Ours is an age in which researchers are paid to make and break the images of politicians. Ours is an age when many eminent beings scrunch their true private lives into one shut hand, even while the other hand leaks image-making stories to the public that careless, lazy, inept or jaded journalists print, knowing more often than not that what they publish is pap, trash—or worse—lies.

One of the duties of expert writers is to expose the secrets of public figures.

This may be repulsive to you by nature. You might say, don't we all have secrets? Don't we all have stories we don't want told? Don't all of us have a right to privacy and to keep these stories buried?

The answers, in my opinion, come down to simple yes's and no's. Yes, probably most of us have our secrets and, yes, even more likely we don't want them told. We've confronted ourselves in private and decided to go on. Or we've locked away those secrets, deciding by intellect or instinct that unexamined lives are worth the living, because unexamined lives are less torturous to live.

But I'd have to say that the correct response to that third question—don't we all have a right to keep stories about ourselves buried—is yes and no. Those who have led private, nonpublic lives have the right to secrecy, a right to keep stories buried, so long as they have broken no laws. But if their dirty little secret is that they've molested a child, or mistreated animals, or driven motor vehicles while stimulant controlled, they've forfeited the protections of privacy laws and the troubling side of their troubled selves very well has become a public matter.

So too does the right to privacy disintegrate once an individual has made an entrance into public life. Individuals who write novels, enter politics, create empires of any sort on earth, share private thoughts in a public forum and so on do so at the peril of their secret lives. The passions and sins and misdeeds of public figures are as much a part of them as exploits and successes and all that has given them fame. No less true is the fact that some people also forfeit their privacy when unfortunate or calamitous circumstances thrust them into the public eye. A good example of this is when a few years ago Ryan White was denied a welcome at a Kokomo school because he had been exposed to the AIDS virus through a blood transfusion.

The problem, of course, is that the public at large is one giant tick that engorges itself on the bloody, the unseemly and the lurid story. The public can't get enough of the John Wayne Bobbits, the O.J. Simpsons and others in that all-inclusive category of "celebrities." And because the press is big business—we're reminded time and again—we've come to see a story on singer Lyle Lovett's sleep-in at a hotel with a woman not his wife (he denied anything untoward happened) in the papers such as the *Indianapolis Star* and *USA Today*—which credits the *National Enquirer* for breaking the story. Rather than elevate the public taste, our supposedly distinguished publications have elected to pander to it, but that's a topic beyond the scope of this chapter.

What is within the parameters of the limits of expertise is the troubling trend I see, whereby authors who have become experts on the lives of certain individuals are stopped in their tracks from writing what they know in popular biographies. Especially bothersome is that of late, several public figures whose fortunes and reputations have been made through the print media have used their money and fame to quash books about themselves. Armand Hammer, Saul Bellow and J.D. Salinger have all tried to halt publication of such books. Extremely disturbing is the tendency of courts to forbid journalists from quoting extensively from the letters of their subjects following Salinger's objection to such publication on the basis of their having supposed literary value to him—being his own creation.

WHEN YOU BECOME THE EXPERT

Once you have established a reputation as an expert in a particular subject, you may be interviewed by the print media to elicit your opinion. For example, every time a fraternity death becomes national news, I can count on getting phone calls from a dozen or more newspaper reporters. My own experience was that once the big publications interviewed me and my name went into various computer datebases, others ever hence were going to do so, too. Most interviewers have been competent, ethical and fair, but a few have not. I've seen mistaken information from college reporters who attended my talks appear in university newspapers. And I've seen instances where reporters have cited an inflated figure on the number of hazing deaths given to them from uninformed sources that do not keep the case-by-case records on fraternity hazing deaths as I do.

Such errors have taught me to halt an interview if I have any reason to suspect that a reporter's professionalism may not be all that it could be. And I've given interviews on occasion with the stipulation that reporters read back what they've written—after I've given them an assurance that I will ask them to change only incorrect facts, not opinion.

I have two points here. One, once you are in a position that editors and the public take your expert opinions seriously, you need to guard against having your expertise questioned because a reporter somewhere has misquoted you. Two, because I have seen firsthand how sloppy some reporters can be (and how professional the majority of reporters are), I advise you to intensify your efforts to verify quotations from other experts and to strive for complete accuracy in everything you write.

I take strong exception to Janet Malcolm's statements in her book, *The Journalist and the Murderer,* which claims that all journalists are confidence men and women who seduce and betray their sources. After publication of a *New Yorker* piece by Malcolm about psychoanalyst Jeffrey Masson, Masson charged that the writer had made up quotations that she attributed to him. Indeed, these quotations proved not to be on tape, although Malcolm tried to excuse her actions by maintaining that Masson had said such things with the tape recorder off.

Now I'm not going to spend a lot of time here preaching about the importance of quoting people honestly and keeping accurate notes. Consider me an advocate of both practices.

But it's also important to avoid the common mistake in which journalists get information from experts and then unintentionally alter what they say during the summation and/or paraphrasing of points. The difficulty arises when journalists, in their attempt to make difficult material comprehensible, put an expert's words into a context that changes the content of what was said.

A second problem is trickier. That's when a journalist, often a magazine journalist, or author takes information from an expert and incorporates it into a piece that has a flippant, irreverent tone. If, in such a context, a journalist misinterprets what an expert has said, it is unlikely that the interviewee is going to be forgiving.

The only solution is careful fact-checking by the writer and by the publication. However, because today's lean magazine staffs at the less wealthy publications cannot possibly check every fact in every issue (the way Rodale's wealthy health book and magazine divisions routinely do), it is essential that you, the writer, check every fact to the best of your ability.

When I first wrote for publication in the sixties, I was told over and over not to show my copy to the subject. The fear was that the subject would go over the reporter's head, might slap an injunction, and so on. But after years of experience, I've come to regard such advice as suspect.

In cases where what I am writing is strictly factual material, I have no problem in showing copy to a subject. For example, I have checked my material with educators I talked to about women's education, physicians I interviewed about specific health problems, and psychologists I talked to about behavorial issues and theories. In fact, I asked them to initial the pages they have read to protect myself in the unlikely event that what they have said later turns out to be an intentional falsehood or incorrect. I remember one case for a Rodale Press chapter in which an embarrassed doctor took back a recommendation for a treatment for gout he had given me on the phone, because he could offer no scientific evidence for his theory. In several instances doctors claimed I had oversimplified their statements and asked me to add some material, which I gladly did.

In cases where my tone is flippant, or in which the interviewee-expert is actually presented in a less than favorable light, I never give the subject the finished pages for inspection. What I do is call the expert and go point by point through the material, summarizing the flippant or unfavorable parts, and reading verbatim the neutral facts. At the end of the conversation, I risk unpleasantness by letting the subjects know the tone and nature of what I have written, treating them the way I hope I'll be treated if someone writes a negative piece about me.

CHAPTER TEN

Marketing Your Work

I t is not enough to master the art of writing to achieve success as a writing expert. You must learn to market yourself and your work.

The task of becoming a professional writer requires you not only to develop expertise in one or more areas, but also to learn how to sell your expertise. Some specialties, no doubt, are easier to turn into marketable articles than others. If you are an expert on nutrition and can write about diets that work, recipes that keep people slim, and new ways to prepare fast meals that taste great, you're going to have an easier time convincing editors to buy your stuff. Likewise, if you can write about sex—behavior, technique, and what men and women want from each other— you'll sell and sell. I promise you.

But that doesn't mean you should give up if, like me, you love writing about social issues, the arts, natural history and science. You and I will have to work harder than the writers selling pieces on diet and lovemaking, but there are markets that will welcome us too. You just have fewer of them, that's all. But you've met challenges before, I'm sure.

ENVISIONING MARKETS

As a freelancer the first step is to come up with a topic or (more likely) many topics that fascinate you enough that you want to write like an expert on them. At the present time I am intrigued with such unrelated and perhaps unlikely topics as rodeo clowning, writer bulletin boards online, snowshoeing, university presses, gifted children, baseball prior to 1950, personal finance, and the art of writing personal essays. You might find it helpful here to create a similar list of your own. Maybe it's cooking light, or sailing, or classic automobiles, or sex therapy—whatever. Putting down your interests is the first step toward selling articles based on specific ideas drawn from these topics.

The second step is to spend an hour or two in a store that sells dozens of specialty magazines and to take home a stack of those that you'd like to write for. I make a point of leaving some time free to browse in some favorite magazine emporiums whenever I'm in New York, Chicago or Los Angeles. Living near Indianapolis has its advantages, but great magazine stands isn't one of them.

Another favorite activity—one I particularly enjoyed when I lived in a remote cabin twenty miles from *any* store (let alone one selling a variety of national magazines)—is to study *Writer's Market*. I make a list of magazines that appear to publish articles in fields I consider to be my expertise and write for copies of those publications, including the appropriate payments with my letters, and request their editorial guidelines.

I learned that there were inroads to some magazines that I wouldn't have expected. For example, I wrote dozens of stories for *Satellite Orbit* on sports and celebrities, but with a few exceptions stayed away from writing technical pieces about satellite dishes because the research took me too long to make the project profitable. The trick is to match what you know with what the publications need—or what you can convince their editors that their readers need.

One of the things I've learned as an editor is that far too many freelance writers send their proposals to a magazine they've seen listed in *Writer's Market* without bothering to get the ink-and-print product itself. That would be like a single person reading an advertisement in the personals and sending a proposal of marriage without bothering to meet the individual who advertised. Every magazine uses a different focus to position itself in the marketplace. You may not be a member of the audience that the magazine's staff tries so hard to please, but you must think like you are, fashioning the article's tone, slant and content with the values of specific readers in mind. As an editor I don't have to read more than four or five sentences to determine that a writer has used some sort of mail-merge software to send the same query letter to many magazines—changing only the salutation and address information.

For example, if you read *Arts Indiana*'s table of contents page, you will make certain deductions about the tone of the magazine. For example, one issue listed an article entitled "South Bend by the Grace of God." The tag underneath it reads: "Notre Dame novelist Valerie Sayers is a South Carolinian by birth and a Hoosier by academic appointment." From it, as editor, I hope you will deduce that our readers like to read about novelists who've come to the state's colleges to teach writing. You may rightly conclude that the lifestyle and education of our readers are several notches above run-of-the-mill publications. And I hope you'll notice from that article's title and tag that I prefer a breezy, cheeky, smart tone without being smug.

Another issue of *Arts Indiana* had an article titled, "How to Watch Dance." Later the magazine ran a piece on the ethics of computer artists. Every month I try to publish at least one piece that serves our readers by educating them in some area of the arts—whether literary, performing or visual. The rule of thumb in such articles is to give readers the equivalent of a verbal road map so they don't get lost watching, say, a ballet performance. But I want the writers to include a handful of tips and inside information or stage gossip that even a reader who is a ballet veteran will appreciate having.

When I take off my editor's cap and become a freelancer, I read other publications for both business and pleasure—including out-of-the-ordinary association magazines, company publications, travel and airline mags, and alumnae periodicals. I am proud that I've written for *GQ* and *Outside*, but I have no objections to cashing the checks of smaller publications. I analyze the contents of these publications, then submit material that is consistent with what they have already published—but with some sort of fresh spin to attract the editor's eye.

Want to score a hit with me—or any editor worth the name? Tell me what I'm *not* publishing—and why I should be.

ARTICLE PROPOSALS THAT SELL

The best article proposals I've read as an editor are in the form of conversational letters. The idea, after all, is not to write the piece. The idea is to convince a person in charge—the editor—that you have an idea that readers will enjoy and learn from. But that's not enough. Within the confines of that single-spaced, one-page (two pages maximum) letter, you'll also have to offer convincing evidence that you qualify as enough of an expert so that readers will stay with you from word one to the end of your article.

This doesn't seem difficult, does it? Yet many otherwise capable writers lose out on opportunity after opportunity to prove they can write articles because they forget that query letters *are* letters. They write stiff and formal memorandums that make editors want to forget their very existence the minute they stuff an unsigned rejection slip into the envelope provided. People who write perfectly decent letters of complaint to the laundry that turned all their shirts pink as cotton candy somehow send in queries to editors that have no warmth, no energy, and ultimately, no appeal.

As an editor I'd rather see a query letter ending with the question—"Hey, what do you think?"—than endure yet one more formal "I await your response." The best query writers, I tend to think, are those people whose friends actually look forward to getting their newsletters at Christmas. Their proposals are chatty without being presumptuous. They make their points and quit. And they argue successfully in a single paragraph that no one else on the planet has the expertise, enthusiasm and desire to do a better job on a piece.

One of the best article proposals I've ever read was this one by Ellen Michaud, a nationally known health writer, who fired it off to *Philadelphia Magazine*.

> *If you'll forgive a personal question—do your eyes bulge?*
> *They do if you're one of the country's 53 million cigarette smokers.*
>
> *Don't believe it? Take a look in the bathroom mirror. Turn your head a little to the left, then a half-turn to the right. Notice those puffy upper lids? See the tiny protuberance along the lower lid? And how about that sweeping curve from corner to corner? If that's not a double astigmatism— bug eyes—it's smokers curvatae.*
>
> *You may think that Boston terrier eyes are cute. You also may think that shaky hands are a sign of intelligence or that a smoker's sticky, oxygen-sucking laugh is sexy. Lauren Bacall has a great one.*
>
> *But it's at your mother-in-law's funeral that the panic*

begins to hover around the edges of your consciousness. "We all gotta go sometime," she'd say with a wave of nicotine-stained fingers. "I just get to know what'll finish me off."

She knew all right. She didn't know that pain could flutter the edges of your brain.

Federal studies indicate that 47.7 million people are searching for a way to stop smoking. The smoking cessation market is so large that "habit control" is a national growth industry. In Philadelphia alone . . .

—you can have your left ear stapled by an anaestheologist at Germantown Hospital;

—you can get hypnotized by Damon and Grace at the Sheraton Valley Forge;

—you can manage stress at a Stop Smoking Center in one of three convenient locations;

—you can go one-on-one with a psychologist at Philadelphia Guidance Clinic;

—you can gradually withdraw with SmokEnders at any one of a dozen locations.

On and on. And you'll pay between $15 to upwards of $400 for the privilege.

"But How Can I Quit?" is an unabrasive service piece of 2,500 words that focuses on ten popular stop-smoking programs in Greater Philadelphia. A chart compares cost and methodology, as well as success rates after thirteen months. The article includes the insanities experienced by smokers who try to stop—along with anecdotes from program graduates and dropouts.

Coming from an ex-smoker who was stapled, modified, poked, educated and hypnotized before I'd quit, my underlying theme is that no one program is right or wrong. The right person must be matched with the right program at the right time.

Hypnosis worked for me. I sit here at the typewriter smoke-free and fifty pounds heavier than I was as a smoker. Blame it on 437 bags of Reese's Pieces.

As a freelance writer I've written for the Washington Post, Parents Magazine, McCall's, Working Mother *and* Savvy. *Give a call if you're interested in the piece.*

The articles editor at *Philadelphia* was intrigued. Michaud got the assignment, and the clip now reposes in her portfolio. She didn't submit it to any other publications, but you probably recognize that with a little reworking she could have pitched a similar piece to any number of women's magazines, men's magazines and airline publications—among others.

I like to envision writers with their sweatshirt sleeves rolled to the elbow as they write their queries late at night with the dog fed and all lights out next door. Good letters encourage that sense of a real writer at work. Letters that are too formal or worse, banal and cliché-ridden, make me think of suffering graduate students sweating blood while writing dissertations to appease (not please) unfriendly academics.

Which would I rather read? Hey, what do you think?

THE PERFECT QUERY LETTER

Perfect query letters are to the point and get your editors worked up to where they want to collaborate with you. These letters have one or two paragraphs that succinctly state your idea in its simplest, purest form. And they usually end with the credentials of the writer for doing the piece. This isn't name-dropping—it's just good business sense, letting a leery editor know that you've had the talent and gumption to write for some other publications.

Include your clips with your letter. If you can't send samples of magazine articles that you've written, don't despair. The next best thing is to demonstrate that you have expertise in a particular area. For example, at *Arts Indiana* I have assigned a "clipless" former museum curator two pieces on visual-arts subjects that turned out well for us.

Be sure you discuss expenses as well as fees when you negotiate with an interested editor. Unlike some writers, never "guesstimate" expenses. If the project requires travel, look up the price of plane fare online, call a mid-sized motel or hotel at your destination for their corporate rate, and estimate all other expenses, usually adding 10 percent to whatever total you reach for incidentals.

The bottom line is the bottom line. You can't write like an expert if your research is inadequate. No one can expect you to write without incurring expenses.

Nonetheless, you'll sell more pieces if you can save your editors some expense moneys. It stands to reason that you can do more articles, for less money, when you contact sources by phone instead of in person. Leaving your office takes money and a time commitment. When it's important to set a scene, I leave my office to conduct interviews; when I'm writing how-to pieces and other types of service journalism and it isn't important that I meet sources in person, I almost always conduct the interviews over the telephone. There were days at Rodale when I would interview twenty-five doctors in a single day. In person I was fortunate to do three interviews in one day.

Be careful what you propose in your query letter, it just might be assigned to you. Before you write the query, estimate carefully how much time it will take you to research and write a piece. The worst thing that can happen is to have your interest in a subject flag long before your research has been completed. If you think you won't stay enthusiastic about an idea, do yourself and your editor a favor—don't propose it.

PUT YOUR JOB SKILLS TO WORK

After you've mastered the art of query writing and have gotten used to the nice feeling you get depositing a good number of freelance checks, chances are you'll start pondering whether or not you can make the jump to full-time professional writing.

In the opinion of Sarah Edwards, co-author of *Working From Home*, writers who wish to quit their corporate day jobs have the best chance of succeeding in a home-based business like freelancing "if they have an expertise that is extremely valuable." Let's say you have a breezy writing style and are anything but a technophobe, choosing to spend your evenings performing twenty different activities on your computer. Consider approaching computer magazines, or contact book companies like IDG Books Worldwide in Indianapolis asking to share your expertise with readers who love their best-sellers like *DOS for Dummies* and *Macworld Photoshop Bible*. "It depends how much demand there is and how many other people are trying to meet that demand," says Edwards.

Carole Hyatt, the nationally known co-author of *When Smart People Fail* (Penguin) and author of *Shifting Gears* (Firestone) agrees, adding that sometimes people are able to write about their hobbies with real success. One trend she has observed re-

cently is people leaving what they had thought were their voca-
tions to pursue livelihoods in their avocations. "They blend their
work skills with their hobbies," the New York-based Hyatt told
me in a phone interview.

On the other hand, if a publication covering your hobby is
low-paying, you may not have any trouble lining up work—but
the renumeration isn't likely to be enough to justify a decision
to give up that regular paycheck. Hyatt warns that it's important
you don't delude yourself. Not all hobbies and avocations are
equally interesting to publishers. Let's say that you are an English
teacher and your main interest in life is writing poetry reviews.
Hyatt notes that it would be career suicide for someone to pursue
a fulltime writing career in the field of poetry since few such
periodicals pay anything at all—let alone enough to cover the
expense of your home office and car payment. In that case, however, ask yourself what sideline publications might prove lucrative. "Do you like the form of writing?" asks Hyatt. "Then what
are the aspects of what you really love and how can you blend
that with something saleable, marketable, and on the cusp of a
trend?"

Poet Gloria G. Brame—an Atlanta resident who is also one of
the most reliable freelance writers at *Arts Indiana*—also en-
dorses such advice. She quit a well-paying job at Morgan Stanley
on Wall Street to pursue her craft a few years ago. She ended
up meeting an established poet named Judson Jerome who also
happened to be a longtime columnist for *Writer's Digest* until his
untimely death due to cancer. Jerome praised her work but urged
her to try commercial writing for a popular audience to put bread
on the table. He told her that he had overcome financial problems
and had to make compromises to put his finances in order during
his own distinguished career.

Learning that Brame had done lay counseling with people
whose sexual practices were out of the mainstream, he urged
her to write a "big nonfiction book about scandalous sex."

Brame, at first, was reluctant, thinking that she might injure
her reputation as a poet. Judson poohpoohed that notion, and
she realized that she had the writing skills and experience to
handle the difficult topic with taste and insight. Brame, her husband, Will, and a third researcher named Jon Jacobs agreed to
co-author a project called *Different Loving: An Exploration of the*

World of Sexual Dominance and Submission (Villard Books) that took the premise that any sex that brings pleasure to both partners is a normal human drive. The book was published in 1993 and dedicated to the memory of Judson Jerome. "I was able to call on different talents and skills—which made the work sufficiently complex to be steadily fascinating," says Brame who was able to use the work and word skills of poetry in *Different Loving*. "Being accustomed to revising a poem endlessly, I wasn't fazed by subjecting the prose to the same kind of scrutiny to get it right."

THE SPIN ON SPIN-OFFS

As I first mentioned in chapter two, one way to boost income is to recycle your articles and ideas to generate multiple sales. Freelancers call such sales spin-offs, and many swear that spin-offs provide just enough extra income to make the difference between a successful and a failed business.

I recently sold three pieces based upon an evening spent watching a neighbor's fourteen-year-old son at his computer, involved in intellectual activities I would have associated more with adults. One piece was on "computer whiz kids" who relate online to adults in math and sciences. The second was on gifted students who get online what they can't get in public school. The third was about teachers who use computer online services to enhance the quality of their teaching.

The only restriction in pitching spin-off ideas is that you never propose a similar idea to competing publications. That would be like a lawyer representing the prosecution and defense in a trial.

WHAT COMES FIRST—THE BOOK CONTRACT OR THE RESEARCH?

When I speak at various conferences for writers, I often hear from people with enough magazine credits to qualify as writing professionals who are unsatisfied, burning to write a nonfiction book. Their questions come in a flurry. Do I need to write the first one on spec, meaning speculation, possibly spending years of my life without any guarantee that some publisher might be interested? If I simply want to write a proposal instead of the whole book to snag a publisher, how much research is enough? What if another writer is doing a book similar to mine?

My answers differ depending on the writers and their personal circumstances. The amount of research needed prior to selling a first book varies dramatically from writer to writer—depending on whether or not the book is represented by an agent with strong publishing contacts, whether or not the author has special credentials, experiences or connections that make editors compete to get her, and frankly, whether or not the writer is fortunate enough to be doing a book at a time when the subject is considered hot. What I cannot judge by appearances is whether these writers have the stamina to acquaint themselves with the fundamental way publishing works and the perspicacity to make opportunities happen.

Briefly, here is how my fifteen books came into being. My first sale was actually four books in "The Bounty Hunter" series co-written with latterday bounty hunter Tiny Boyles. In 1979 I profiled Tiny for a magazine, and Playboy Press editor Bob Gleason read it and invited him and me (as an expert on bounty hunters) to write an outline and sample chapter for a fictional series. I holed up with Tiny for four weeks to work night and day, sent the pages, and Gleason signed us to a contract.

In 1980, because a Hollywood producer wanted an option on the series, I obtained the services of an agent to represent Tiny and me. The agent happened to need a collaborator to co-write a book with Carole Shaw, the founder and then publisher of *BBW.* I switched agents in 1983 and my new one sold books six through eight (*Strategies of the Great Football Coaches, Strategies of the Great Baseball Managers* and *Recruiting in Sports*) on the basis of sample chapters and outlines I had written.

Electing to go without my agent (who has quit the industry) in 1987, I approached publisher Franklin Watts with sample chapters and outlines for a no-nonsense book on steroids and a biography of track legend Jesse Owens; both sold. I then wrote and placed two additional proposals with Idaho State University Press: a collection of interviews with writers published under the title of *Rendezvousing With Contemporary Authors* and a collection of essays on poet Ezra Pound that I co-edited with Robert G. Waite. My thirteenth book was *Broken Pledges,* sold after a dinner conversation with Jane Hill, then an editor with Georgia-based Longstreet Press, while I was speaking at a conference of student journalists in Atlanta in 1988. Nonfiction book fourteen was a history of a Pennsylvania college; I had answered a newspaper ad for a writer. In your hands you have my fifteenth book, sold unagented after Writer's Digest Books approved the outline. The idea for this book was that of Bill Brohaugh, editorial director, who previously had turned down two book ideas I had submitted.

All authors have sold their books in similar diverse fashion. There is no one surefire way to get a book contract. My way was to keep writing proposals and to keep hammering on publishing-house doors, figuring someone would open them—if only to tell me to "Stop all the knocking!"

WHEN MUST A RISK BE TAKEN?

Should you write a book on spec? In two circumstances, yes, and in all other instances, no. I often tell writers that it's a good gamble to take two weeks or a month to write an article on speculation—provided that they write with a specific publication *clearly* in mind (and rewrite it with a new publication in mind the first or twentieth time it is rejected). I emphasize that almost always I write no more than two sample book chapters on spec. Losing two weeks or a month if an article doesn't work out is acceptable to me; losing two years of work is something I am willing to do only in one exceptional case. If I have an idea for a book that is so compelling that I would feel a loss if I didn't tackle it, I would take the chance and write it, knowing intuitively that if it's good, it will see print. If you have a book concept that won't let you rest, do it. Remember, however, that few, if any, published authors would choose this option for anything less than the book of their dreams.

To get publishing credits early in my career, I wrote eleven pieces on speculation; all were published by the first publications I sent them to. But reality arrived and I went on a long streak of acquiring rejection slips. I stopped writing on speculation and learned to write a proper query letter. Today, if I were beginning over I'd write ten or twelve articles on speculation and not give the time spent a second thought—so long as I was also sending out query after query at the same time to get into the flow of what it's like to be a working freelancer.

How many book proposals have I written that failed to go anywhere? Some fifteen the last fourteen years have sunk without a ripple. Two are still in my files, and I intend to perfect them and submit them to publishing houses I failed to approach earlier. I've discarded the rest—agonizing when some of them (a book on Motown's Berry Gordy, for example, and three separate biographies of old-time baseball managers) were developed by other writers as marketable ideas. Those failed proposals are gone, unlamented. I haven't thought about them ever again until writing this chapter. I've never thought stewing improved anything— not even the taste of tomatoes.

WHAT IF YOU'RE NOT THE FIRST?

Which brings me to the last question I often field at conferences for writers. If you've started a project—say a biography of a public figure—what do you do if you learn in the course of research that someone else is doing the same book? My answer is that it depends on two things. If you already have a contract, talk the situation over with your editor and make an informed decision together with the publisher as to whether it's wise to continue. That way you can make whatever revisions in your game plan are necessary if you do proceed to write the book. If you don't have a contract, and you read in R.R. Bowker Company's *Forthcoming Books* about someone doing the same research you're doing, ask yourself honestly if your project is different enough from your rival's that both can compete in the marketplace. If the answer is yes, keep going. If the answer is no, accept the crushing inevitability as my friend Alanna Nash had to do in the late eighties when she learned that *Golden Girl*, her then biography-in-progress of anchorwoman Jessica Savitch, would come out a few weeks after another book on Savitch by rival Gwenda Blair. However, Nash not only survived the competition, but prospered, getting paid down the road for a paperback and movie rights.

You don't need a doctorate in economics to figure out the latest trend in book publishing. Publishers are trying to meet the demands of readers who want to make millions fast, lose weight quickly, buy real estate at bargain prices, and knock the fuzzy socks off of members of the opposite sex. This makes your job as a writer more difficult if, like me, your aim is to sell creative, quality nonfiction, investigative journalism, biographies, and how-to books for writers.

Publishers themselves are in a bind. Consumers who didn't blink when professional basketball tickets started selling for fifty dollars are griping mightily at paying twenty dollars for a book that will give them a week's reading pleasure or more. Nonetheless, in spite of all dire predictions, the book industry hasn't collapsed. While the multimillion dollar advances to the likes of Marlon Brando and Newt Gingrich disturbed professional writers whose advances, in comparison, seem like mere crumbs, the news isn't all bleak. The advent of small publishing houses that specialize in quality titles, the specialty houses such as Rodale Press's health book division and Franklin Watts's young adult line, the ever-increasing number of commercial trade books put out by university presses such as Indiana University Press, and the special imprints owned by mega-book corporations offer opportunities to publish that make it still worthwhile for writers to invest their dreams, passions and talent.

BOOK PROPOSALS THAT DEMAND TO BE BOUGHT

The realities of the marketplace drive publishers now more than ever. That means would-be authors must convince acquisition editors, the representatives of the publishers, that their books not only will be well-written but also well-read. One problem you'll encounter is that many unqualified people have had enough gumption to sit in front of a keyboard so that editors have been staggering for years under the sheer weight of manuscript submissions in the so-called "slush" or unsolicited pile. Hence, you may be aggravated by the three weeks to three months or more it will take you to get a response from a publisher on your book proposal. And you need to be aware just how well-written your entire proposal must be, lest a first reader scan your first couple hundred words and toss your proposal into your stamped return envelope with a rejection slip attached. It also should be reason enough to scan your local bookstore for titles that are similar in scope to what you are proposing and to consider giving smaller publishers a shot at purchasing your book—saving yourself time and frustration by excluding the giant houses whose publishers buy agented book properties almost exclusively. I also recommend familiarizing yourself with the descriptions of individual publishers offered by the *Small Press Record of Books in Print*, *Writer's Market* and *LMP (Literary Market Place)*.

How long is a proposal for a nonfiction book? Between twenty and thirty-five pages plus a sample chapter or two.

What goes into a proposal? All of the following:

1. Craft an arresting introduction that drives up the interest in your proposal. The editorial staff may finally say no to your book, but they surely will say no to your proposal if the first sentence, the first paragraph and the first page don't throw a loop around their necks and draw them toward you.

2. Write a thoughtful analysis of the marketplace that exists for your book. What niche do you see it occupying and why? Give facts and figures on the possible audience and why they would reach eagerly to snatch your book off the shelves. This should involve considerable research on your part. Seat-of-the-pants figures and unsupported generalizations ("Every Baby Boomer on the planet will want to buy it") have no place here.

3. Include a summary of the book in a page or less that is calculated to excite both the editorial and sales staff of a publisher. This is a proposal you are writing. Propose to them. You wouldn't offer a proposal of marriage that had less than your heart in it, would you? I always pretend that my proposal is in the hands of the sales force when they are trying to convince a bookstore owner why my book should be offered to customers. Following the short summary, follow up with five to ten pages that expand upon what you have said. This must be well-written. You must convince everyone that you can think, write, and sell at the same time.

4. Come up with a thoughtful two-to-three page presentation of how this book needs to be positioned in order to sell. Why is it needed by the audience you are trying to reach? What is available to this audience now from the competition or the same publisher? Why would your book be better and sell more copies?

5. Sell your expertise. This is not the time to hide your light. The publishing house needs to be excited about your qualifications. You must sell yourself before a publisher will want to sell your book. Make this section as long as a page or two. Exclude anything that would give editors a negative impression of you. If you have sold articles or a book, this is the time to show off your track record. You may prefer to write about yourself in the third person here to avoid sentence after sentence of I-I-I.

6. Sell the book some more. Go into the book a little more

from the editor's point of view. What is the theme of this book? How will it be organized? How do the parts (chapters) make up a unified whole? What are the dynamic aspects of your book that a reviewer cannot help being impressed by?

7. Write a ten to twenty-page chapter-by-chapter summary of the book you wish to write. This is where many authors fall short. Do not try to write this summary until you have a grasp on all the chapters in your book. A proposal that is fairly strong but has a couple of poor chapter possibilities is going to turn off potential buyers. If you have punchy titles for your chapters, provide them. Anticipate questions that your editors will have and answer them. Remember, these are summaries, not sample chapters.

8. Indicate the manuscript length in words and the time needed to research and write the book. Most first and second books by nonfiction writers go 70,000 to 90,000 words. Try to deliver the book in twelve months or less unless there is some compelling reason why it is going to take longer. Today's publishers want a chance to earn back as soon as possible the advance they are paying you.

9. Finally, your editor is going to want to know what visual features you see going into your book. Specify the type and number. What will be the costs of obtaining the art or photographs? Do you have someone to do the illustrations? If so, what are this person's qualifications? Are you still interested in doing the project if the publisher wants to use a freelance vendor of its own to do the art or photos? Will you provide the captions or labels for the pieces of art? Do photographs have to be obtained at great cost from a company that holds the rights to them? Do photos require models, a photo shoot or any other special requirements?

Be aware that the manufacturing costs of putting out a book go up with the number of illustrations, photographs, charts, maps and other visual aids that an author sees as essential. Give long and careful thought here. You don't want to include any costs that might tip the balance scales against a publishing house buying your book.

GET IT IN WRITING
Unless you have an agent, the editor is going to come to you with an offer of an advance and royalty percentage, plus other

rights if they apply such as audiobook rights or movie rights. It's up to you to get concessions and promises from the publisher before you sign a contract. You are not insulting the editor by negotiating or having a lawyer read the fine print. The contract for this book, for example, was read by my contract attorney, Bruce Munson.

There are basically two ways to go here if you decide that you would like an agent to handle your book. You can purchase one of the several commercial guides that contain the names of agents willing to read proposals, or you can look at reference books such as *LMP*. Some agents charge a fee for reading proposals and some do not. If you cannot make a substantial case that you are a professional writer, my advice would be to wait until you've gotten an editor to show interest in a proposal before you spend time and money contacting agents. Just because a publisher is interested, however, is no guarantee that an agent will sign you up as a client. Some agents are already booked to the maximum and won't add clients lest they shortchange the ones they already have. Other agents specialize in certain genres of books. However, the fact that you already have a publisher interested in you goes a long way toward establishing your credibility.

GETTING CONTROL OF YOUR WRITING LIFE

If you would write a book or write articles week-in-and-week-out to earn a reasonable living as a writer, you must get organized. Expert writers must control time and information and the space around them. Failure in just one area can make your career crash and burn.

But even if you are like the messy half of *The Odd Couple*, you can put your writing office in order. I have four tips you cannot ignore.

1. Never regard time spent organizing your life as wasted time. Take all the time you need to get organized. On the other hand, time spent looking for lost files, lost photographs, and lost phone numbers of sources *is* wasted time.

2. Concentrate on putting one section of your office at a time in order. That way you reduce frustration as you see yourself making progress.

3. For environmental reasons, recycle what you toss. So much

of the waste generated by writers is paper and is easily recycled.

4. Allow twenty to thirty minutes every working day to clean your work space so you never again have the messy office blues.

YOUR OFFICE

Keep possessions in your work space to a minimum. You are in a business where storage-keeping and accumulation of materials is inevitable. If you start filling every nook and inch of available space, you will soon be out of room. Don't fill your office with toys, souvenirs, replicas of art, photographs of your dog and so on. Put in what you need to reflect your needs and personality, but promise yourself that you'll take out one old object every time you bring in something new. My biggest fault is keeping too many books too long.

Visualize your closets, attic and other storage areas empty. Jot down a list of what needs to go into these areas. Try not to leave anything out. Are you going to be short several shelves for stored books or records? Make a note to pick some up—along with any hooks you'll need to store such items as duct tape for sending packages of notes to editors. I swear by plastic crates, the stackable kind, for keeping lots and lots of folders at my fingertips when writing a long project like this book.

One caveat. Never let another member of your household share your office. Not only does it interfere with your productivity, but you will not be able to satisfy Internal Revenue Service guidelines for claiming a home-office deduction. I recommend only inviting people on business into your office.

Unless you own a Victorian mansion, chances are you don't have enough square feet in your office to suit your needs. Screens and partitions can help, making one area of the office a place to hack away on the computer, another place to keep your fax and phone, and a third area to mull over research.

You'll also need shelves for supplies. I have a notepad alongside my supply shelves to remind myself that I'm getting low on something. You may wish to do the same if you seem always to be running to the supply store when you should be writing.

Try to take advantage of all available space. I have many portfolios, and they fit nicely in between file cabinets—out of sight. I had unused space behind my copier, and I filled it with novels that I don't ordinarily need to look at on a daily basis.

The Weight of Paper

To be successful as a writer you must control the flow of paper that comes into your life. The solution is to develop your own efficient systems of handling paper before it starts to overwhelm you.

You have three choices to make. You can deal with the paper immediately. You can file it, or put it aside in some logical place and deal with it later. You can shunt it off to some illogical place and needlessly clutter your life.

In the end, to survive, you undoubtedly will someday decide that the only logical answer is to be smart and to organize the way you deal with paper.

Keeping Track of Your Files

I used to have trouble with my system of filing, because I simply filed things alphabetically. One drawer might have been "A-E," another "F-K," and so on. This system was hard to follow; I filed items on hazing in the same "F-K" drawer with my folder on Indiana basketball coach Bob Knight and writer Ken Kesey.

My solution was to use one file drawer for a larger subject and to place only file folders pertaining to that entry inside the drawer. For example, I have a file drawer marked "Expert" for this book, a drawer marked "Sports" for my freelance sportswriting and a drawer marked "Arts" for freelance arts-related files. Within these file drawers I insert several dozen folders clearly marked with headings that mean something to me. (Never mark them with vague headings like "miscellaneous" or you'll dump anything and everything into them, defeating the purpose of segregating your materials.)

Inside the folders I place clippings from newspapers and tear sheets from magazines, press releases, pamphlets, notes to myself, etc. I also have cardboard file drawers for business letters. These I keep out of sight, hauling them out only when I need to file new letters or check old correspondence. I file them in logical categories by person or institution.

Keeping Track of Sources

When I worked at Rodale Press as a senior writer, one thing I admired very much was the efficient way they kept files on the many thousands of doctors, dentists, chiropractors, nurses and health-care experts that are regularly interviewed. We writers and editors could press a few computer keys to find an expert under many categories—by name, by location, by specialty and so on.

You or I don't have the money that Rodale Press has to hire researchers, but we all can have an efficient filing system. For some freelancers, a simple file-card system serves well to keep tabs on editors, information sources and vendors such as computer consultants and typists. Or, you may prefer to use your computer to track your dealings with contacts and clients such as editors. Be sure to keep a copy of your files on a backup disk in the event there's a hard-drive crash.

On my computer I list editors, experts and sources with their names, addresses and the occasions that I have contacted them. For example, I keep track of article queries sent to my editors at *Writer's Digest* and other magazines.

I also keep a record of my dealings with sources such as the date and nature of interviews conducted with them. When you are interviewing several thousand people a year for a book or multiple articles, you must keep these types of records or find yourself hopelessly disorganized.

Other Files You'll Need

I try to file everything—letters and other information—the day it comes in, but that's not always possible. In that case, I make use of "To File," "To Read and Sort" and "To Answer" file folders that will keep things neatly until the next day or two when I can get to them.

In addition, I keep a photo "morgue" of people that I have photographed for regional and national magazines in case I can resell them. I also keep a half-dozen headshots of myself to give reporters or institutions that request one, saving me the time of enduring yet another photo shoot. I also keep clippings of articles about myself and my work that have run in national and regional publications to photocopy whenever needed for business purposes.

Keep Files Current

If you have pack rat tendencies, you'll need to clean your files out at regular three- or six-month intervals. On the inside of my file cabinets, I keep a small taped paper letting me know the last time I cleaned a certain drawer. I am likely to spend more time updating some files than others, depending on their importance to my writing life.

When you write a book, the volume of paper you'll acquire can be daunting. When the book is published, you will be tempted to pitch many of your files. Should you? The answer depends upon your subject. Since anyone can sue for libel whether they have a good case or not, I have decided that what makes sense for me is to keep my files for one year after my book is taken off a publisher's list of its books in print.

Once you have a policy, stick to it. Some investigative reporters keep their records for two years after publication, pitching them then as a matter of policy. Some keep them for as long as they think there is even a remote chance they'll be sued or have their research challenged.

PUTTING TIME ON YOUR SIDE

Sometimes you learn from mistakes. One of the hardest things for me to learn as a freelancer was to estimate the time a project would require. I accepted projects that seemed at the time to offer a decent amount of money—but when I was well into the assignment, I learned that I was working for far less than $25 an hour, my absolute bare minimum charge. The project that finally taught me the value of doing a time estimate was the college history I wrote. I failed to research some important considerations that made this project a drain on my finances and energies. My hard lesson, I hope, is your easy lesson. When you have a project, estimate how many hours your project will take you to research and write—and multiply that total by 20 percent to account for any factors beyond your control.

At the time you decide to earn all or a large part of your income from writing as I have done on and off for four decades, you'll need to keep adequate financial records to run your business and to satisfy the record-keeping requirements of the Internal Revenue Service. The bottom line is that proper record keeping saves you money.

You will be spending a good part of your writing income each year on office supplies, electronic equipment and miscellaneous expenses. You should be able to take all deductions that are right and proper under the law, but you must keep proper documentation in the event of an Internal Revenue Service audit. You cannot run a business by simply piling your receipts willy-nilly into a shoe box; you must keep accurate records.

Chart your workdays for five days, keeping track of everything in an appointment book. At the end of the week examine all that you have done, marking them "necessary," "somewhat useful," and "unproductive."

Likely you'll be appalled by what you learn about how much precious time gets wasted. Unnecessary phone conversations, meetings that accomplish very little and socializing add up to many lost hours. Evaluate what you find. Decide what you want to change. Then be ruthless. No one is going to issue you any more time to replace what you've lost.

Speaking of time—you've been reading long enough. It's time to put all you've learned to the test. See you in print.

INDEX

More Great Books For Writers!

Writer's Market—Celebrating 75 years of helping writers realize their dreams, this newest edition contains information on 4,000 writing opportunities. You'll find all the facts vital to the success of your writing career, including an up-to-date listing of buyers of books, articles and stories, listings of contests and awards, plus articles and interviews with top professionals. *#10432/$27.99/1,008 pages*

The Writer's Ultimate Research Guide—Save research time and frustration with the help of this guide. 352 information-packed pages will point you straight to the information you need to create better, more accurate fiction and nonfiction. With hundreds of listings of books and databases, each entry reveals how current the information is, what the content and organization is like, and much more! *#10447/$19.99/352 pages/available October 1, 1995*

How to Write Fast (While Writing Well)—Discover what makes a story and what it takes to research and write one. Then, learn, step-by-step how to cut wasted time and effort by planning interviews for maximum results, beating writer's block with effective plotting, getting the most information from traditional library research and on-line computer bases, and much more! Plus, a complete chapter loaded with tricks and tips for faster writing. *#10473/$15.99/208 pages/paperback/available September 1, 1995*

The Writer's Digest Guide to Good Writing—In one book, you'll find the best in writing instruction gleaned from the past 75 years of *Writer's Digest* magazine! Successful authors like Vonnegut, Steinbeck, Oates, Michener, and over a dozen others share their secrets on writing technique, idea generation, inspiration, and getting published. *#10391/$18.99/352 pages*

Thesaurus of Alternatives to Worn-Out Words and Phrases—Rid your work of trite clichés and hollow phrases for good! Alphabetical entries shed light on the incorrect, the bland and the overused words that plague so many writers. Then you'll learn how to vivify your work with alternative, lively and original words! *#10408/$17.99/304 pages*

Writing for Money—Discover where to look for writing opportunities—and how to make them pay off. You'll learn how to write for magazines, newspapers, radio and TV, newsletters, greeting cards, and a dozen other hungry markets! *#10425/$17.99/256 pages*

The Writer's Digest Guide to Manuscript Formats—Don't take chances with your hard work! Learn how to prepare and submit books, poems, scripts, stories and more with professional look editors expect from a good writer. *#10025/$19.99/200 pages*

Roget's Superthesaurus—For whenever you need just the right word! You'll find "vocabulary builder" words with pronunciation keys and sample sentences, quotations that double as synonyms, plus the only word-find reverse dictionary in any thesaurus—all in alphabetical format! *#10424/$22.99/624 pages*

Freeing Your Creativity: A Writer's Guide—Discover how to escape the traps that stifle your creativity. You'll tackle techniques for banishing fears and nourishing ideas so you can get your juices flowing again. *#10430/$14.99/176 pages/paperback*

Writing the Blockbuster Novel—Let a top-flight agent show you how to weave the essential elements of a blockbuster into your own novels with memorable characters, exotic settings, clashing conflicts and more! *#10393/$17.99/224 pages*

20 Master Plots (And How to Build Them)—Write great contemporary fiction from timeless plots. This guide outlines 20 plots from various genres and illustrates how to adapt them into your own fiction. *#10366/$17.99/240 pages*

Handbook of Short Story Writing, Volume II—Orson Scott Card, Dwight V. Swain, Kit Reed and other noted authors bring you sound advice and timeless techniques for every aspect of the writing process. *#10239/$12.99/252 pages/paperback*